Voices from the
SAN ANTONIO
MISSIONS

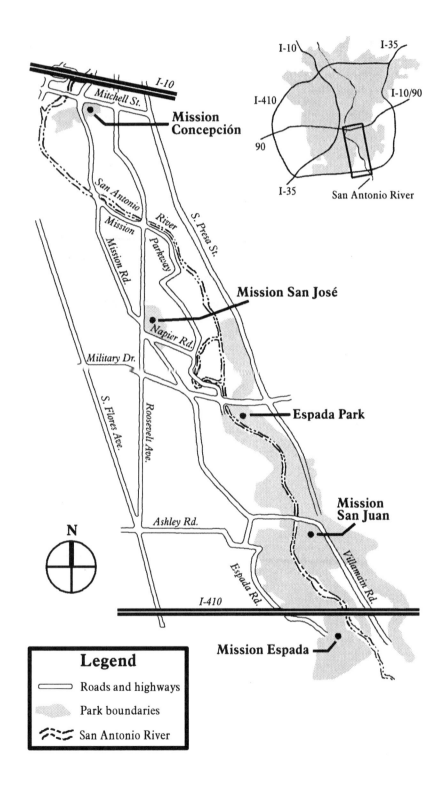

I-10

I-35

I-410

I-10/90

90

I-35

San Antonio River

Mitchell St.

I-10

Mission
Concepción

San Antonio

River

Mission

S. Presa St.

Mission Rd.

Parkway

Mission San José

Napier Rd.

Military Dr.

S. Flores Ave.

Roosevelt Ave.

Espada Park

Mission
San Juan

Ashley Rd.

Villamain Rd.

N

Espada Rd.

I-410

Mission Espada

Legend

Roads and highways

Park boundaries

San Antonio River

Luis Torres

Foreword by Dora Guerra

Texas Tech University Press

This book was set in Aldine 721 and Snell printed on acid-free paper that meets the guidelines for permanence and durability of the Committee on Production Guidelines for Book longevity of the Council on Library Resources. ∞

Illustrations by Lisa Camp

Book and jacket design by Lisa Camp

Printed in the United States of America

Library of Congress Cataloging-in-Publication Data
Voices from the San Antonio missions / [interviewed by] Luis Torres.
    p.   cm.
    Includes index.
    ISBN 0-89672-378-X (cloth : alk. paper)
    1. Spanish mission buildings—Texas—San Antonio—Conservation and restoration. 2. Historic preservation—Texas—San Antonio.
3. San Antonio (Tex.)—church history. 4. Interviews—Texas—San Antonio. I. Torres, Luis, 1936-
F394.S2V65 1997   97-709
976.4'351—dc21   CIP

97 98 99 00 01 02 03 04 06 / 9 8 7 6 5 4 3 2 1

Texas Tech University Press
Box 41037
Lubbock, Texas 79409-1037 USA
800-832-4042
ttupress@ttu.edu

*To the people of the communities surrounding the
San Antonio missions, whose lives are an example of quiet
dignity and perserverance in the face of life's challenges*

Contents

Foreword

In any body of study, there builds a comfortable familiarity with venerable scholarship and its authors, whose names represent valid and respected research. And just as the fabled prison inmates who eventually were able to reduce their telling of a joke to calling out its assigned number, historians and other cognoscenti in a particular subject area need only mention an author's, institution's, or archive's name to bring to mind a particular body of work. Such has been the case with the San Antonio Missions. Mention Henry and Mary Ann Noonan Guerra; mention the microfilm collection at the Library of Our Lady of the Lake University; or mention Bolton, Castañeda, Habig, Leutenegger, Almaraz, Fox, Ivey, Cox, or Hinojosa; and informed listeners nod knowingly.

Pages upon pages have been filled about the why, when, and wherefore of the missions. Geographers have traced the routes of the original missionaries and described the topography they encountered. Ethnographers have told us about the native tribes whose lives were forever changed. Archaeologists working with puzzle pieces found above and below ground have given us insight into time frame and lifestyle as defined by the tools, weapons, pottery and other artifacts from mission sites. We have learned about the building of acequias and their dams and about mission farms, who worked them, and what crops they raised. Architects have waxed poetic about mission structure, orientation, cross ventilation, decoration, stone work and the like. Musicologists have shared their findings about the music and instruments introduced to natives in the missions, and how these were transformed with time. These myriad voices, sounding in testimony, have been gathered and synthesized by historians into a prismatic saga of the missions and their role in the past.

In the pages that follow, Luis Torres, long a gatherer of voices, has turned the prism by just a fraction and has captured an additional beam of light that bridges voices of the past with those of the present, thereby illuminating a continuum and currency of life in and around the missions. The eighteen interviews he presents in this meticulously gathered oral history pull us into the lives of ordinary families for whom, generation after generation, the missions have been central, in some cases since as far back as the eighteenth century. His work defines the closeness of the union between the missions and their people, and how each has affected the other.

Viewed solely as structures, the missions become mere artifacts. Their life and energy have always come from the people whose lives have been tied to them from their founding. When politics forced their parishioners to flee, the missions' life was drained from them, and decay set in. It has been people all along who have been the missions' lifeline and pulse, and this oral history heightens our awareness of that long standing symbiosis.

But Luis Torres's work adds yet another dimension, it goes beyond showing us the connectedness between the missions and their people. His work is also a social history. It chronicles and documents who the mission people are today, and shows us the rhythm of their lives. It tells us how they view themselves in relation, not only to the missions but also to the larger community around them. At the end, the reader reaps the bonus of many delightful or perhaps totally surprising details that might have gone unrecorded for posterity.

For example, the distinction between being "from town" and "from the mission" is resounding. When asked, many interview subjects didn't say they were San Antonians; what they said was that they were "from the missions." We are less than half a decade away from the twenty-first century, and still the distance between the San Antonio community and their own looms large in the minds of mission dwellers, almost as if the mission communities were circumscribed by actual geopolitical boundaries.

Susie Bustillos Chávez in her interview delineates a further demarcation when she talks about her childhood school. When schooling was no longer offered at the mission's granary, it affected mission folk deeply to have their children cross a whole street to a school they viewed as beyond the familiar boundaries of their world. That school across the way seemed in another world indeed, especially when mission children felt ostracized precisely because they were from mission communities, which for years had been predominantly Mexican-American.

Claude Guerrero tells us how "many people in the neighborhood were related to each other." Having gone through numerous marriage records in my personal research, I see a continuum, a social pattern deriving from the eighteenth-century custom of their ancestors' to marry within the community.

Another social pattern from the early part of our century that comes to light through these interviews has to do with marrying outside the missions community. It was acceptable to marry a "town girl," but town girls didn't give up their outlander status readily. Just as American women living in foreign countries might choose to return to the United States to give birth in their native land, town girls married to "mission men" frequently insisted on having their babies in San Antonio, in their own parents' homes, reinforcing the separation of communities. What emerges as a result of this study is a picture of a group of San Antonians whose past is deeply entwined in their present, and whose true self-identity is still not quite San Antonian.

As a native San Antonian, I have always felt a strong connection to these missions. Each of my visits to them transports my spirit to the days when ancestors of some of these interviewees were forging their lives because of and in unison with the missions. This knowledge has always struck a chord within me and has set my nerve endings atingle. However, I can't say my father was born in the mission's granary like Susie Bustillos Chávez can, nor can I say like Claude Guerrero that I was born three hundred feet from the mission church. By their standards, I'm definitely a "presidio girl."

What Luis Torres has given us here—a sharp picture of the human condition in and around the San Antonio missions—deepens and enriches the works that have preceded his. Missions historians can boast that one of their cadre has yet again enlarged our appreciation of these American monuments by spotlighting what is most valuable of all—their living history.

Dora Elizondo Guerra
Head of Special Collections and Archives
The University of Texas at San Antonio Library
December 10, 1996

Preface

The five San Antonio missions—Mission San Antonio de Valero, known as the Alamo, and Missions San José, Nuestra Señora de la Purísima Concepción, San Francisco de la Espada, and San Juan Capistrano—were founded between 1718 and 1731 as part of Spain's effort to secure the vast territories it claimed in the northern reaches of the Viceroyalty of New Spain, whose center of government was Mexico City. Unable to populate that area with Spanish settlers or their New World descendants, Spain expected the missions to Christianize the native inhabitants, educate them in the ways of the European, and make them worthy subjects of His Majesty, the King. Together with the Presidios, military garrisons to protect the missions and to supplement the Spanish presence, the missions were expected to hold the territory for Spain until proper settlements could be established.

The work of the missions was supposed to last some ten years, at the end of which, with the Europeanized natives coming into the same rights and obligations of every Spanish citizen, the mission church would be secularized—that is, removed from the hands of the missionary and placed under the secular clergy as a regular parish—and the mission lands divided among its inhabitants. For a number of reasons, among them high mortality among converted Indians and a steady influx of nonmissionized ones, the San Antonio missions never were able to function as expected. The task anticipated to last one decade extended for many, and it was not until the 1790s that secularization began. The final steps in the secularization process were ordained not by the government of the King but by that of the new and independent Mexican nation in the 1820s.

Over the following century, the missions suffered abandonment and decay, so that by the 1930s they were, for the most part, in ruins. Fortunately, since then, as a result of the efforts of countless tireless individuals and dedicated organizations, their decay has been arrested and in some cases even reversed. The first among the missions, San Antonio de Valero, has, for all intents and purposes, lost its character as a mission; instead, as a result of the famous battle fought there, it has become a shrine of Texan patriotism. The Daughters of the Republic of Texas (DRT) have been its guardians and administrators since 1905.

Beginning in 1983, and after long and arduous negotiations, the remaining four missions were brought together in the San Antonio Missions

Mission San José. Courtesy of the National Park Service, San Antonio Missions National Historical Park.

Mission Concepción. Courtesy of the National Park Service, San Antonio Missions National Historical Park.

Mission San Juan Capistrano. Courtesy of the National Park Service, San Antonio Missions National Historical Park.

Mission Espada. Courtesy of the National Park Service, San Antonio Missions National Historical Park.

Mission San Antonio, The Alamo. Courtesy of the The Institute of Texan
Cultures, San Antonio.

National Historical Park, under the administration of the National Park
Service (NPS). However, the Catholic Church, represented by the Archdiocese of San Antonio, retains an active interest in the missions and
exercises control over the mission churches, each of which is supposed to
house an active congregation.

As might be expected, over a period of nearly three centuries the missions
have become an integral part of the fabric of life in San Antonio. This study
began as an attempt to capture what was still available of the history of the
San Antonio missions from oral history sources. It quickly became obvious,
however, that the material collected was as much about the San Antonio
community that surrounds the missions as about the missions themselves.

Acknowledgments

Many people were instrumental in making this work possible, and I wish to make sure that they are properly thanked. First and foremost, my appreciation goes to the men and women of the San Antonio community who were willing to sit down with me for formal interviews on the subject of the missions. Many of them also provided photographs that accompany the text.

I also received invaluable cooperation and support from Dora Guerra, special collections librarian at University of Texas San Antonio (UTSA); park historian Rosalind Rock, chief of professional services Mark Chávez, and assistant superintendent Alan Cox at the San Antonio Missions National Historical Park; Tom Shelton, photo archivist, Diane Bruce, librarian, and Laura Howard, photographer at the Institute of Texan Cultures of UTSA; Sister María Carolina Flores of the Old Spanish Missions Historical Research Library at Our Lady of the Lake University; Martha Utterback at the Daughters of the Republic of Texas; and Judy Zipp, librarian at the San Antonio *Express-News*.

Above all, I want to thank those closest to me, Don Schecter and Billy Jack McKinzey, who functioned as critics, proofreaders, and sounding boards, and who were willing cheerleaders and morale boosters when difficulties seemed to overwhelm the project.

Luis Torres
San Antonio

Introduction

Oral history is something of a Cinderella among the various approaches to the discipline of history. All of us are used to the traditional approach, which focuses on the major figures and the documentary evidence surrounding a period or a specific event. Not everyone, however, is familiar or comfortable with the possibility of seeking to understand a portion of the historical continuum by looking not at the big picture but at the smallest possible component of it.

Fortunately, over the last several decades, historians have both broadened and narrowed their approach: broadened to include entire segments of society that were once either totally ignored or given short shrift; narrowed to include the realization that, although it is good, healthy, and enlightening to approach a topic from a global or broadest-possible point of view, it is just as important to see it from the point of view of minor players, or of the man- or woman-on-the-street.

The San Antonio missions have been around since the 1700s. There is no doubt that the available documents related to them—legal and ecclesiastical documents, the correspondence of Spanish royal and church officials, the property inventories, the written reports of the *visitas*, the periodic visits of higher officials of the missionary orders—are important. But, how much would we give today to have the text of a candid interview with one of the Franciscan missionaries who spent long years on this often lonely frontier, with one of his Indian converts living in the totally new environment of the mission, or with one of the soldiers stationed to help defend the mission compound and train recently nomadic people in the use and handling of European weapons?

The insights we could gain from such interviews are now irretrievably lost to us, as is the viewpoint of all the succeeding generations around the missions but the one or two generations closest to ours. Oral history is usually a mop-up operation fraught with frustration. As the oral historian surveys the chosen field, he or she is constantly encountering the names of individuals who would have been excellent sources but who have died within the last decade, or even within the last couple of years. In the small number of months that it took to survey the San Antonio community and compile a list of possible interview subjects for this project, several potentially interesting sources died; others suffered incapacitating strokes or succumbed to the frailties of old age and ended up either in the hospital, too sick to be interviewed, or inaccessible in a nursing home.

Still, just the contact with some remarkable individuals has made the work interesting and worth pursuing. The eighteen individuals interviewed here represent a broad sample of the San Antonio community. They range from humble folk who have spent most, if not all, of their lives in the mission communities to people who have traveled widely and whose children have routinely studied abroad; from the children of migrant farm laborers to the offspring of prominent parents.

Even if they had nothing to say about the San Antonio missions, these interviews are small social history gems for what they reveal about the San Antonio community within which, after all, those missions survive: about community dynamics and tensions, for example, or about the tremendous changes that have taken place over the last two generations. But the interviews do have something to say about the missions. To this author, perhaps the most fascinating single thing to come out of the interviews was the discovery that only four generations ago there was still a family in the Mission San José community (Anita Bustillos Rivera's) whose members routinely used the expression *"vamos pa'l [para el] presidio"* (let's go to the presidio) when they wanted to indicate they were going to the center of the city—the *presidio de San Antonio de Béxar* back in the eighteenth century.

Several of the people interviewed have lived all or most of their lives within the mission communities. A number of them document the fact that, as one subject put it, the missions belong to all of San Antonio, not just to people of Indian or Spanish/Mexican blood. The ancestors of those groups may have been at the missions first, but other ethnic groups quickly mixed into the community even prior to secularization, and the missions have also played an important role in the lives of their own descendants.

Two interviews (Margaret Benavides, Jesse and Zoila Sánchez) document the demise of the parish at Mission Concepción, the only one of the four mission churches that does not have a "living parish" using the site. Also included are interviews with the son (Robert Walker) of a contractor (Rufus Walker) who carried out many restoration and conservation projects at the missions; with the son (Donald W. Harris) of a formidable woman, Ethel Wilson Harris, who focused immense drive and dedication on Mission San José; with a husband and wife team (Henry and Mary Ann Noonan Guerra), whose broad civic involvement has benefited the missions in countless ways; with a Catholic priest (Monsignor Balthasar Janacek), whose assignment for the last several decades has been to represent the interests of the Archdiocese of San Antonio in the missions; and with two outstanding younger individuals: the first female state park superintendent hired by the Texas Parks and Wildlife Department (Betty Bueché) and someone whose early contact with the missions led to a career in historic conservation and preservation (Ross Hunt).

METHODOLOGY

The project originated with a request by the National Park Service (NPS) for an oral history component to be included in a cultural landscape report of the San Antonio missions—a global look, from their foundation to the present, at the four missions that today form part of the San Antonio Missions National Historic Park. The original report has been expanded for publication, but the author wishes to acknowledge the NPS for agreeing to the inclusion of material from that oral history component in this publication.

The study began with an attempt to determine a prospective pool of informants regarding the San Antonio missions. To begin with, key individuals within the San Antonio community were identified who might be able to identify others as good subjects for interviews. Some twenty-five of these original referents were contacted, informed of the purpose and scope of the project, and asked to identify possible subjects, describe their connection with the missions, give a brief description of the person, and, where possible, provide an address, telephone number, or other means of establishing contact.

The result of this survey was a list of eighty-four names. Some entries contained relatively complete information about the person, including address and phone number; others were just names. Considerable detective work went into trying to locate these individuals and having at least a preliminary phone conversation with them to ascertain their connection with the missions and their willingness to be interviewed. Each person contacted, as well as each person actually interviewed, was asked to name others who might qualify for inclusion in the list of possible subjects. As a result, the list quickly grew to around one hundred names. Of the persons contacted, only five or six proved uncooperative or unwilling to be interviewed. A few of the individuals on the list were deceased or inaccessible.

A cull based on initial information about each individual narrowed the list to some thirty-five names. The NPS regional office in Santa Fe was then given the opportunity to identify individuals they would prefer to have interviewed before a final selection resulted in the eighteen interviews that were conducted for inclusion in this work. There are, of course, many other people in the San Antonio community who would have been interesting to interview. Various circumstances, however, made it impossible to include those interviews.

ABOUT THE INTERVIEWS

This project was begun, from a different point of view and with different proposed methodology, by Richard Flores, who had to bow out when professional commitments made his participation impossible. From his initial efforts, Flores turned over four untranscribed interview tapes to form part of the present study. One of these had to be discarded because technical problems made the tape unintelligible. The subjects were located again; the ruined interview was done again, and material from additional conversations was added to the original interviews. I hereby wish to acknowledge Mr. Flores's contribution and to thank him for it.

Prior to the present study, the NPS had commissioned some oral history work in connection with the construction of a new visitors center at Mission San José. One of those interviews was with one of Flores's subjects, and he located and provided the transcription of it. The text of that interview was merged with Flores's own interview and the additional material collected; the result is included here. The original interviewer was José Zapata, at that time with the University of Texas at San Antonio's Center for Archaeological Research, now with the Texas Parks and Wildlife Department. I wish to recognize Mr. Zapata here and thank him for his contribution.

Each interview took from one to two-and-a-half hours and was conducted either in the subject's home or in a place of his or her choice. The interview was recorded and later transcribed. Most of the interviews were conducted in English, but several were conducted in Spanish, or in the mixture of Spanish and English that is characteristic of the Hispanic community in San Antonio. The latter are, of course, presented in translated form, except for a few phrases of the original language that have been preserved where they either make things clearer or contribute a special flavor to the conversation.

What is presented here is the written form of a conversation. Although every effort has been made to remain true to the rhythms and patterns of the subject's speech and what appeared to be the meaning of the subject's utterances, the transcriber (author as translator and editor) had to keep in mind that the text would ultimately be read, not listened to. Conversational speech contains hundreds of pauses, useless words, interjections, *non sequiturs,* and so on that would be maddening if preserved in written form. As many of those as possible have been eliminated in the transcription and editing. For the sake of continuity, the author has felt free to move sections of the conversation around in order to keep references to one subject together or to improve the flow of the transcript.

By its very nature, oral history represents the experience and point of view of the subject of the interview and thus contains its own biases and distortions. One could conceivably circumvent this problem by checking out each statement against appropriate documents or other sources. For the purposes of this study, such an approach would be impossible; not only would it make the investment of time and effort required impossible to handle, but it would also destroy the flavor that makes these interviews both charming and interesting. The subjects in this collection are not presented as paragons of factual interpretation or as representing some ultimate historical truth. They are simply individuals who have lived with and around the San Antonio missions for a significant part of their lives and are willing to share that experience with others. Their ages and other information provided in the introductions to each interview are current with the date of that interview.

NOTE

1. It is important to note that the San Antonio Mexican-American community does not always observe the traditional Spanish usage in giving a person's family name, something which undoubtedly came about as a result of daily contact with a larger Anglo community that has difficulty understanding that usage. Traditionally, in Spanish, one uses a *nombre de pila* or baptismal name, a middle name, then the father's last name followed by the mother's last name. Thus, José Enrique, the son of Juan Valdez and María García, would list his name as José Enrique Valdez García. Although the usage is not uniform in San Antonio, one might find him giving his name as José Enrique García Valdez, thus allowing him to preserve both his parents names but making it easier for Anglos to identify him correctly as "Mr. Valdez." In addition, the traditional Spanish usage for married women to append "de" and their husband's last name to their father's name—thus, Josefina Pérez Santiago, when married to José Enrique Valdez García, would become Josefina Pérez de Valdez—has almost disappeared.

Susie Bustillos Chávez

(left, with Rose Anguiano)

Susie Bustillos Chávez (SC), *eighty-eight years old, was born and raised in San Antonio. Passionately interested in her family's history, she has traced her line back to the 1790s. Her ancestors at one time owned extensive sections of lands that were part of Mission San José and Mission Espada. The property on which she currently lives, on Bustillos Drive near San José, came to the family through her mother's side. She was a Huizar, related to Pedro Huizar, who is credited with sculpting the "Rose Window" at San José [See Apendix B]. This interview contains material contributed by José Zapata, Richard Flores, and Luis Torres, and was collected between June 1993 and August 1995. It was conducted in both English and Spanish. During part of the interview, SC's niece* **Rose Anguiano** *(RA), daughter of SC's sister Adela, was also in the room.*

Where were you born?

SC: On South Flores Street, 3115 South Flores. My mother was a town girl, and she would take us to be born on South Flores, but I lived at the mission until I was five years old.

Were you born at home?

SC: At my grandmother's, with the help of a midwife.

Do you have any brothers and sisters?

SC: Oh, yes. Do you want me to name them all for you? The first was Cornelio, and then Elena, and then Juan (we called him Johnny), and then me, Jesusa or Susie, Adela, Erineo, Carmen, and Eufemia.

How many is that?

SC: Eight.

And are they all still living?

SC: No. My brother Cornelio passed away, and Elena also passed away, and Adela also passed away. Gosh! And Erineo also passed away. My God, there's only four of us left!

Did they pass away while in their youth?

SC: No, not in their youth. I believe my brother was about eighty. Lena was about sixty-two. How old was Adela? [Directed at RA.]
RA: My mama was seventy-five.

What about your father? How old was he when he passed away?

SC: Eighty-one.

What was his year of birth?

SC: I think it was 1874.

And your mother?

SC She was born two years after him, in 1876.

And your father, where was he from? Was he also from San Antonio?

SC: Yes, he was from the mission. He was born in the *galera*.

I'm not familiar with that term.

SC: That's the granary.[1] Got him there! [Laughs.]

Where did your father attend school, or did he?

SC: He went there, in the granary. There was a school there, and that's where he went.

Up to what grade did he attend?

SC: I think it was the third or fourth. Because back then, well, you know . . . but he knew how to write.

Did he know English?

SC: Yes. Oh yeah, he knew how to tend to business, about land, and all the good things. He was a farmer. They had lands, you know. They had a lot of property.

What about your mom? Where was she born?

SC: She was born on South Flores. Right here, in San Antonio.

Did she go to school?

SC: Yes, she went to school. I think she went up to the fifth grade. She knew how to read and write and spoke English, too.

Do you have any idea where she went to school? Was it also in the mission?

SC: No, she was from town.

And what kind of work did she do?

SC: She was a housewife; my daddy never wanted her to work.

Any interests besides the home or housework?

SC: No, just the house and the family: sending us to school and back, making the tortillas, beans, whatever . . . taking care of us!

Where did your mother and father meet?

SC: When my aunt Elogia and my uncle José Chávez got married, they invited my mother, and that's where they met, at a wedding.

And how old were they when they met?

SC: I don't know, but they got married in 1901. I think she must have been twenty-two or twenty-three, somewhere in there.

RA: And he was about twenty-six.

That was kind of old, wasn't it, for that time period? I thought that back then they married much younger, say, sixteen, seventeen.

SC: I suppose. My grandma married at about fourteen or fifteen.

Let's talk about your grandparents on the Bustillos side now. Your grandfather, do you recall what year he was born?

SC: No.

How old was he when he died?

SC: When he died, Grandpa Mingo [Domingo], I think he was sixty-nine, wasn't he? [Directed at RA.]

RA: Yeah, but you have it right here. [Points to the family register.]

SC: He was born April 22, 1845, and he died on May 20, 1917.

And where was he born?

SC: My grandpa? He was born here, at Mission Espada. The Bustillos practically owned all of Espada, and the Huizars, San José.

Did he attend school?

SC: I think he did, but I don't know for sure.

Do you know if he spoke English?

SC: Yes, he did.

What was his occupation? What kind of work did he do?

SC: They were farmers, too. Like I said, they had a lot of land, and they planted corn and beans. They would be at the market, every night, selling their products.

And your grandma, his wife? What was her name?

SC: Eufemia Huizar.

When was she born?

SC: [Refers to the family register.] It was on May 5, 1852, and she died on May 5, 1919. May 5! How she loved to dance on the Cinco de mayo![2]

And then on your mother's side, what is the last name?

SC: My maternal grandfather was Jesús Villalpando Flores. And my grand-mother was Carmen Chávez. She came from among the first families of Canary Islanders to settle here in San Antonio.

Where was [your grandfather] born?

SC: He was born here in San Antonio on May 18, 1834. And he died on January 24, 1925. I think he was ninety-one.

How about your grandmother?

SC: She was also born here in San Antonio: María del Carmen Chávez [refers to the family register], born August 16, 1838. And she died January 30, 1922. They were married March 20, 1854.

So you've done a complete family tree?

RA: Yes.

Are their grandparents listed there as well?

RA: Yes, it goes back to the Floreses: Juan José Flores, who was born in 1804, married to María Virginia Villalpando . . .
SC: That's his father.
RA: Jesús Flores's parents.

And what about Carmen's parents? Who were they?

RA: She was a Carvajal . . . María del Carmen Carvajal Chávez

Did your maternal grandparents speak English?

SC: Ah, yes, my grandmother spoke English, and I think my grandfather, too. A little English. Poorly, but they spoke it.

Susie, is there anyone in your family tree that you can identify with certainty as an Indian?

SC: Not that I know of. Of course, there's no doubt that all branches of the family have more or less of their share of Indian blood, but there is no one that we can identify as a pure-blooded Indian.

Were you baptized here at San José?

SC: No.

Where, then?

SC: At San Fernando Cathedral.

Where did you go to school?

SC: I went to the Morrill School. It used to be on Sayers, but they razed it, and they've built a new one right across the street from where the old one used to be. That was when I was in the seventh grade. In those years, those from the mission, all my brothers and sisters, were in the fourth or fifth grade. And then they moved us all down here, and those in the seventh grade over there. So that I went by myself to that school. Two miles I had to walk to school.

There were no buses back then, were there? And this area wasn't part of the city yet, right?

SC: Oh, no, no; this was just an alley, that's all we had here. But then in the following years, as kids began to pass grades there were more Mexicans in the school. But when I started, the school was exclusively Anglo at first. And, man, did I find discrimination over there! [Laughs.]

You had a hard time?

SC: Well, they didn't want to have nothing to do with me, you know, because I was Mexican. And, that's all. [Laughs.]

But you already knew English?

SC: Oh, yes, we already knew English. From the time we were very small, my mother would teach us English.

So what was your home language, as you were growing up? Was it Spanish or English?

SC: Spanish.

But your mother would still teach you English?

SC: Yes, that's right. My father was very reserved, but my mother was the one who would get us to practice our English. At times we would ask her to teach us Spanish,[3] and she would take a book out and also teach us to read Spanish.

So she was more than a housewife, she was a teacher as well. What else did she teach you? Music?

SC: She taught us how to sing. She sang "La Golondrina" beautifully.

You mentioned before that you all used to live around the mission.

SC: We lived there, we lived near the mission. You know where the church is? And where the bathrooms are, the toilets?[4] Well, right in the back. That was our house, back in there. And my grandma's was next to it. My grandmother lived partly in the granary, and partly in something like that little house that's there. You've seen that little house?

Yes, I have.

SC: Well, my grandma's was right there, one of my grandma's, but it burned down over the years. And then, my father wanted to move over here, to these properties, and he brought over the house that was there.

Because these properties were also his?

SC: Yes. And my grandma told him, "If you're going to take it, be sure not to set it towards the bottom of the riverbank, because you'll always have problems with the water."

Why? Does it flood?

SC: Yes, here, down Bustillos Drive. She said, "Set it on the hill." And that's where he set it, right where it is. This was my grandmother's property—Grandmother Huizar, not Bustillos. The reason they named it Bustillos was because most of her children were men, so when they divided the properties, that one went to Basilio Bustillos, and this one to Francisco, and so on. So that's how this became Bustillos Drive. And it would go down to the river; it curves around the little store, and then it goes where that Kiddieland is. I remember when they took our house from over there and moved it here. It was the second house on Bustillos Road.

I'll never forget when my father was about to move over here. I remember I was five years old.

Were there many people living here in the Bustillos Road area?

SC: No. There was a little house, but they moved it to the back. That was the only house [on the property]—then it was called an alley, el Callejón de Bustillos—but that was the only one. Then, when my Daddy moved the house in 1912, we were the second house on this side.

I don't remember them putting the house on top of something, some wheels, or something, but I remember it coming out, over by where the granary is. And I remember the mules with the house coming out; we were standing there waving it goodbye! Then it got on Mission Road and they brought it over here. It was 1912, so I was five years old, because I was born in 1907. *Ahí venía la casita, y todos diciéndole adiós.* [There came the little house, and everyone was saying goodbye to it.] I don't know how we got it over here . . . maybe in a wagon.

And that house no longer exists?

SC: Just one room. My sister had it, but then she had it remodeled. The room is there, but they added more around it.

You must have had lots of friends, I guess, when you were growing up?

SC: Oh, yes. The entire mission. [Laughs.]

What kinds of games did you all play?

SC: My mother would teach us many games. And we played hide-and-go-seek. Man, did we play hide-and-go-seek. [Laughs.] We'd get stuck with thorns, and we'd just rub them off. Do you know where the theater is now?

Which theater? The drive-in or the amphitheater?

SC: The drive-in. The first thing my mother told us [when we moved here], "I don't want you to go over there, because there is a well, a water well, and if you fall in there, you can drown." I remember we used to play around there. In fact, my sister—her mother [pointing at RA]—got lost there where the theater is. There used to be a lot of huisaches and a lot of brush, *y se perdió. Y Mamá grita y grita: "Donde está Dela?"* [. . . she got lost. And Mother yelled and yelled, "Where is Dela?"] And my mother, I tell you, was frantic. We were screaming and calling her name, until there she was, just as cool as ever! [Laughs.]

And my father used to play where they . . . what's it called, where they process the corn? The mill, where the mill is. Well, he said they used to play there, and dig around in there, but they never knew it had been a mill until the WPA came and dug it out.[5]

Which grandma was this who lived in the granary at San José?

SC: It was Grandma Eufemia Huizar and her husband Domingo Bustillos. They all were born there: my grandmother and her family. And then all of her children: my father, my Uncle Martin, my Uncle José, all of them. And until recently I still had a cousin who had been born there, but he passed away about three years ago. Jesús Chávez; he was the last one.

But every time my mother was going to have a child, and she had eight, she'd go over to her mother's house in town. And we'd ask her why she hadn't stayed at the mission, because we'd have liked to have been born in the granary. She said, "No, no. I didn't want you being born underneath all those rocks; there's nothing but rocks at that place." And she didn't like that; she was a town girl.

Then your relatives were still residing in the galera after you moved here?

SC: At the *galera?* I remember one of my uncles still lived there, and I remember somehow there was a second story. There were stairs on the side, you know, and I used to see him going up. That's why I can tell you that. And my mother would say, "Don't go into the *galera!*" But we wanted to see, because we saw him going up the stairs; he lived up there.

Why didn't she like you playing in there? Because it was too dangerous?

SC: Too many rocks. She was afraid they'd fall over. But that's where my grandmother got married, in the granary. That was the homestead of the Huizars.

RA: She had her reception there, right?

SC: Yes.

RA: She got married at the mission church.

SC: Yes, she was married in the church, and they had their reception at the granary, and it's always been said in the family that they danced till dawn. God! It must've been a big wedding inasmuch as both the Huizars and the Bustillos were well off . . . , you know, because the Huizars owned nearly all of this [gestures widely with her hands to encompass her neighborhood]! This is Huizar land, and the Bustillos owned Espada.

So, when they secularized the mission and redistributed the land, the Huizars were awarded the granary and some other plots, isn't that so? The land was divided among those that were still living there?

SC: Yes, that was theirs. That was their homestead, but the granary was given to Antonio Huizar because of services that his father, Pedro Huizar, had rendered. That's the reason they gave him the granary when he asked for some land.

He requested this from the Mexican government, right?

SC: Yes.

So that members of the Huizar family lived there continuously right up until the early 1920s?

SC: My grandmother was still living there, and I remember that when my grandfather died, we got to sleep with Grandmother while we were at Grandpa Mingo's vigill [Laughs.] *Pero yá viviamos acá.* [But we already lived over here.] So I remember the granary, and they had a beautiful fireplace where you could see the coffee pots . . . *pués grandotes, porque la gente de antes venían al velorio toda la noche a tomar café.* [. . . great big ones, because in those days people came to the wake and stayed all night drinking coffee.] That I do remember. And the people were arriving from all over the place.

RA: Did they have him there . . . in the kitchen?

SC: No, they didn't have him there in the granary; they had him in the little house. And when the hearse came . . . well, they didn't have much to do, just take him from the house and into the church. That was it. But then, they put him in the hearse. They had money, on account of the properties they had. It was a beautiful hearse drawn by beautiful horses that were kind of gray. They put him in there, and it was glass, so you could see inside. And they started to go to the cemetery. You've been to our little cemetery?

No, I haven't. How many people lived in the granary aside from your grandmother?

SC: It was just them. I don't know if my Aunt Juanita lived there in some rooms. And Escalera, he was an adopted son, lived there, too. My grandmother lived in one part, and Aunt Juanita and Escalera lived in another. And then they all moved. They built a house on the side, but they still had part of the granary; there where they [now have the model that tells the story of the mission], that part was her kitchen. They still kept two rooms over there for the kitchen, and she had a table, and a lot of food. There were steps, because it was a two-story arrangement, and when one of my uncles moved, he lived upstairs. He was the last one to live in the granary.

But when my grandmother lived there, they didn't sleep there anymore. They slept in the little house that they made on the side, but they had their kitchen over at the granary. They still kept two rooms for the kitchen.

Was the mission church still being used when your grandmother lived there?

SC: Oh yes, grandmother was married there. And she remembered when it [the dome] fell. It was 1874, when my father was born. She said it was after the Christmas Eve mass. It rained and rained, and she said all of a sudden, after midnight, they heard something, and that's when the dome fell. So she got to see that.

You've seen pictures of when the dome fell, haven't you? Yes, inside. Well, I saw when they were working on the [reconstruction of the] church. They had big posts, you know, iron and all, where they were rebuilding the dome. And my cousins, Domingo Bustillos and Leopoldo Bustillos—they passed away, both of them—they were working for the WPA. Many men did in those days, and those two cousins also.

My cousin Leopoldo used to sit right here where you're sitting. And he would tell me this story: He said when they were building the tower here in the church—you know where the lights are? The lights we have in the church?—anyway, he said Domingo was working up there, and he slipped and was left hanging there on the scaffolding. [All laugh.] And he said Domingo looked down from up there and said [assumes a mock-dramatic voice], "Leopoldo, pleeease!" [Laughs.]

And whenever I go to church now, I look up, and I can imagine him swinging up there! [Laughs.] Poor soul is dead now!

How has the mission changed since you were a little girl?

SC: Well, there was a *cerca*, a fence, by the church. And [pointing to a photograph], you see these little fences here? I remember that, because that's all cemetery, all of it [cemetery] grounds. Juan Huizar, he's the one that's buried there. He used to tell them that he wanted to be buried near the church. Of course, the others are buried there, too.

He would pray to Our Lady of Guadalupe every time he would go on a business trip to the coast, or to get things from Laredo. He would kneel in front of Our Lady of Guadalupe, and he asked for him to have a safe trip. And he would say, "I will be here giving you thanks when I get back." And he said he wanted to be buried there. *Viene siendo mi abuelo materno.* [He was my maternal grandfather.]

When I was a kid, we'd go to rosary at the mission. Back then there was a lot of boys around. One night, one of 'em said, "Say, do you want to see some skeletons?"

I said, "Yeah, I want to see some skeletons." That was when they were digging around the church.

After the dome had fallen, they buried people in there, inside the church. My grandma would tell my daddy that when cholera struck, as soon as anyone complained they would be bundled up and they would put them there, in the church. Anyway, when that boy asked me, we said, "Yeah, we want to see some skeletons."

So he said, "Okay, some of you watch for the priests, for Father Bonaventure, because he'll be here to say the rosary after a while. And the girls and the boys that want to come see the skeletons, come on this way. But if the priest comes, you come running and tell us." [Laughs.]

Do you know where the sacristy is, and the door that leads into the main part of the church? Well, we got in the sacristy, went through the sacristy and into the church. And he said, "I've got some matches here, come and see!" There were two skeletons there, and they were huge!

And I can still see them so plainly! [Laughs.] That's why I sometimes pray for them at night. [Laughs.] They were like this: [indicates arms crossed over the chest]! And you know how these bones are [points to her forearms]? There was dirt in between the bones, you know, nothing but bone and dirt.

That was during the time when they were restoring?

SC: Yes, during the restoring. And later, I asked the priest, "What did they do with them, Father?"

"Oh," he said, "Tommy Borland and I, we took them out, Susie, and we gave them a nice burial. We took out the bones, and put 'em there, in front of where the crosses are, right there."

As you were growing up, the walls around the mission compound didn't exist, right?

SC: I got to see some rooms right here [pointing at a plan of the present mission compound].

View of the interior of Mission San José, looking through the door toward the altar, during the WPA reconstruction of the early 1930s. The roof has collapsed, and the north wall is missing. Courtesy of the The Institute of Texan Cultures, San Antonio, *The San Antonio Light* Collection.

In the middle, more or less, of the west wall.

SC: But they were already falling apart.

So, none of these walls was standing; I'm referring to the west, south, and east walls of the compound?

SC: No. I just saw part of this west wall. One could see big rocks there.

RA: She has told me before that there was a well.

SC: Yes, there was a well; that's where we got the water. My mother used to go over there and carry it to wash. Then my uncles built the one that was near the house, the little rock house. [Refers on the plan to the area north of the present gift shop.] They really built it deep.

Did they line it? Build it with rocks?

SC: Oh, yes. I don't know anymore what you call that, but I used to know what you call it in Spanish, you know, when they line it with rocks. We used to have a well here, at the back of my sister's house on Bustillos Drive. The uncles made it, too, and it was a good well. I bet you it still would have water if we would clean it.

RA: Oh yes, all of us used to get water from there. [Laughs.]

Did anyone live over there, towards that side?

SC: Oh, yes, there were houses right here. And there was also a school. I remember seeing the school. Let's see: this is the entrance over here, right?

The present one.

SC: This is the visitors entrance. Well, the school was about right here [pointing to an area at the southwest quad, about one hundred feet east of the west wall and about fifty feet north of the south one]. My oldest brother went to school there. I remember that Sara Huizar would come, you know, to help my mother, and my mother had my brother all ready—white shirt and all—to go to school, and she'd come and take him. We were all standing on the porch, and I could see her taking him to the little school. It was a white building.

RA: She's told me that her father, that would be Francisco Bustillos, used to tell her that they went to school in the granary, that there was a Fabiana Huizar, one of the young girls, that taught them school in the granary.

SC: That must have been before the school I saw. The first school we had here was in the granary. And I think Elogia was also a teacher.

RA: And, even after they moved, they used to spend a lot of time over there, because they would go to church a lot, and then they would visit the grandparents.

The school that you recall: you didn't get to go to that school, did you?

SC: No, no, when we moved over here to Bustillos Drive, I was five years old, but I remember it very well.

Do you remember if it was set on the ground, or if it was on cedar posts?

SC: It was on cedar posts. It was a wood frame house, and the door wasn't facing the granary; it was on the other side.

And do you have any idea who taught there, or who was in charge of it?

SC: Well, the first teacher who taught in the granary was Fabiana Huizar. But then, when they made this school, I think there was a lady, Miss Poor, you know; she lived on Hart Street.

I'm trying to get a feel for the community at San José. It sounds like it was pretty tightly knit, that everybody knew each other.

SC: Oh yes, yes. And there were a lot of relatives. The school was for all the children of the mission.

Do you remember if it was run by the state, or the city, or the church?

SC: I don't know, but it was a pretty good school. And Cornelio would go with a shirt, whiter than snow. [Laughs.]

And Mission Road ran all the way through what is now the compound?

SC: Yes.

Was it paved? Did it have blacktop?

SC: Yes. it had blacktop, asphalt.

What about Pyron Road?

SC: Pyron Road didn't have asphalt. It was like gravel, when I lived there.

Do you remember who lived in the houses at the mission?

SC: The houses when I lived there? The Guerreros, lots of Guerreros. [Looking at a map of the mission.] Oh yes, the houses. Where do you want to start? We'll start at the granary, you know, *la muralla* [the wall]. There were the Hornegas, but they were newcomers. There was Don Felipe Guerrero here where the entrance is, and there was Don Eduardo Guerrero, Santana, all of the Guerreros.

RA: And Claude?

SC: No, *el papá de Claude* [Claude's father] . . . They all used to live here. Because one of them got married to a Huizar, I think.

RA: One of the Guerreros?

SC: Yes, that's how come they got the property. But when the government, the WPA came, [they all had to move out].

So the Guerreros lived along the south and east walls?

SC: Yes. There was also Venegas, who used to live there. When they bought that land for the reconstruction, Venegas didn't want to sell, but the state condemned it, and he had to leave.

He lived right around the middle of the west wall?

SC: Yeah. You could see the little house that had been left there all by itself; he had to take it out. But Venegas, he didn't want to go out. His little house was still there, and he was mean! He finally had to move out, and that's when he built that pretty house that burned not long ago on Mission Road.

Did you marry there at the church at San José?

SC: No, I didn't. I got married, my first time, at Perpetual Help, because that's where the priests were. [Laughs.] The priests wouldn't come here all the time, so oftentimes we'd have to go wherever they were.

So Chávez is your married name?

SC: My maiden name is Bustillos, and I married—in just a little while I'll tell you something that will make you laugh— and I married a Chávez in Mexico, but he's no relative of ours. We are Chávez from my grandma, who was among those that came from the Canary Islands. And this Chávez that I married came from San Martín Hidalgo. A very good man, but he was no relative, you know.

And where did you meet him? Here in San Antonio?

SC: Yes, I met him here, at the dances. I didn't want to have nothing to do with people from Mexico. Oh my! [Laughs.] I had had a boyfriend from Monterrey, and, oh, he was a good-looking guy! He owned a factory that made combs over there, and he wanted to get married with me. He was already coming to speak to my father and mother. And Dad said, "I'm telling you, if he's from Mexico, I don't want him here!" [Laughs.]

So I had to tell him no. And his family was about to come over from over there. So I didn't get married.

I married another man, and I had bad luck with him. But then I married Arturo Chávez . . . and he was from Mexico, too! I told Daddy, "Daddy, he is from Mexico."

And he said, "Well, he doesn't look like he's from Mexico. He's got his ways from here. He's a good man! You marry him, if you want to." [All laugh.]

So he looked like a Tejano? [All laugh.] What did you do when you were dating?

SC: Oh, we'd go to the Nacional. We loved that! And we'd go to dances. Oh gosh, we'd dance all night.

The Nacional? You're talking about the movie theater?

SC: Yeah, and there was another one, but I can't think of the name.

RA: But where were the dances you frequented?

SC: I used to go on Losoya Street, to the Ponsiano; that was a big one. And a dance hall that was close to the river over here, from Hart Avenue on in. That also was a big one! And then, this one that used to be there at the mission, by the entrance that's there now. There used to be a big hall there.

Is that the one that belonged to the Guerreros?

SC: Yes, we went there. We could hear the music all the way over here. Gosh!

What kind of music did they play?

SC: Jazz music! Horns and . . .

Big bands?

SC: Oh yeah, big bands.

RA: And didn't the Guerreros have a dance hall there?

SC: Yes, at the entrance, where we go in now. Yes, a big one. It was beautiful. At first there was just a small one, a very small dance hall. And Santana Guerrero and his wife Ester, she played the piano and he the violin. And oh! [laughs], we were at it all night!

It was music nonetheless.

SC: Yeah, we loved it, and it made us happy!

RA: She's told me she remembers about the acequia they used to have to cross to go to the grandmother's house.

What was the acequia like?

SC: *Como un riíto chiquito* [like a little river] . . . The boundary line was the acequia.

RA: But the one you used to have to cross to go see your grandmother . . . ?

SC: It was right there at the back, near where old lady [Ethel] Harris built her house, near the theater. I think it's the same one that goes to the mill, that carried the water for them to grind the corn.

Was the mill still operating?

SC: No, and I don't think at Daddy's time either. He said they used to play in that area and they would dig up bricks and things. When the WPA came, that's when [the mill was reconstructed].

And in those days when you were growing up, what was the acequia used for? Did the people use it for irrigation?

SC: No, because they had wells right near their house. My father, they used to have a farm at Espada. They would plant corn and beans, and, during the time of the crops, they would take it to the market. Every night they would come with wagons full of corn, and all the people from the mission would stop them and buy corn. Then, they used to take it at one o'clock in the morning to the market, and I remember him coming home with his pockets full of money . . . *bastante dinero* [quite a lot of money]. He never did work for nobody. He either farmed or received rents from his property.

Of course, right here on Bustillos Drive, when we first moved, it was all corn, beautiful corn on both sides. But the good farm was near Espada, because that one had the irrigation ditch.

What else grew in the area?

SC: We had green beans, and my daddy used to hire people to help him; he paid so much a bushel. One time we told him, "We don't want you to hire [anybody else], we're going [to do the work]." And they had just irrigated, and with the heat, all of a sudden I saw black, and I fainted! And my dad said, "See, that's why I don't want you all around here!"

We got a little money, but... never again. He didn't want us; he'd hire other people. The work is too hard when you're not used to it. The cotton was south of us.

RA: Did you ever pick cotton?

SC: No, but if you want to lose weight, [that's the kind of work to do]! [All laugh.] It really gets your back. I remember my sister Lena would put down her sack of cotton and lay on it and complain, "Oh, my back!" That was a hard job.

How active were you with the church when you were growing up?

SC: Well, we used to go to catechism; my mother always sent us to catechism. All of us. I made my First Holy Communion in the sacristy. That's where we used to have Mass [when I was a girl].

Were there any nuns there when you were going through catechism?

SC: No, a father. Some priests would come: Father Hector and some other priests would come from Perpetual Help. But that's all. And Mass ... when I was small, they would only have Mass every other Sunday. We didn't have Mass every Sunday. We were too far out of town; we were in the wilderness! [Laughs.]

What year would that have been?

SC: Well, I must have been seven, eight years old when I made my first Holy Communion, so that was in 1915, 1916, or thereabouts.

So there were no priests who were at the mission [on a permanent basis] at that time?

SC: No. The priests, like I said, Father Weiner and them, they used to come from Perpetual Help. But when my grandmother was there, the priests were different. They came from that building for the priests at Concepción [St. John's Seminary]. *Venían los padres* [The priests came] and they gave first communion and married all the ones who were not married. Where the rose garden is now, I remember them crying out: *Vénganse todos: los que no están casados, se van a casar.* ... [Everybody come here: we're going to marry the ones who are not married yet.]

RA: When did you have Mass? Wasn't it every Sunday?

SC: No, we had it every other Sunday. Like, when my son was born, I lived in Elmendorf, *iba a llegar el obispo, e iba a hacer barrida... a hacer bautismos y confirmaciones* [the bishop was coming, and he was going to do a big sweep: baptisms, confirmations, etc.], so my son was baptized when he was only fifteen days old and confirmed at the same time! *De una vez todo!* [Everything at once!]

Then some years later, when I came home from school, I taught catechism there; I'd ring the bell, so that the entire mission community would come! [Laughs.]

You used to teach catechism when you were in middle school?

SC: Yes, and we used to sing in the choir. Did you see the organ on this old photo? In 1923 we had this *gringa* playing the organ. She would pump it down below, and the choir would be singing and singing.

And my sister Elena said to me, "Go tell her that we want to sing in the choir!"

And I said, "No, you tell her, you're the oldest!" But Elena never wanted to be the first. So I went and said, "Miss Flack, we wanna sing in the choir."

And she said: "Well girls, sure! How many?" And it was all of us! We were . . . what? Five sisters! So, from there we started to belong to the choir.

Did you sing in English or Spanish?

RA: In Latin, right?

SC: Oh yeah, I can sing you the whole Mass in Latin.

Oh, I forgot about that. [All laugh.]

RA: When the priests gave you the homily, was it all in English?

SC: They gave it in both: Spanish, and a little English. One time, one of the fathers, Father Eustace, he was young and just starting as a priest. And he said, "Remember that during Lent, you don't have to eat a whole lot. In the morning, don't eat more than one *hueso!*" He said, "don't eat more than a bone," when he meant to say a *huevo*—egg! [Laughs.]We just broke up! Well, he kept on going, and, after Mass, once we were outside, he said, "Susie, come over here. Why were you all laughing?" So I told him. He said, "Oh my goodness, I hope they don't start eating bones." [All laugh.] Poor soul, he always remembered that. Oh, that Father Eustace!

When did the church become active?

SC: Oh, it didn't become active, really active, until '30, '31, when the Franciscan fathers came.

When they built their house?

SC: Yes, otherwise they would have to bring them in from Perpetual Help or from where the priests are schooled, next to Concepción.

RA: Saint John's Seminary.

SC: Yes, we didn't have no priests around here. But now we have a wonderful priest: Father Arturo Ocampo. You don't know him? Oh, you should meet him.

RA: Father Arturo comes into the family through the Bustillos.

SC: But you ought to hear his sermons! Other priests, and much older, too, I see them recite from notes. Not him! He doesn't use any notes. He gives a sermon . . . [claps her hands in admiration]! I wish you could come and hear him.

When did you start getting involved in the church? I think you said you were part of some committee . . .

SC: Oh yeah, that's when I was older, though. That was in 1970, but I've always been at the mission, with the priests and everything. [Laughs.]

RA: They had the Madres Club, and she was the president at that time.

SC: Oh well, they had the Altar Society, you know, and they were *gringas*. And then Maria Rivas said, "Susie, let's join; let's tell them we want to join the Altar Society."

So I said, "Go and tell them!"

And when she told one of them, she said, "Oh, no, we don't want no Spanish in our Altar Society." So we decided to create our own, and we went to Father Felician, and we told him: "Father, this and this happened, so we want to . . . ."

And he told us, "Go ahead, girls, start your own." And it was the Madres Club that we founded.

What year was that?

SC: That was in '42, I think. And we had a *jamaica*, a spring festival fund-raiser, and they had another *jamaica*. . . . [Laughs.]

Who made the most money? [All laugh.]

SC: Oh, we built that little room that they still use for the San Vicente de Paola. We built that, with the money that we raised. Then Miss Luna said that she had talked to some of the ladies from the other society, and, after some time, they began saying we should join them. So I finally went in and joined the other society. But, I belonged to the Madres first.

RA: And she used to teach summer school also. Remember the summer school that you used to teach?

SC: Oh, it wasn't just summer school. It was a little school that I started. [Laughs.]

You started a school? When was this?

SC: I think it was in 1933, somewhere around in there.

And where were classes held?

SC: At my house, my mother's house. And all the fathers of the kids from the mission brought them over by car. In fact, I went to a fiftieth wedding anniversary Saturday, and when the wife was a little girl, she didn't know how to write her name, and I taught her, and she always remembers. She says, "Susie, you're the one that taught me how to write my name."

More recently, I also used to belong to the Old Spanish Missions Committee. When we started in the Old Spanish Missions Committee, we didn't have nothing at the church. Father Lambert came, and he said, "I'm gonna ask for six things for this mission." First thing he asked for was an air conditioning system, and it's true that the bishop installed it. He paid for it; I don't know how many thousands of dollars. Then he asked for a little room for Our Lady of Guadalupe. Then, he said we needed the walkways paved with something.

And those *viejas* [old ladies] started out, "Well, we want to see the color of the bricks that are going to be used on the walk!" Oh, those *viejas* gave the poor priest such a hard time! [All laugh.]

What *viejas* are you talking about?

SC: The ones from the Conservation Society. Yeah, and he asked for the Angelus bells, and he got 'em all. But we used to go to the meetings, which were far away, and poor Father Manuel, the *viejas* were very mean to him, very mean.

Do you remember Los Pastores here?[6]

SC: I was the Gila [one of the characters in the play] when I was a little girl!

RA: You weren't with the ones from Guadalupe?

SC: No, no, no. I was with the Guerreros, Bustillos, and Huizars.

RA: Did the Guadalupe ones come later?

SC: The Guadalupe ones started just seven years ago. No, we had this when
I was . . . let's see . . . I think I was fourteen years old. Ah, they were
good Pastores. Ay, I wish you could have heard them. And they had a
Guerrero girl singing. My brother, you know, Johnny, he was in it, too.
You know, *todos misioneros* [all from the mission].

One of my brothers told them, "If you want a good singer, you should get
my sister."

So one night . . . oh, it was cold . . . they came to our door, and they said
"Francisco,"—that was my father—"we hear that you have a girl that
knows how to sing, and we have five other girls . . ."

I was listening, and I thought, "Oh, boy, this is going to be good!" And there
were two or three boys my size, *y el ángel era Daniel Ayala* [and the angel
was Daniel Ayala].

And I used to go everywhere with them. Now they have too many girls in
the Pastores, and I don't like that. [In my day,] they were not girls, they
were men, and the only girl character was the Gila. And the Señora
Guerrero had the book, and when I was working with the pottery, she
came by and said, "Susie, it's *you* I'm going to leave this book to." So I
used to sit until one, two o'clock in the morning copying it, but there's
no telling what they've done with that book.

RA: Where did you have the Pastores when you were little?

SC: Wherever they called us! We were on call! [Laughs.] We went to San
Juan, we went to Espada, here at the mission [San José] in the sacristy,
and many other places. My uncle was the *padrino* who went with us, and
the roosters *empezaron a cantar, y nosotros todavía estábamos de camino*
[started crowing, and we still were on the way] until seven o'clock in
the morning. And from there we went to church. I remember sitting at
the Mass and falling asleep, *y empezé a soñar de gallinas* [and I started to
dream about chickens], but when I opened my eyes, I was in church!
[All laugh.] And they had such a beautiful *nacimiento* [manger scene]!

RA: And the Posadas? [7]

SC: No, we didn't have Posadas.

RA: But in *abuelito's* (grandfather's) time they did, didn't they?

SC: Yes, then they had Posadas. They started at the mission at eleven o'clock at night, and since we were the last house, we could hear the singing all the way as they came closer. And then, Felipe Guerrero would yell at our door, *"Oiga, Francisco, levántense."* [Hey, at Francisco's house, get up!]

And my dad used to tell us, *"Si vienen a cantar aquí, ustedes se callan la boca; no vayan a abrir ni puerta ni ventana!"* [If they come to sing here, you all keep your mouths shut; don't open any doors or windows!]

When did Los Pastores start in your parish?

SC: I don't know exactly, but the Guerreros and the Huizars started it. Probably when my mother was young. I liked them better than the ones from Guadalupe.

NOTES

1. The only Spanish use of *galera* that would seem to apply here would be in the synonyms of the words *tinglado* and *cobertizo*. Both are defined as a covered passage, a hovel, or a roofed area to provide shelter from the rain.

2. Cinco de mayo is a Mexican national holiday commemorating the battle of Puebla in 1862, during which the Mexican forces defeated the French army, an event that led to the ending of French intervention in Mexico.

3. As did many mission children, SC and her siblings knew Spanish only as a spoken language.

4. In the reconstructed Mission San José compound, restrooms are in a section of the wall near the church.

5. The Works Projects Administration (WPA), a Depression-era public works program, did archeological work at Mission San José and reconstructed the mission church and compound.

6. La Pastorela is a traditional Christmas play, originally lasting some five hours in performance but often presented in abridged versions. It depicts the efforts of the shepherds at Bethlehem to find the manger, the scene of the Nativity, and the actions of a variety of evil characters to prevent them from doing so. Since the shepherds are the main characters, the play is also referred to as Los Pastores.

Los Pastores at Guadalupe church started in 1913 under the leadership of Don Leandro Granado, who came to San Antonio from the Mexican state of Guanajuato. The group started performing at San José in the 1950s, sponsored by the Conservation Society.

7. Posadas refers to the traditional reenactment of Joseph and Mary's search for lodging in Bethlehem. The participants, whether members of a congregation or simply residents of a particular neighborhood, go to a different home on each of the nine evenings preceding Christmas, often with people representing Joseph and Mary leading the group, ask for lodging—*posada*—and are turned down. Singing accompanies this tradition, as does the praying of either a novena or the rosary. The observance culminates with the Misa de Gallo, the "Cock's Crow Mass" or Midnight Mass on Christmas Eve, when the couple finally gets the lodging they seek at the manger in Bethlehem.

Claude Guerrero

Claude Guerrero, *seventy-seven years old, is the same Claude Guerrero mentioned in Susie Chávez's interview. Mr. Guerrero was born at Mission San José, was raised there, and lived in the mission neighborhood until 1986. A quiet-spoken man, he now resides in south San Antonio, near I-35 South and Somerset Road. This interview took place on July 19, 1995.*

What can you tell me about your parents?

They were born in the latter part of the nineteenth century, about 1893-94.

And were they local people?

Yes, born and raised here, and so were my grandparents.

So you're a third-generation San Antonian, or does it go further back?

Oh, it goes back much further. My daughter has traced back the family history, and it goes as far as the 1700s.

What kind of work did your father do?

My father was an aviation mechanic. Later on, in World War II, he worked at Kelly Field. He started out as an auto mechanic. He was the driver for the first automobile that was bought to bring tourists from the train station to the Hot Wells Hotel. There were no mechanics at that time, so he had to learn to fix the car.

But, in essence, he must have taught himself, because at that time there were no trade schools where one could learn auto mechanics.

Yes, he taught himself, and in fact, at that time there were not too many tools available, so he had to make do.

Well, I can understand automobile mechanics, but how did he get into aviation mechanics?

According to what he told me, a motor is a motor, except that in aviation the gasoline used is higher octane, and I supposed he learned it like he learned to work with cars. He worked at Stinson Field.

How many children in your family?

We were three boys. I'm the oldest, and then there were George and Arthur. They're still living, but they're in poor health. We didn't get much education, because we grew up during the Depression, and we had to go out and get whatever work we could to help the family. I even ended up in Arizona in 1936, working in a CCC [Civilian Conservation Corps, another Depression-era agency] camp.

Where in Arizona were you?

In Winkelman. It's about eighty miles northeast of Tucson. It was gila monster and rattlesnake country!

What kind of a project were you working on?

We worked on erosion control, and also fixing highways. At that time they were just gravel roads. Nothing as romantic as a national park!

When did you leave school?

After the fifth grade. I was supposed to go [through] high school, but during the summer I started working around the Harlandale area, doing yard work and anything that came up. One time I mopped a kitchen for twenty-five cents [laughs], but twenty-five cents was a lot of money in those days. People today don't know the value of a dollar. It was hard to find work. I even worked at Mission Cemetery and did lots of different kinds of work.

Did you do that until you retired, or did you end up doing some other kind of work?

No, I went to truck driving, working for lumberyards, and eventually I found myself in the Navy during the war. I never expected that. Everybody was usually drafted into the Army, but the Navy. . . . They asked me what I wanted to do, and I said the Army, but when they finished with my papers, they said, "Navy!"

You probably had never seen much water except for the San Antonio River until then, had you?

I had never seen a ship before, except perhaps in the movies; had never seen one that I could stand there and look at. But I found myself on a big aircraft carrier in the Pacific.

And how long were you in the Navy?

A little over two years—two years and about nineteen days, something like that. Just until the war ended. I was married already. My daughter was seventeen months old when I was drafted. But that didn't make much difference to them.

After the war ended, I came back to San Antonio and started over again. That "cruise" in the Pacific was something unexpected. My old ship is now in Corpus Christi, the "Lexington"; it was involved in eleven battles. Every time I go there, I go and visit it.

What can you tell me about growing up near the mission?

I was born about three hundred feet from the church, and that neighborhood was my home until 1986. Then I lived in a house about one hundred feet from where the wall is now. [Looks at a map of the mission grounds today and points to a spot along the Roosevelt Avenue wall.] I had an uncle who had a bar about here.

The church was in ruins then, but what we called the chapel, the sacristy, was intact, and that's where we used to go to church, just off where the altar is today. And back here there used to be a pottery.

The house where we lived later was owned by a man called Venegas, and the reason it was there was that he refused to sell and move out. He held out for a long time; he would sit in there with a rifle. Later my dad bought a property that eventually ended up on Roosevelt Avenue and Huizar Road. I don't know what year it was when we moved.

Did your parents own the house, or were they renting?

That house they were renting from Mr. Venegas.

Tell me more about what was left of the mission buildings when you were growing up. Was the granary standing?

The granary walls were intact; they were standing, but the roof had caved in. At night we would go in there and sing and talk, and in the winter, we would set a tire on fire for warmth. The property belonged to a man named Sauceda, and he had a fence built around it. He later sold it to the city or to the Conservation Society. In fact, you've seen that display that's in the granary now? That model? Well, that model used to be right outside the granary. I don't know where it came from.

Did Sauceda use the granary for anything?

No, but he used to own a lot of property all over San Antonio. He was well off. And the property from there to where Roosevelt Avenue is used to belong to the Reyes family. I think Sauceda was related to the Reyes in some way.

Many people in the neighborhood were related to each other. I had five uncles: Eduardo, Felipe, Mariano, José, and Jorge Santana, and they all had children. And I had an Aunt Lucía, too, but she died. She was walking in front of the church carrying a watermelon, and she dropped dead.

There was also the Pacheco family, Bustillos, Guerrero, Venegas, Hernandez, Vallejo, and there was a lady who came from Mexico. There was a man named Sánchez who owned a service station, and the Casillas family, and some Mireles. There was also a Stewart family.

So the neighborhood was mostly Hispanic, but there were some Anglos, too?

Yes, there were some other Anglos. O'Neil Ford used to own a house near where they have the *charreadas* [Mexican-style rodeo] today, out Padre Drive. It was a small community, maybe a hundred people, but we all knew each other. We had the usual entertainments, you know, ball games and such, and there used to be a dance hall behind my grandmother's house. A lot of people used to go there on a Saturday night.

What do you remember of the condition of the church at that time?

The only part that was used was the chapel, where we had Mass. We used to have a priest come out from St. Gerard's on weekends. The church had no roof. I believe it was in 1925 when part of the tower fell down.

When I was young, they had a long cable rigged from the bell to a tree near the west side of the granary, and you pulled on the cable to ring the bell.

But, wait a second, usually in a church like that you can ring the bell from inside the church or, at least, inside the tower.

Well, not here. I don't know why that was. It was a real big bell. When it rang you could hear it all the way to Hot Wells. The people claimed that it had gold that had been melted into it, that people had put in rings and whatever they had to contribute to the bell. Anyway, sometimes, when they pulled too hard, the bell would flip over, and someone had to go up there and turn it around again. If any of us was around, they'd give us five cents to climb up there and do it.

There was a wooden circular stairway that went partway up, and from there the steps continued on the sides of the tower, and then when you got to the top there was a space where you could climb through. But you had to be careful when you did it, because there was no railing or nothing to hold on to. You would grab hold of the bell and push it, and once it was halfway over, you'd let it loose. But we were young, and we'd take our chances.

One incident I remember concerned my Uncle José, who used to be the caretaker at the church. Then, they removed him and named another man by the name of Tom Teague, who took over. Anyway, the culture had the tradition—and they still do it—of ringing the bell in what they called a *doble*, two times [to announce a funeral]. Of course, Teague didn't know anything about the traditions, because he was not from the mission community. So, when somebody died, my uncle went out and started ringing the bells in the usual way, but old man Teague came out mad, because my uncle was interfering. They argued and argued, but they couldn't understand what the other one was saying, so they finally ended up fighting! Finally they had to explain to the man what to expect, so there wouldn t be any more trouble.

Where did this Teague come from?

He used to live out on Napier Road.

But how did he get the job?

I think the bishop used to give it to one person and then the other. They used to charge for tourists who wanted to visit the church. They used to have what they called a *carretela*, a truck with a high bed and seats built on it, and it was used to bring tourists out to the mission. They used to come from downtown. There weren't too many of them at that time. Certainly nothing like what we have now. Cornelio Bustillos told me that that money was used to help the poor widows in the community.

At that time there were a lot of gardens around the mission, and up to the south side and down to where the Mission Drive-In Theater is now, there used to be an Italian family that employed a lot of people growing vegetables: cabbages, carrots, and things like that.

When you were growing up, was the acequia still functioning?

No. They used to irrigate the fields in that area where the Mission Drive-In is, but they did that with pumps.

What about the convento, where the archways are today— was that area used for anything?

No, it was all in ruins, just like it is today. I don't know why they never did put a roof over it. You know, the old-timers never used to talk too much, and when we were children, we were supposed to be quiet and not to ask questions.

And you couldn't see any traces of walls or other structures?

Just in one place. [Shows on the map.] Right here, where the main entrance tower is today. Some of the Casillas used to live there, and they used a corner of what must have been a building. They had a fireplace in there. But I don't remember whatever happened to it. That must have been

Musicians lead the congregational singing at Mission San José's traditional Sunday mariachi Mass in this photo taken on October 1, 1989. The mariachi Mass continues to be the mission's most popular weekly religious event. The church is usually packed for it, and, after the Mass, the musicians entertain parishioners and guests in the adjoining convento garden. Courtesy of the The Institute of Texan Cultures, San Antonio.

around 1927 or something like that, but all of a sudden, I don't remember it being there anymore. It must have fell down, or something must have happened.

How long did you live in the mission neighborhood?

That was from when I was born until 1986. I don't know how many years that is. And my Dad lived there all his life; when he died, he was seventy-two.

What happened when the reconstruction project began with the WPA in the '30s?

What happened was that they bought up property. Like my grandmother. She used to live [inside today's compound], and she ended up over here, across from where people park today. My Uncle Felipe and my Uncle Eduardo ended up nearby. Emilio and the others were over on Napier Road. The Mireles and Pachecos also had to move, and some of them kept that property until two years ago. The people who had to move didn't get any money, just another house in exchange.

So, in essence, what they did was trade you property outside what became the mission compound for what you had owned before?

Yes, but later they bought people out outright.

How did the people feel about this having to move?

Well, nobody complained very much. Of course, the people believed that that was their place, because they were the last ones left there.

People weren't too happy about moving, but they moved nonetheless?

Yes, you'd hear somebody complain once in a while, but nothing organized. But anyway, they stayed in the neighborhood. A lot of people might say: why move all those people from there? But it takes a lot of money to preserve that mission, and the church couldn't do it.

When you were a kid, was there a regular priest at the mission?

No. The priests from St. Gerard's used to come over and have Mass or CCD [Catholic Christian Doctrine] classes, First Communions, or whatever else the congregation needed, but they were not there all the time.

So you had all the activities of a congregation right there; you didn't need to go elsewhere for anything.

No, they used to come in the afternoon, when we were out of school. I remember when the Franciscans came; I think it was around 1938 or a bit before that, but by then the reconstruction was done and the stone walls were up. A lot of the people who live in the area now are people who came in after the war from places like Floresville and others nearby. But some of the relatives of the old families still live on Bustillos Drive.

Anita Bustillos Rivera

Anita Bustillos Rivera *is now ninety years old. Although she grew up in the Mission San Juan and Mission Espada communities, she is connected to Mission San José in several ways. For one, she is related to Susie Chávez and her Bustillos clan. For another, she is the grandmother of Father Arturo Ocampo, the current parish priest at San José. Although she has had medical problems since she was first interviewed, she remains lively and strong of will. She lives with her daughter in south San Antonio between I-35 South and Nogalitos Street. Mrs. Rivera was first interviewed by Richard Flores in June 1994. Luis Torres did a follow-up on August 23, 1995. The interview was conducted in Spanish; it was transcribed and translated by Luis Torres.*

Do you know where your ancestors came from?

Well, on my father's side, his grandparents came from Madrid. They brought them here from Spain to work. We once had an argument about whether the Huizars or the Bustillos had come first. Some said one and some the other, but I don't know for sure.

How old were you when you lived near the missions?

I must have been around twelve years old. We moved into my grandfather's house when he died. My father worked for the county; he was a cook. I made my First Communion at Mission San Juan when I was thirteen or fourteen. The mission then had a lot of *nogales*,[1] but today it has none. I went to school at Mission Espada.

Where was your house located?

At San Juan it was at a place called Arroyo de la Piedra [Stone Creek], where there was a bridge [that went over the creek], but the creek does not exist anymore, because it has been covered over. Just before you went over the bridge to Espada, there was a little hill where an aunt of mine lived, and we lived just a short way beyond that.

Between the river and the little rise where our house was, there was an acequia. From there we went on foot to the Catholic school at Espada, which must have been about three miles, I believe. Sometimes we went to Mass at San Juan, which was where we lived, but sometimes we went to Espada, because that's where we went to school. At Espada they gave us hot chocolate and doughnuts every time after we had communion.

At San Juan there was no school, but there was a lady who undertook to give us catechism lessons. And for our First Communion, she made us all similar dresses out of a material like what you use for sheets, because she did not want to have differences between those of us who were poor and those who had a bit more. We wore tennis shoes on our feet, and she also made some simple but pretty little crowns for our heads. All of us looked the same!

And the merchants from the stores at Bergs Mill helped with the party celebrating our communion. They set up big tables under the pecan trees, and everything was beautiful. They brought sodas and things to eat.

Later on, we moved from there.

What about your house at San Juan?

My mother used to live in the house that is directly in front of the church at San Juan. My oldest brother was born there. And my aunt, my father's sister, lived in the house that was just down the road from the church. My uncle, her husband, was called Ignacio Benavides; she was Fernanda Bustillos. My oldest sister was born there also.

How did the mission buildings look then?

Well, pretty much like they do now. I've been to look at the house where my mother lived, and it is barely one big room with painted walls, no partitions or anything.

The Bazán family lived nearby. They had a store just over the bridge. Their neighbors were Italian, but I can't remember their name. The Bazán sons also lived nearby. There was also a family by the name of Kunz. And beyond the tracks, there was a cemetery that I think was very old.

It was a peaceful life. I had uncles—Gutierrez and Oliva—and they had their gardens with tomatoes, beans, and other vegetables. They sometimes hired us kids to help them take their things to market.

And did they use the acequia?

Yes, they used the acequia for irrigation. And over at Espada, there were some [stone] arches, and the acequia ran over the top of them.[2] There was a mill nearby, and the water there was very sweet. We got drinking water from there, too. The women took their laundry down there to wash also, and the kids played in the water.

Once it rained a lot, and the river overran its banks, and its water joined the water of the acequia. The floodwater came to just below our house. It was like a sea of water, and a lot of people drowned that time. After that, they had to build a new bridge, because the flood swept away the old one that was near the corner where the Bazán family's store stood. One of the Bazáns was Adán, who killed my Aunt Antoñita.

Heavens! I shouldn't be saying such things! She was my father's first cousin. Oh, that was a notorious case; he was in prison for fifteen years.

Did you ever visit San José?

Yes, when we were kids we visited there, and we used to play on the steps that go up to the bell tower. What I remember most about San José was that there were a lot of prickly pears; *era una pura nopalera* [it was prickly pears everywhere]. Prickly pears were hanging even from the walls. Not in front of the church, but where they had *talleres* [workshops, in the convento area]. I used to think: Why don't they clean the place up and take away those *nopales*? [Laughs.]

Do you remember trees around San José?

Yes, I seem to remember trees, but I think they were mesquites. Around San Juan, though, they were pecans, great big pecan trees. The mission compound had nice shade then. Now all the trees are gone and there's nothing but sun.

Was there a priest then at San José?

I know that they had Mass every Sunday, but we didn't go to Mass there, because we were closer to Espada. My uncle Francisco Bustillos's family, however, all went to San José. The girls were younger than me, although one of them, Elena, died already. She was about my age. San José was closer for them.

And my grandmother lived in a little green house behind the church. She was called Socorro, and her husband was Francisco, or Pancho, Aguilar. He was not my mother's father but rather her stepfather. My mother's father was called Charlie White; the family lived in Piedras Negras, but she was born on this side [Eagle Pass]. I think she had half-sisters there, but my mother told me that he was murdered down there. My mother inherited some city blocks from him. Her name was Adela White.

Did you put on *Pastorelas* at the mission?

Oh yes, they used to have them at all the missions. At San Juan, when they put them on, nearly all the shepherds were my uncles: my Uncle Francisco, my Uncle Martin, my Uncle Domingo Bustillos, who was their father. And the devil was played by another uncle. I can't remember his name now, but I used to call him *mi tío viejito* [my little old uncle]. Those were beautiful Pastorelas! Not like the ones today! And they also decorated very colorfully for the Posadas. When the people approached, you could hear all the noise, and the bells ringing.

The shepherds, wearing capes, are confronted by the Hermit (right) at a performance of the traditional Christmas play *Los Pastores* (The Shepherds) at Mission San Jose, December 18-19, 1971. Courtesy of the The Institute of Texan Cultures, San Antonio.

And Posadas?

Oh, Posadas they had especially at Espada. All of us from the school used to go on them singing, and one man played the violin and another the guitar.

Were the houses far apart? Were there houses on the mission grounds?

No, they were not too far apart. On the mission grounds the only houses were the ones where the little sisters, the nuns, lived, and the one where they had their meals. Then there was a place where they sold souvenirs, and a large room where we rehearsed when we were going to sing. Nowadays all of these are fallen down.

And did they have processions?

Oh yes, especially to honor San Isidro Labrador when we had periods of drought. They went in procession around the mission walls to pray for rain, and they would take San Isidro around and pray the rosary. Once, just as they were coming back in, big black clouds gathered, and we had rain.

You've said something about when you went to San Antonio.
When we went into the city, my aunt used to say *"vamos pa'l (para el) presidio."* [We're going to the Presidio].
　　And I used to ask her, "What does that mean?"
　　And she would say, "Well, it's the center of town." I thought it was a jail, where they kept prisoners [an alternate meaning of *presidio* is "penitentiary"]. I think she meant the Alamo, but she used to call it the presidio. She never would say, "Let's go to San Antonio" or "Let's go to the center of town." She would say, "Let's go to the presidio."

And who was that aunt?
Antoñita Gutiérrez was her maiden name, but by her husband, García, so she was Antoñita Gutiérrez García.

She was your aunt on your father's or your mother's side?
On my father's side.

Around how old was this aunt at that time?
Oh, she was probably around fifty years old.

Was she born here in San Antonio?
Oh yes, and she had several sisters. They were the daughters of my Aunt Trinidad Bustillos Gutiérrez.

You say she used to say *"vamos para el presidio"* when she meant "vamos al centro (de San Antonio)"?
Yes.

And do you have any idea why she used to say that?
Well, I was around fifteen at the time, and I thought that perhaps there had been a jail downtown, and that was why she said that.

Did her sisters use the same expression?
Oh yes, they all did, and when I asked why they called it that, they said, *"Oh, ansina le decíamos antes! Era un presidio."* [Oh, that's just what we used to call it a long time ago! It used to be a presidio.]

[Mrs. Rivera's daughters, who are present, ask]: What did that mean?

Well, this is very interesting, because "presidio" was the name the Spaniards used for the military garrison stationed at San Antonio during Spanish colonial days. It was called the Presidio de Béxar. So the name did not come from a prison in downtown San Antonio but from the old military detachment there, although the other meaning in Spanish of the word is just that, a penitentiary or jail.

Did your family have other connections with the downtown area?

I was baptized at San Fernando Cathedral, and it was more beautiful then than it is now. I don't know if I remember correctly, but behind the main altar there was stained glass all the way to the floor. Later on they took away a lot of things and decorated it differently. I didn't like it as much.

NOTES

1. In Spanish, *nogal* is a walnut tree, but in Texas Spanish usage, *nogal* is a pecan tree.
2. Reference is to the Espada aqueduct, which still exists.

Dionicia Díaz Chávez

Dionicia Díaz Chávez, *age eighty-three, is related to Susie Chávez by marriage. Although she grew up in the San Juan/Espada neighborhood, she now lives with her daughter near Bustillos Drive, a short distance from Mission San José. Mrs. Chávez provides fascinating details about life in her childhood neighborhood, particularly about school days there. The interview reveals her as a fighter who has always been able to stand her ground. Although battered recently by several strokes, she has fought her way back from partial paralysis to mobility (although curtailed) and to normal speech. The interview was originally conducted by Richard Flores in June 1994 and contains additional material collected by Luis Torres on August 28, 1995.* **Rose Anguiano** *was present during the first interview. The interview was conducted in Spanish and English and was transcribed and translated by Luis Torres.*

How are you related to Susie Chávez?

DDC: Susie and my husband are cousins. His father and her mother were brother and sister.

RA: We always used to call her [points to DDC)] *tía* [aunt]. It was tradition when we were growing up to call our parents first cousins "uncle" or "aunt." We didn't dare call them by their first names.

Were you born in San Antonio?

DDC: I was born in Mason, Texas, but my grandparents lived in San Antonio. Then my grandmother got real sick, and my grandfather wrote my mother to come, because she was dying. Mother stored her furniture with some friends in Mason, and we were supposed to go back, but after my grandmother died, she couldn't leave my grandfather alone, so we stayed here.

What year was that?

DDC: 1918, and I stayed here from then on.

And where did you live when you moved here?

DDC: At Espada Mission. Well, not right at the mission, but close by. But we still called it Espada Mission. I was telling Rose that all of the Bustillos were land rich. They had property. I don't know if you're familiar with the area around San Juan, but they owned land in Bergs Mill from Ashley Road all the way to Sabinal Road along the river, and then all along Ashley Road and Sabinal Road down to Espada.

RA: Then, in 1836, that's when the taxes came in . . .

DDC: They started selling land, but also a lot of people started coming in from Mexico, and they squatted on the land and eventually got it through squatters rights. That's how the Bustillos lost a lot of their land: in those days they'd take a horse [in exchange for] an acre of land.

What were the missions like when you moved there? Were they falling apart?

DDC: No, they weren't in tiptop condition, but they were not falling apart. The nuns lived there, and we went to school with the nuns. You know, where they have those student priests now. But there were no lights, no water, no nothing. And the roads were just dirt roads. When cars came through, sometimes they needed two or three teams of horses to pull them through.

How many other families lived in the area?

DDC: There were quite a few others. The Gutierrezes lived there. They were related to the Bustillos.

We used to go to school in the mornings, and the boys had to be there in the wintertime by 7:30 so they could start the wood stoves in the classrooms. We had about four nuns at that time, and they had the first three grades in one room. Across the street from the mission, in that old tumble-down building, that's where the big kids had their classroom: seventh, eighth, and ninth grades. And when you got to the ninth grade that was it. Eleventh grade was graduation, but we did not have the last two grades.

At recess, the girls weren't allowed to play with the boys. It was a two-story house, and the priest lived upstairs—he came there on weekends—but on the first floor we had our crafts room. We had to sit there and learn to crochet, embroider, and so on. One time, one of the boys broke his foot, and he could not go out and play with the other boys, so they put him in there with us during recess. The other boys used to tease him about it, but I taught that boy how to crochet! [All laugh.]

How old were you when you moved here?

DDC: I was six years old. Mother had four kids at home. Our postman was coming to San Antonio for a vacation about the time we had to move, and he had a car, so he brought us. Of course, everybody knew everybody then, so he told Mama, "Well, if you'll just pay for the gas, I'll take you all." We loaded up a few clothes, and we came to San Antonio. He took us to Grandpa's house.

I remember how my grandmother was real, real thin and had such bony hands! And I was her grandchild, but I wouldn't go near her!

What was her name?

DDC: Her name was Eminencia. She was a Chávez, but her married name was Tijerina. I don't know, but I sure don't want to go back to those old times! Dirt roads, and all . . . .

RA: Didn't you used to go swimming in the acequia?

DDC: Yes. You know, Mother, after she had been here a while and got her a job, she bought this little place, a quarter of an acre, and the ditch ran along the back of it. And many a time did we take baths in there! With Octagon soap, yellow soap! We lost many a bar in the water because it ran pretty good.

How deep was the acequia?

DDC: Our section was deep. We had four kids, and everybody used to come to our place. We'd tie a rope to a tree and jump in there. It went up to our necks. And that was the irrigation ditch that all the farmers used. All the people would get together once a year and clean that ditch. When they got to our place, they'd say, "That's a deep place. Don't get in there; you'll drown!" [Laughs.] All our neighbors were farmers.

What did your grandfather grow?

DDC: My grandfather quit farming. He got him a job at this place called the White Horse Tavern. It was a restaurant and nightclub, and he was the caretaker there. And Mama got her a job there as cook. She had to be there by seven in the morning to start breakfast. Then after she'd cooked breakfast, she'd wash dishes and then start lunch. And then she had to be back at 3:30 to help with the evening meal; she didn't get home until 11 p.m.

But we had this little old lady who took care of us. Grandpa's house was here, and hers was nearby, so she'd come in in the morning and help us get ready for school. Then Grandpa would go to work. And in the afternoon, she'd come in and make us take our school clothes off. I really think my grandpa was living with that old lady! [All laugh.] I have a feeling that they had a lot to talk about! And, you know, that never entered my brain until now!

RA: You were telling me once that you all had your little jobs that you were supposed to do after school.

DDC: Oh, yes, all the older kids had something to do. They had to pick beans, or pull carrots, all kinds of peppers, or whatever they had. They were farmers in the area, you know. And the Grafs had everything: they had vegetables and everything. We picked whatever was in season. The only thing we didn't do was pick okra, because we were too little.

I was telling Rosie that we didn't have running water, no bathrooms, only outside toilets, and no electricity. And in school, we had no drinking fountains. Each classroom had a bucket and a dipper. The boys had to go and get water in the morning, and everybody drank out of that community bucket. It wasn't like today, when everybody has to have a paper cup that you throw out!

RA: Where did they go and get the water?

DDC: There was a well nearby on the mission grounds.

What other buildings were in use aside from the church?

DDC: They had the school right there where the mission is now. They had two classrooms there, and then across the street they had another one for the big kids.

Are those buildings still there?

DDC: They've deteriorated now. And every morning, we had to leave the house at seven so that we could be in school by eight o'clock and we could go to Mass. Then, everybody marched back and we had to salute the flag and sing.
RA: So the priest was there everyday?
DDC: He'd come in. He stayed there over the weekend. The road used to run right in front of the church. Now it's behind the church.

Were other buildings there that aren't there anymore?

DDC: They're in ruins. There used to be a little grocery store. The owners later moved downtown and had a plumbing shop, but now they're all dead. There was that one store, and that was it. The rest all came afterwards, at Bergs Mill in the San Juan neighborhood.

But lots of people there had cows and chickens and all, and there were people who would kill a cow or some chickens and put them in their little wagons and go peddle them in the neighborhood. And everybody would run out and get some. But they couldn't buy too much, because they didn't have iceboxes.

What do you remember about the trees and bushes that grew around the mission?

DDC: Well, they were mostly mesquites and hackberries, but on the mission grounds it was mostly mesquites. If you ever got in bad with a boy, or got in a fight, they would take your cap and throw it up in a mesquite.

There were about three German families in the neighborhood, across from Sabinal Road. They had big farms, and their kids would have their little wagons to go to school in, buggies, you know, and they would stake out their horses and let them eat while they were in school.

They went to school there, too?

DDC: Yes, and there were two Italian families, and, I think, three German families, and the rest were Mexican.

The classes were in English, I take it?

DDC: Yes, they were in English. When we came there in 1918, none of the kids in the first grade could speak English. None of them. Of course, I was raised with Anglos, and I could speak English. And they would ask me, "How do you say this in English?" And I'd tell them something crazy! [All laugh.]

What nuns were there at your school? Do you remember?

DDC: They were Incarnate Word nuns. One of them, Mother Pauline, she was raised on the west side, and she knew the parents of the older families; she'd gone to school with some of them. She was Mother Pauline as a nun, but her real name was Guadalupe Fierros. Her family lived just off Flores Street. And, although we had to call her Mother Pauline or Sister Pauline, my father-in-law and other people his age would come up and say, *"Hola! Cómo estás, Lupita?"* And we thought that was so funny! But all the old folks knew her.

Those nuns were good instructors. In the old church, they had this altar railing, and we had to know the history of that altar railing. It was made out of wood and had twelve openings, and each opening was decorated with a three-leaf clover. The clover was supposed to be the Father, Son, and the Holy Ghost, and the twelve openings were the twelve apostles. I used to be able to name all the apostles. Listen, they drilled it into us!

We used to have some nuns that came from Germany, but the ones we liked the best were the ones that came from Ireland. One time we got a bunch of new nuns from Ireland, and Mother used to do their washing. We'd take our little red wagon and go and pick up the dirty clothes and bring them in. And they wouldn't pay Mother. Instead, they were teaching me how to play the piano.

The first piano teacher I had was German; I think I would have learned to play the piano with her. But the next one, she was from Ireland, and she played Irish jigs. I was about eight or nine years old, and I got real good at dancing the Irish jig, but she never did teach me much about playing the piano! [Laughs.]

RA: Did they give you lunch there?

DDC: No, no, you had to pack your own lunch. One time, I remember, they bought us some playground equipment: a swing, a slide, and some croquet things. And at lunch, the sisters would go eat at their house, and then they'd come back and watch us. In the meantime, we'd eat ourselves.

Sister Superior Alma and her class at the Mission Espada school, January 12, 1941. Courtesy of the The Institute of Texan Cultures, San Antonio, *The San Antonio Light* Collection.

There was this German family I've told you about, the boy was a great big old guy, and Mother Pauline tells us, "Now, everybody take turns at the swing." I think it was ten swings you could take. And the sisters had put down a pile of sand where we came down from the swings.

My sister and I were eating our beans and tortillas, and the German boy was on the swing. So I said, "Okay, Cornelius, it's our turn now. We're nearly through eating lunch."

He got off the swing and, you know, he picked up a handful of sand and said, "Here's your sandwich!" And he put all that sand on my tortilla. That's when the Mexicans and the Germans had it out!

How did people get along in those days?

DDC: We generally got along real good, but when he put that sand on my tortilla, we had a big fistfight. He was a big, tall guy, but I beat the socks off him! Cornelius ran off because I was chasing him, and he got on the slide. I was climbing up the ladder, and he was going down the slide, so I told my sister, "You stand there at the end of the slide, and when he comes down, you knock him over." So she did, and that's when we had it. And the Mexican kids made a circle around us—we were fistfighting—and they wouldn't let his cousins through when they tried to help him.

After school we had to go and say the rosary, and the boys would line up on one side and the girls on the other. And who turned out to be my partner that day? Cornelius!

And years later, my son Freddie was in the Air Force Reserves, and he was going to Brooks Air Force Base for their meetings. He came home one day—he was sixteen or seventeen—and he said, "Mama, there's a sergeant out there, a great big, tall guy, real husky, and he asked me what my name was. I told him, "Fred Chávez."

And he said, "What's your daddy's name?"

"Jesús Chávez."

"And what's your mother's name?"

"Dionicia."

"Well, I'm going to make it tough on you, young man. Your mother beat the socks off of me when I was a kid, and you're going to pay for it!" [All laugh.]

And the darned fool believed him! For a while, he wanted to quit the reserves. Then I found out it was Cornelius Ripps, so I said, "You go back there, and you tell him, he might be a sergeant, but I can still whup his butt!" [More laughter.] So he went back and he told Cornelius, and they had a good laugh about it.

There were some Masperos . . . they were Italian. They were twins. And my brother was crippled, so they were always trying to gang up on him. I had more fights over my brother! We used to have to wear hats to go to school, because women couldn't go into church for Mass unless their head was covered. The Masperos were Italian, but they could speak real good Spanish, and, since my name was Díaz, they would tease me with a singsong:

> *Dionicia Díaz*
> *Come sandías*
> *Todos los días!*
> [Dionicia Díaz
> eats watermelons
> every single day!]

Just to tease me. And I would tell them:

> *Masperos*
> *son más perros*
> *que gatos!*

[The Masperos
are more dogs
than cats!]

[All laugh uproariously.] And you know that years after, whenever we saw each other, they would come and put their arm around me and ask, *"Todavía comes sandías todos los días?"* [Do you still eat watermelons every day?]

And I would tell them: *"No, pero tú todavía eres más perro que gato!"* [No, but you still are more dog than cat!] We never had a grudge against each other, but we sure used to tease each other!

How many years did you go to school there?

DDC: I went there from the first grade through the ninth. And the Irish nuns were still there when I got a scholarship to go to Incarnate Word. But I went one year and then couldn't afford it. I was staying with my sister. They had boarders at school, but Mama couldn't afford it, so the first year I stayed with my sister. But then she and her husband got a divorce, so I didn't have anyone to stay with, and I had to come home.

Life was rough then, I guess, but of course we didn't realize it! Everybody was in the same boat.

From what you tell me, it sounds like you've always been a fighter!

DDC: Well, maybe not a fighter, but I've never allowed anyone to take advantage of me or abuse me. I had ten children, five boys and five girls. One time, I took the three oldest boys to Harlandale to get their hair cut. At that time, many places used to refuse to give service to Mexicans, and we often had to take the boys all the way over to the west side to find a barber. Anyway, we got to the barbershop around four o'clock, and I went in and told the barber that I'd like for him to give the boys haircuts. He said, "Well, where are they?" So I called the boys in. He took one look at them and said, "I'm sorry, but I'm closed."

I told him, "Your sign says that you're open until 5 p.m.," but he insisted that he was closed. So I told him, "I know why you're 'closed'; it's because we're Mexicans. Well, mister, you are really going to be closed!" Then I went outside, told the boys to sit down, and I stood at his door for an hour. Anybody who approached looking like he was going to come in, I would block their way and tell them, "I'm sorry, but he's closed!"

And if they said, "But he looks like he's open!," I'd tell them, "No, that's a mistake; he's really closed."

I also had my battles with the local schools, because they didn't want to accept some of the kids. And when I tried to get other neighborhood people to support me, nobody wanted to stick their neck out, so I had to do it alone. Boy, I took my chances! [Laughs.]

You'll excuse me, but that sounds to me like a fighter! [All laugh.] How long did you live in the mission neighborhood?

DDC: I lived there until I got married, and I got married in '29, so I guess I lived there seven years. Then later, I got the notion that we should move back there, so we built a house and lived there twelve more years. We rented on Bustillos Drive for a few years, and then I went to work at [Kelly Air Force] Base, and then we bought this property and built the house.

Is the house still there?

DDC: Yes, my daughter lives there now.

RA· Has Espada Mission always been open as a parish?

DDC: Oh, yes, as far as I can remember. There was a parish there in 1918. We used to have priests come over from Perpetual Help, the Redentist priests; I don't remember when they started getting the Franciscans, because we moved by then.

What do you think has changed the most about the missions, about Espada?

DDC: Well, it's more populated now; there's more people living there. There used to be just a few houses there, but now they are on both sides of the street. And the roads have also improved.

Do any of the old families still live there?

DDC: Oh, yes, certainly, many of them. See, they were property owners, so the property has gone from one generation to the next. Some of their old houses are still there.

[Shows a photograph.] That's my husband. We were married sixty years. It was five years yesterday since he passed away. He used to say that he should get a great big medal for putting up with me.

RA: Did you meet him there [at Espada]?

DDC: Yes, they lived across the street from us, but, see, he was sweet on my sister; they were about the same age. And he'd come over to visit my brother, who was crippled, and play with him. My sister would be in the kitchen fixing something, and he would go in there and chat with her.

They lived on one side of the road and we on the other. Their land adjoined Mama's farm.

Have the acequias pretty well dried up now?

DDC: Oh, no. At San Juan they have, but not at Espada.

Does anybody take care of the acequia today?

DDC: I don't know. There used to be a German family that lived there, the Grafs; I think they bought from the Bustillos, because their land was in between that of the Bustillos. They always planted there, so they made a big pond. With the irrigation ditch, everybody had certain days to irrigate; everybody got two days. They'd use the water those two days, then you would put your floodgate down and then pass it on to the next person. The Grafs made their pond and had floodgates on it which they could open, so they always had water.

And who controlled this procedure?

DDC: There was always one person in charge of it. And every year, I can remember that they would come over with trucks and picks and shovels and clean the acequia. They'd shovel all that mud out.

RA: How far was that from the mission?

DDC: It was some distance. There are two acequias: the one by the mission was dry, but the other was working.

Have you heard of the Los Pastores presentation at Guadalupe Church?

DDC: Oh, yes, they used to have Los Pastores also at the mission.

Do you remember who performed it?

DDC: There was a group of them that got together. I think they got their script from Guadalupe. They had a bunch of people playing devils. Were they supposed to be keeping people away from the Nativity scene?

They were supposed to keep the shepherds away.

DDC: Well, my husband was one of those, one of the devils. And each devil had a name. They had staffs, and they had swords, and they had masks made out of tin. Yes, Daddy was one of them.

What year did he perform, do you remember?

DDC: Let's see: '29 . . . [tries to calculate using the births of her children as benchmarks]. Well, Danny was born in '39 . . . see, we had ten kids. I used to say that they came like this *chorizo mejicano* [Mexican chorizo sausages], one link after another. Every two years I had a kid.

We lived there at the mission, you know. They built us a little house when we got married. And during the Depression, I'm telling you, it was hard. And my husband used to work a farm with his daddy, farming on shares.

We were paying on this house . . . it was just a two-room house, a bedroom and a kitchen . . . and we paid on that house five years, ten dollars a month. You could find a place anywhere for a dollar, dollar-fifty, but we paid five years, ten dollars a month. And one time we had a huge disagreement with my husband's mother, who was holding the mortgage, so, after Danny was born, I told Jesús, "You can stay with your parents; I'm not having any more babies by you. I can go out and work by myself." So that's when we moved to Colorado City. We were out there six months. Then we came back and started living on this street.

And those were the years when he was performing in Los Pastores?

DDC: They'd go out on those Pastores, and then they'd go out after that; they'd all get drunk and come in tipsy. I haven't seen one of those presentations in a long time. The one at Espada was directed by a man called Nicanor Martínez.

This one at the mission, they'd start it around December 15, I think, and each one of the parishioners would have a Pastorela, and then the one on the 24th was the big one; that's when they took the Baby Jesus and put him in the manger and all. But all that time, there were Posadas going on, where they'd go from house to house. We used to have a good time! [All laugh.] They had a couple selected to be the *padrinos* [godparents] to the Baby Jesus.

Were the priests involved in this?

DDC: No, it was just the people. I don't remember ever having it at the church. It was always just families. People would go out and solicit for participation. And they usually ended up by the acequia. There used to be a big stone house there, owned by a sister and two brothers. None of them were married, but they had this big, big yard, and that's where they ended up on Christmas Eve. Everybody would pitch in.

Another fellow who directed for a while was Tomás López. It was a lot of work, but people didn't realize that it was so much work. I guess it brought the community together.

I remember during Lent, when they made . . . *como se dice*, . . . *la capirotada* [a bread pudding concoction made in Mexico and among Mexican-Americans during Lent], we kids used to get so disgusted. All of them made this bread pudding, and I can remember us kids going from one house to another with a bowl. Then we'd get a bowl of it, and we'd say, "Well, it's time for dog food!"

RA: You didn't like *capirotada?*

DDC: It was good, but everyone made it, and they brought it from one neighbor to another, so you got tired of it pretty fast!

RA: I guess it's like with tamales at Christmas today. Everyone is making them, so you get a lot of them all of a sudden.

DDC: But you know, in that little community, you'd send a bowl of it over to someone, and they would never return your plate back empty. They'd put something on it.

Whatever happened to the Indian families that were in the missions? Did you ever hear stories about them?

DDC: When we came here, there were no Indians there anymore.

Did you hear stories about them, or about what happened to them?

DDC: No.

No one ever talked about it?

DDC: Not to me. No [not back then]. Now, my mother-in-law could tell you stories that would make your hair stand up on end. And Mama didn't believe everything that she said. I would go tell her—Mama used to live down the street from us: "My mother-in-law said thus and such."

And she would say: "Oh, your mother-in-law is crazy!"

But I wish now that I had listened to some of her stories. She could tell you some of the most horrible stories . . . about *brujería* [witchcraft], and home remedies, and all this other stuff. If any kid got sick, my mother-in-law went there; if any woman got sick, there she was. She had this book. It wasn't a Bible, just a book, and it had all the prayers for the various sicknesses and for the dead. Anybody would get sick, my brother would come up: "Ay, Doña Elogia, so and so is dying!" And there she'd go with her book . . . her glasses falling down her nose, and that old book falling apart . . . she'd go over there and pray for them.

Emilio Guerra

At eighty-five, going on eighty-six, **Emilio Guerra,** who was born and raised in the neighborhood where he still lives, continues to work at "this and that." He also runs his general store at Bergs Mill, as he has for the last fifty-five years. Although his card calls it "Bergs Mill Grocery and Service Station," he has not sold any gasoline there since the times of rationing during World War II, when he found that the rationing authority would not give him enough of an allowance to make it worth his while. Mr. Guerra was interviewed on July 27, 1995. The interview was conducted in Spanish.

Mr. Guerra, what is your real name? Your daughter told me Emilio, your notary's certification permit here says Jesse E., and your card reads J. Emil.

My baptismal name is Jesús Emilio Guerra. I am a twin; I've got a twin sister. And I was the firstborn son of Emilio Guerra, so they named me after my father. My sister was named María after my mother. I was born in 1910, and in those days it seems that a majority of the male children were named Jesús, because of our Catholic connection and the devoutness of the women, and correspondingly, a large number of the female children were María. My grandmother was the midwife when we were born.

When I went to get my birth certificate at the courthouse, my grandmother came with me as a witness, but those *pendejos* [expletive] at the courthouse had apparently never registered me even though I was born right here, just a few blocks from the missions. I took my baptismal certificate, which had me listed as Jesús, but they would not accept that. They said that was not "documentary evidence." So I had to register myself all over again, and now I only use the initial "J." and go by Emilio.

I was born here, baptized at Mission Espada, and confirmed and married at San Juan. When they moved Ashley Road over by Stinson Field and left this short street that ends here at my store, the city people asked me if I wanted the street named "Jesús Guerra," but I told them to use Emilio instead, so now it's labeled Emilio Guerra Drive. But my Social Security and other official records have me as Jesús or Jesse.

By the way, why is this area called Bergs Mill?

That's because just down the road here, where the old bridge is, there used to be a water-powered woolen mill. A lot of the members of Román Martínez's family in this neighborhood used to work there. But by the time I saw it, the mill was abandoned and run down. The owner was a man by the name of Berg, and therefore the name Bergs Mill.

And your twin sister? What happened to her?

She died at age thirty-three; she never married.

And what did she die from?

I'm not sure, but I think, like so many other girls, she used to take something from the drugstore to lose weight, and whatever it was caused a reaction in her blood.

Our mother's maiden name was Olivas, and my paternal grandfather was Rafael Guerra. This property where I live now belonged to him; supposedly he bought it in the 1800s. He came originally from Tamaulipas, somewhere between Mier and a town called San Pedro, which they later renamed Ciudad Alemán, in honor of the Mexican president. The town was called Los Guerras, because the family owned a lot of property around there. This was in the 1850s.

Apparently, he moved freely between Mexico and Texas, until he married into the Sáenz family, because the girl he married—my paternal grandmother—was Concepción Sáenz. The Sáenz family—her father, Don Florencio Sáenz, and his family—came from the Rio Grande Valley, where they, too, had a lot of property in Starr County. In fact, there is a town down there called Roma-Los Sáenz. Their children were born some on this side, some on the other, of the river, but I can't remember which ones were which now. I used to have a family album that had all that lineage written in it, but I loaned it to a relative, and they lost it.

All of this I found out after I grew up, because my grandparents never talked to me about it. In the old days, if grownups were conversing, they usually shooed the kids away. They wouldn't even let us listen. But I've heard that in the 1890s, when they came up to the San Antonio area from Starr County, the journey took them three months, because they brought their cattle and everything. In those days, there were only trails down to that area; there were no proper roads.

And what happened with your father and mother?

My mother died from burns when my sister and I were a year and seven months old. The house where it happened is still standing near the highway. It's a small place, just a kitchen and two rooms. She was lighting a wood stove. In those days people used kindling to start a fire and, although kerosene was not that common, there was some around. Supposedly she put kindling in and then doused the kindling with kerosene, but apparently there were embers underneath, and the thing exploded on her.

Some people say it was an accident, but others have told me that it was a suicide. They say that my father used to chase women, and he would walk right past our house with them. Even my grandmother, his mother, admitted to that. But anyway, people say she killed herself over my father. My paternal grandparents took me and my sister in after my mother died and raised us, but when my father became a widower, people around here did not want him around. We also did not get to know much of the Olivas family, because my mother's father, Don Sabino Olivas, didn't want anything to do with my father's family after her death.

Well, you certainly have a colorful family tree!

And it doesn't stop there. There's also a family story that my maternal grandmother's mother, Conción Gutiérrez . . .

Do you mean Concepción?

No, no, Conción. Anyway, she never married, but, *sabe quién* le"hizo un bien" [do you know who "did her a favor," i.e., got her pregnant]? A circus clown by the name of Espinosa. How old are you?

I'm fifty-nine.

Oh, well, then compared to my eighty-five, you're a youngster! In those days, there was little to do outside the community. As a kid, I remember not going into San Antonio shopping more than once a year. We would go in a wagon pulled by mules to Market Square to sell produce and buy provisions. We would leave here around 10:30 or 11 at night and we wouldn't get there until 3:30 or 4 in the morning. My grandfather was a truck farmer, and he would take his vegetables in to sell.

Anyway, one of the big entertainments of the year was when a traveling circus would come through with clowns and acrobats and whatnot. They would set up a tent at San Juan and another at Espada, or play one place for a while and then move to the other. They came once a year, or every six months, usually when it was warm weather. And one of the clowns from a traveling circus was the one who got her pregnant! And that's where my grandmother, Josefa Espinosa, came from. She was the one who married Don Sabino Olivas, and from that marriage came my mother.

Don Sabino was a big, rough man, well over six feet tall, and I used to be scared of him. I still own part of his ranch with some cousins. The land was back behind the acequia and had no access to the road, so they had to buy an acre from Mr. Rilling—he's the fellow that Rilling Road was named after—so they could have access to that land.

Hearing you talk, I get the impression that in this neighborhood, everyone is related to everyone else.

Well, not in our case, because the Sáenz, Guerra, and Bazán families were "strangers"—they moved here from somewhere else. But there are other families that have been around much longer than us. Unfortunately, although they had a lot of land around here to start with, they got to the point where they would sell an acre of their land for a gallon of wine. That's how a lot of the German families around here got into the neighborhood. But, the stupid idiots then had to go to work for the new landowners for fifty cents a day!

I've had a lot of disagreements with some of the Germans. They call us foreigners and wetbacks; they don't know what else to call Mexicans. If there are any "Native Americans," we're it, because we've been here more than 100 or 150 years. The Indian was here first, and we're the product of the mixture of Indians and Spaniards. Wetbacks? You can cross the Rio Grande sometimes and not get your feet wet, but you can get your back a lot wetter crossing the Atlantic Ocean like they did!

Where did you go to school?

To begin with, I went to the Espada Mission school, which was taught by the nuns. But I never graduated, because we were too hungry. One had to go out and work as early as possible to make a living. But later on I took and passed the GED, and in 1986 I enrolled as a freshman at Palo Alto College. I was seventy-six at the time. That was different! It wasn't like the old days, when all you had to do was bring Teacher a nice apple and you got good grades. I really had to work. I've also taken courses at the Universidad Autónoma de México in San Antonio. I decided to take Spanish, because I felt that my Spanish was terrible, especially my written Spanish, so I tried to improve that.

So, how many years did you go to school with the nuns?

Seven years, and after that, I went on to about the tenth grade. In the meantime, my grandfather had died, and then my grandmother, so I was an orphan all over again with my sister. And my real dad was murdered not long after that by a fellow named Cerda over some woman.

So being a ladies man finally got him killed?

He was running a *zacatería*, a feed store where they sold hay and grain for mules and horses, chickens, and so on near Market Square at 1224 West Commerce Street, about where Santa Rosa Hospital is now. At that time, most of the transportation was still horses; there were just a few cars around, but we had a little truck that we used for delivery. And he also had a billiard parlor down there, which I ran for him.

This was around 1925 or '26, and my grandmother was still alive. I was sixteen or seventeen. The woman he was involved with had a restaurant called El Centinela [The Sentry], where they served Mexican food. Anyway, the Cerda brothers ran what was called Arrow Livery. At that time there were no taxis, but some individuals who had the money would buy a couple of motor cars, and if you needed transportation, you talked to them and arranged to have them take you where you needed to go. *Y también "bootleguiaban"* [They were also bootleggers] whiskey, because in those days Prohibition was in effect, and everything was supposed to be dry. That started in 1917, as I remember, and continued until Roosevelt came to office in 1932 or '33. Anyway, the Cerdas got into a fight with my father and beat him to death in the middle of the street. After that, my grandmother only lived about another six months.

And what kind of work did you do when you started working on your own after that?

I used to do this and that. For a while I had a couple of old trucks that I would work with, but I had to spend the night fixing them so they would be able to run the next day. And I had to do that by lamplight, because we didn't even have electric light. It wasn't until 1920 or '21 that we finally got electricity out here. Roads were just dirt; *era un mugrero bárbaro* [it was just dreadful filth]! The mailman got here on a horse and buggy because automobiles had a hell of a time getting here. Henry Ford was the one who made "people" out of us poor folk, because before that, Studebaker and the other automobiles were meant only for millionaires.

What was the condition of the missions when you were a boy?

In those days, the San Juan compound was closed, and there were a lot of small houses within. The entrance was from the front; today it's from the back. But I don't remember much about it. By 1915 to '18, most of those little houses were gone. There were a bunch of Italians that came in around that time—you see? Those are what I would call foreigners! They started buying this and buying that, and the poor Mexicans were driven out.

I remember during the Depression that you could get a *costal*, a certain amount of provisions per person: a pound of lard, a pound of beans, and so on, and they put you to work cleaning up the roadways and doing other things. I had to go on that for a while to be able to help my sister. After that, WPA came in, and they paid you $2.25 per day. Some of the WPA people dug around the mission at San Juan and found a lot of Indian bones. And at Espada they did the same. They had fifteen to twenty men working daily, and the government paid them for the work.

By then, around 1932, I had a little truck, and I used it to sell firewood. Around that time was also when construction was really taking off in Alamo Heights, building all those homes, and a number of us hired our trucks to lug stone and other materials. I got paid 40 cents a day, plus $1.25 for the truck. But that's what you do to make a living.

When the war started, I got a job at Stinson Field, and I became an aviation mechanic. I used to test plugs and rub banana oil on the wings of planes, because to start with they were made out of very thin plywood covered with some sort of material similar to bed sheeting. In 1939, I started to work at Kelly and worked there about four years. By that time, rationing was already in effect, and you needed coupons for gasoline, for tires, for a lot of things. So I went to my boss and told him that I lived only two blocks from Brooks, and that if I could be transferred there, I would not need coupons for any of those things, so they moved me. I was there for another eight years.

Have you seen much change at the missions in the time you've lived here?

Well, not really; the missions are still where they've always been. The only thing that's different is that they've done some reconstruction work on them to prevent them from falling down further. Beyond that, I haven't seen much change.

Have you been very active here in the San Juan Mission congregation?

No. I used to be very devout when I was a kid, but to tell you the truth, I only go to church nowadays when I get married, and I've been married twice. My wife is always at the church, but I tell her that's only right, because women are bigger sinners than men! [Laughs.]

Janie Garza

Janie Garza, *age fifty-one, is a petite woman with an easy smile and a ready laugh. Although born into a family of migrant farm laborers, she was raised at Mission San Juan in a house that still stands in the mission compound. She currently resides in the Mission Espada neighborhood, but is a member of the Mission San Juan parish. Janie was active as a neighborhood representative in the period preceding the establishment of the San Antonio Missions National Historical Park and opposed the coming of the park. She was interviewed on July 14, 1995. The interview was conducted in both English and Spanish.*

I hear you called Janie sometimes and Juanita other times. What is your *nombre de pila* [baptismal or given name]?

My given name is Juanita Garza, but I go by Janie everywhere. I think the only person who calls me Juanita is our parish priest. *El quiere que hable español!* [He wants me to speak Spanish.]

I understand that you were raised in this community of San Juan mission and are a resident here now. Is that correct?

I recently moved back here as a parishioner, because my residence is really in the Mission Espada community. But I moved my membership to this parish because I hope, when I die, to be taken out from this church at Mission San Juan.

I've heard of planning for the future, but that is the first time I've encountered that kind of future planning!

[Laughs.] I know that may sound silly, but death is always next to us! Didn't you know that?

For certain none of us is going to escape it, and I guess you're right: if you want certain things done, you'd better plan accordingly. Tell me something about your parents and grandparents.

My parents were born here in San Antonio. My grandfather that I can trace was from Nuevo León and Tamaulipas; he was my grandfather on my father's side. As far as I know, on my mother's side, they were also born here. I'm trying to trace my family.

And your paternal grandmother, where was she from?

That I don't know. But I was born and raised here.

Were your parents raised in this mission community?

As far as I can tell, they came originally from La Parrita, Texas, east of San Antonio, in the direction of Sulfur Springs. I haven't been able to verify that. They were cotton pickers, and they would migrate sometimes.

How big a family were you?

We were five girls and one boy, but I also have an adopted brother.

How many of them are living?

All of us!

According to tradition, once a year on St. Francis's Day, women at the Mission Espada parish "wash" and dress the images of the saints at the mission church. The garments on the figures are changed every two months. In this photo from June 1941, Beatrice DeWitt sews a garment on the image of Our Lady, while Martine Sandoval washes the image's face. Courtesy of The Institute of Texan Cultures, San Antonio, *The San Antonio Light*

Parish festival at Mission Espada, October 4, 1982. Courtesy of the Old Spanish Missions Research Collection, Special Collections and Archives, and Our Lady of the Lake University.

Indian dancers dance in front of the mission church at Espada during the parish festival, October 4, 1982. Courtesy of the Old Spanish Missions Research Collection, Special Collections and Archives, Our Lady of the Lake University.

And you are what number among them?
I was "the last of the Mohicans!" [Laughs.]

So your oldest sister is how old?
I would say about sixty-five.

What is your occupation?
Right now, I am the clerk for the parish priest here at the mission. I do his typing and office work.

Are you single or married?
I'm single.

Tell me something about your childhood. You've told me that you used to live in what they call "the tufa house"[1] here on the grounds of the mission?
Well, I think they should call it "the Janie house" instead of the "tufa house." [Laughs.] What can I tell you about that?

Well, for example, how old were you when you lived there?
From age four or five until I was about twelve years old. For three years after we left the tufa house, we lived in the Kunz house until we left the community. That was a house that was right behind the tufa house, one that the national park had to tear down. They bought the land and tore the house down.

So the Kunz house was a separate structure, not joined in any way to the tufa house?
No, and it wasn't in the mission compound, either. It was outside the mission. When I was a child, the whole place was very, very different. We used to have the whole neighborhood come through the compound and out the back for their recreation, because we used to do our swimming in the San Antonio River.

Our parish picnics were held at Dillon's, which is about two or three properties down from here. Our parish festivals were always held here in the compound; what is now the museum used to be our parish hall, where we used to make our *tamaladas* [*tamal*-making feasts].

What kinds of trees were they?

There were pecans, mesquite, *lo que le dicen álamos, y uno que otro huisache* [cottonwoods and a few huisaches]. But most of them were pecans, with a few palo blanco. *Y cuando se venía el tiempo de la nuez* [And when it was pecan harvest time], oh, my gosh, you should have seen the people!

How did your family come to the tufa house . . . or the Janie house?

[Laughs.] It's a long story. My mom died when I was very young, and my father couldn't take care of me, so I was given to my godparents to raise. This is where you take your religion very seriously, and your godparents take over if something happens to your parents.

After a while, my godparents left for La Parrita, and I stayed over there for maybe two or three years. Then my father died, and they returned to San Antonio. They came here to live in the tufa house, with an agreement from the priest that they could live there rent free if they would take care of the mission church and do the maintenance on the compound. So they stayed on here taking care of the church, seeing that it was open, that it was clean.

What were the names of your godparents?

José y Elvira Garza. Actually, he was my father's brother as well as my godfather.

So he was your uncle. Did they have any children?

No.

So you became an only child with them?

Only for a while, because when my father died, they took the rest of us kids in. When they used to go picking cotton, we went as a family and stayed together, so we all knew each other real well. We stayed in the same family. But they raised us.

Oh yes, that's very Hispanic! At my paternal grandmother's house the place was usually full of cousins that she was taking care of or housing for a time.

Yes, thank goodness for that!

Have you any idea how your uncle came upon the job of caretaker at the mission?

I would imagine it was because they would come to church here and the priest knew him. He has died already, but I'll have to ask Mother about it. There are a lot of questions that I haven't asked her!

Would you describe the tufa house while you were living there? Was it one large room?

It was divided. Maybe not in the middle, but it was divided. A small room was our parents' bedroom, and the larger room served as both living room and as a bedroom for the kids. They had added a room in the back that served as our kitchen and dining room. It was small, but we all fit in there somehow.

Was this kitchen/dining room addition connected to the house or a separate structure?

It was connected to the house. Later on, the national park tore it down. We had a wood stove in there that we used both for cooking and to heat the place, because it was not very big.

What was the mission like at the time? What did it look like? You've already mentioned the trees.

It was beautiful, and it was very lively, because most of the evenings the youth of the parish would come to the compound and play volleyball or baseball or whatever. It was like the *zócalos* [main plazas] you find in Mexico. On the weekends, *los señores* [the older men of the community] would bring their beer—we had a well here—and you could hear singing way into the night. We could roam around at all hours and nothing would happen. There was no crime or nothing. It was peaceful and at the same time happy; a lot of people would come, and this was their gathering place.

What about the structures in the compound? What was their condition?

There was nothing on the north side of the church, except perhaps the outlines of the walls. By the tufa house there was just brush and trees, and behind the tufa house there were *labores* [agricultural fields], with the acequia running through them for irrigation. On the other side it was also *puro pasto* [untended land] and the river.

What kinds of crops were they growing?

At the time, the kids would work for Mr. Bazán. He was the one who farmed. He raised onions, cabbage, okra, and other vegetables. I don't remember for sure, because I was very little. My brother used to work for him so he could have money to get sodas! [Laughs.] When the pecan season came, they went pecan hunting, because they could make more money that way. I also remember corn, especially over here in front of the compound, where the well is. It was mostly veggies, and mostly onions.

What did the people do with so many onions?

They were taken to market. We took only what was used at home, but the rest of it was taken to market, at Market Square.

Your father got the house for nothing. Did he also get a salary?

No, he had a job.

What did he do?

Well, among other things, there used to be a dairy back here on Villamain Road, and he used to work there. Milk cows and things like that.

And your mother? Did she have another job aside from the house and taking care of all the kids?

No, she just worked at home.

Where did you go to school?

At Mission Espada. At that time, Mission Espada and San Juan were one parish, together with St. Ann's. One priest took care of all the churches. They would bus us to the Catholic school at Espada from kindergarten through the eighth grade.

Who ran the school?

It was run by Incarnate Word nuns.

You mentioned sports and social activities here. What other parish activities were there?

Well, on Saturdays there was *doctrina* [religious instruction] for the people who did not get to go to Catholic school, right here under the trees. They would have the parish festivals. The men would have their Holy Name Society meetings. Girls would have their Hijas de María [Daughters of Mary Society], and I'm not sure, but I don't think we had Guadalupanas [Our Lady of Guadalupe Society]. And of course they had their choir.

Did they have any kind of *fiestas patronales* [patron saint's day feasts]?
Yes, they had la Fiesta de San Juan.

What kind of celebration was that?
I really don't remember the church services and how they were. All I remember is that they had a festival.

What about feasts like Christmas?
Oh yes, we had *la levantada del Niño Dios* [the raising of the Christ Child].

Would you describe that?
That was done in the home. It's the reenactment of Joseph and Mary looking for a place to stay in Bethlehem. You know: *hacen una Posada, cantan, suena a la puerta, entran a la casa, dicen un rosario* [they do a Posada, they sing, there's a knock on the door, they come into the house, and they say the rosary].

I am saying this, and I can remember how my mother used to decorate the house. She would set up a beautiful altar. You have a figure of Baby Jesus sitting in a little chair before Christmas, with Mary and Joseph. These figures are wooden, or whatever material. Then they take Baby Jesus and put him in the manger for his birth, and they leave him there, maybe put a little dress on him, *y lo dejan hasta el Día de los Reyes* [and they leave him there until Three Kings' Day], January 6.

Then they come back. The altar is still set up as it was from Christmas, *y lo levantan al Niño; supuestamente ya está grandecito, ya lo van a bautizar, y lo sientan en su sillita, y lo dejan sentado* [they raise Baby Jesus; supposedly he's grown now, and he's going to be baptized, so they set him up on his little chair and they leave him sitting], for the rest of the year. Then they take off all the Christmas decorations and everything. Of course, there are special hymns you sing, and *los rosarios que haces* [and the rosaries you say] and everything. You have a festivity, a *tamalada*, special *comida* [food], and you celebrate! [Laughs.] That's the best part.

From what you're telling me, the altar remains, but the special Christmas decorations are put away.

In every Mexican home most of the time you will find an altar. Like, if you go to my house *ahorita* [right now], you'll find an altar. La Virgen de Guadalupe [Our Lady of Guadalupe] is there, a candle, *y todo eso* [and all that]. El Niño usually stays sitting there *hasta que viene Christmas otra vez* [until Christmas comes around once more], and then we put on a special big altar *donde ponemos Mary and Joseph bien grandes y acostamos al Niño* [where we put Mary and Joseph in big statues and lay down Baby Jesus], and you decorate the whole altar like that.

Once Three Kings' Day comes, they raise the Baby up, which we call *la levantada del Niño Dios* [the raising of Baby Jesus], and then you put him back on the smaller altar.

Is this ceremony separate from the Posadas?

No, that would be our Posadas. For us Christmas starts early. *El 16 de diciembre ya comienzas tus Posadas, me parece que son nueve dias* [On the 16th of December you start your Posadas, which go on for nine days] before Christmas, from the 16th to the 25th. You go *de casa en casa, vas cantando, quizás escoges unas tres casas* [from house to house, singing; maybe you pick three houses]. You go from your house, *y vas y cantas; si te dicen que no, vas a la otra* [and you go and sing; if they say no, then you go to the next house], and finally you find a place.

This is the reenactment of Joseph and Mary trying to find a place in Bethlehem, and it goes on for nine days. Then, on the real Christmas, you go to the particular house where you're going to *levantar al Niño Dios*, and you do the whole thing: *levantas al Niño, le cambias la ropita, y dices un rosario* [you raise the Child, you change His clothes, and you say the rosary].

Nowadays, we don't do it as much any more as we used to. In the first place, and I'm ashamed to say, *porque el Niño Dios se nos quebró* [because we broke our Baby Jesus statue], and we haven't replaced Him yet! [Laughs.] But also because usually the people who would do these things would be your grandmas and your grandpas, the older people, and as they've been dying off, the tradition is also disappearing. My godparents used to combine with other neighbors to go through the whole thing. We still go to this particular house on Christmas, but now it's only on the 24th and the whole thing is much simpler. Right now, if I were to be somewhere else at Christmas, in my heart it would not be Christmas, because I couldn't do what I do every year.

Right now *nosotros en nuestra casa* [we in our house], what we do on the 16th is to put a light outside on the porch, either an electric one or a candle, showing that that is the beginning of the Christmas season for us. Dad always used to do that. It shows that the Christ Child is coming.

This arrangement of going from house to house, was it done as a community thing or as something arranged between a few families?

Just among families. *Había veces que no se podía hacer* [There were times when it could not be done outside], so we would just do it inside around the house. It was just a symbolic thing to do.

Any other special traditions or observances that you had?

Our picnics. I can only tell you what I remember as a child. Every year our school would take all the kids from San Juan and Espada who attended the school at Espada, together with their entire families, and we would go and spend the day at Brackenridge Park as a community. And it was the whole school, from Kinder to the eighth grade. That's one thing that I tried to bring back when I was at Espada, so that we could not only work together when we had our festivals but we could have a chance to play together, to sit and relax. But it never took hold. Then I moved to San Juan.

Habían también muchos retiros [There were also a lot of retreats]: the men in the Holy Name Society, for example. They used to go away for three days and have their retreat. *Ahora aquí ya no lo hacen eso* [They don't do that anymore here].

Where did you go to school after you finished at Espada?

If you had the money, the girls would either go to Blessed Sacrament from ninth through twelfth, or you could go to Providence. Those were the only options for Catholic girls. The guys could go to Central Catholic and LaSalle. But if you didn't have the money to pay the tuition, you had to go to public school. I wanted to go to Blessed Sacrament, but we couldn't afford it, so I ended up going to South Side.

And I can tell you that the only real education that I had was from K through eighth with the nuns. In high school, I just floated. There was not the discipline, and they were not interested in whether you learned or not. And what I already knew was enough to take me through the twelfth grade without anybody noticing that I wasn't learning anything new!! [Laughs.]

The nuns taught me very well. I even know how to run meetings properly, because the nuns taught us. Sometimes you go to meetings, and people who are educated and are younger than I don't know how to run a meeting. They don't know *Robert's Rules of Order.* The nuns made us go through mock meetings, where we had to use them and become familiar with them!

Was your education with the nuns in Spanish or in English?

In English.

And were there any rules about not speaking Spanish while you were in school?

[Laughs.] I *knew* you were going to ask that! You know, oddly enough, I just don't remember it ever happening to me, maybe because I've always been a happy person and never wanted to look on the bad side of things. However, I know that a lot of the people that went to school with me—my cousins, for example—remember the nuns hitting them or getting after them for speaking Spanish; they remember a lot of cruelty, but honestly, I don't. Maybe it was because I was too eager to learn the English, or maybe because I was always very little and the nuns liked me. I was their pet. But I don't remember bad times with the nuns.

And there was no Spanish class as such in your course of instruction?

Oh, no, definitely not.

What happened after high school?

I took a clerical course in high school, and afterwards I went to work. And I've been in and out of work since then.

I have been told that you opposed the creation of the national park.

Yes.

Explain to me why.

Well, I opposed it because, as I saw it, the national park was going to give us a lot of rules and regulations to go by, and I didn't see anything that it was going to give us or help us with, to help our environment, to help our housing, to help our community. A lot of people thought that the park would mean community improvement, but the original maps that they drew up showed that there were going to be a lot of parishioners that were going to be asked to leave, because their property was going to be bought. And it was too much.

Before the park came, the River Corridor [see page 106] took out a lot of people from San Juan. I have drawn a map showing the people who used to live here, and *había mucha gente* [there were a lot of people]. The community was big. In fact, San Juan was considered to be bigger than Espada. But now you can see a lot of people at Espada and not so many here. *De la noche a la mañana* [From one day to the next] they were wiped out and told they would have to leave.

What was the River Corridor?

I don't know, because at that time I was not involved, but I figure they were city officials or government officials, who said *se tienen que ir todos los de San Juan* [all the people from San Juan have to leave] from here. There were a lot of houses here. *Mi abuelita* [My grandmother] used to live there. They had lived there for years, and now they all had to leave. And I know cases like Mrs. Annie Kunz; when she had to leave here, within a year she died. The woman had nothing wrong with her; she was just very saddened at being taken from here.

This was being done because the national park was coming in, so I decided, hey, I don't want this. That's why I opposed it, because from the very first they started *llevándose la gente* [taking people away]. At the time I wasn't very much aware of who was doing it or why, but I knew it had to be the government or city officials. A long time before, studies had been done, but they had never told the people that this was coming. Mrs. Kunz and them, they were very surprised to be asked to leave right away. To me it was very sad.

I thought maybe they also intended to take our religion away, by making the missions like they are in California, where *ya no tienen servicios* [they don't have Masses anymore], okay? I heard down the line once that even the bishop was thinking of making the missions ecumenical, so that any religion could come in and perform their services. This is my religion, so of course I'm going to oppose it! I still do.

So this business with the River Corridor had happened before, and what you feared was that the national park was going to mean more of the same?

I thought that these were the preliminary steps for eliminating the community: get the people out, so you can have this park and the tourists can come in and see the missions. A lot of tourists come in and see the Alamo, and they're very disappointed. It's in the middle of the city! People imagine that it should be somewhere out in the backwoods.

When people come to see these missions, they get a better idea of how things were way back when. They can't picture it at the Alamo, because they don't know what used to be there. To me, that's what the national park intended, and maybe still intends: "Hey, let's do away with the community, so that we can show the place to the tourists as it used to be!"

They've already bought land from the Centenos so they can irrigate and plant the way it was done for the tourists. My goodness! We're still doing that at Espada! People are actually irrigating and planting. Why can't they show that? Why does the national park have to "interpret?" Why can't we interpret? I'm sorry to say this, but why do *gringos* have to interpret our culture?

We were talking to the superintendent and telling him that we would like to have some trees here in the compound, and he was saying that the Park Service was going to hire a person to come in and do a study to find out how things were here, *qué palos había aquí, y que esto y que lo otro, y que pa' aquí y que pa' allá* [what trees were here, and this and that, and from here to there]. And I said, "Sir, maybe I'm not hearing correctly, or maybe you just can't see, but just look around you: we're here, we were here then, and we can tell you something! You don't have to pour in a lot of money for someone to come in and tell you that. All you have to do is turn around and ask the people here!"

That is the kind of thing I object to. It's our history, and we can interpret it far better than outsiders can. But the national park has never asked the people for their side of the story. [See interview with Betty Beuché.]

Were your worst suspicions confirmed? Has the actual experience of having the park as bad as what you thought it was going to be?

It's been what I expected. What I thought would happen has happened. Not only that, but when you open these missions to the public, you bring in a lot of nice visitors, but, especially at the two smaller ones, which are isolated, you also open them to unwanted people who vandalize and cause problems. And, you know, we're just a simple community here; we don't have a security force.

Is it fair to blame the national park for the destruction of the San Juan community, when the natural tendency of these rural communities is to disband anyway, to have the people be drawn away to San Antonio or to other cities?

I'd bet that if you were to ask all the people who were here before, "Would you have left if they hadn't forced you out?" they would have said, "No." I would stake my money on that. We were happy here.

Is there anything positive that has come out of having the park?

Well, we've got the VIA [San Antonio's bus system] bus coming through here! [Laughs.] I want to be fair, but that's what I can come up with. All I can see the national park doing is interpreting the missions in their own way, from their own history books, and at times not interpreting correctly what was here.

Perhaps the tufa house would have fallen down already had the national park not helped maintain it. The structures are here, and Father has a house that wasn't there. Those are good points. But there has never been good cooperation between the residents and the national park.

Not that the national park has perhaps not tried. Maybe it's just me and other people feel differently. I don't see the community deciding to meet with the national park and have a *fandango* or a festival, to get together and see how we can better this place. I've never seen the community say, "We want to meet with them." Neither have I seen the national park say, "We want to meet with the community."

Do you think there would be anything left here if steps hadn't been taken to salvage and restore the structures?

Maybe not. I don't know how the archdiocese would have found money to do it, but I'll tell you something: If you leave a house abandoned, it's going to fall apart. Our casita, the tufa house, was never abandoned, so it would have never fallen down. The church was always used: we always had services, we always looked after it. Maybe the museum, maybe the rest of the walls would have fallen. I have no idea. But I figure that if the people had not been driven away, they would have found a way to keep the place going, because this is our church, and you don't let your church fall apart. Some of the reconstructed buildings would not be here, because we would not have put them back up, but what was here would've stayed, because they were being used.

When the park was coming in, you were a member of committees and so on when the negotiations were going on, weren't you?

At Espada, where I was a member then, not here. I was with the Organized Mission Residents.

What was that?

It was a group of residents and parishioners that got together to see that the landowners knew what was going on, and, if they were going to sell or were going to be expropriated, they thought about possible alternatives. I guess, you might say *que dábanos el pitazo* [that we were blowing the alarm whistle].

And how successful was that group?

Well, you go to Espada, and you look around, and you can see how most of that community is still intact. I think it was very successful. But then again, we had a priest over there who was behind us. Here at San Juan, when everything was going on, I don't know if they even had a priest. Maybe if there was a permanent priest he didn't back them up, or he didn't know what was going on. At Espada, we had both a nun and a priest who knew what was going on and who warned us and talked to us. Then we started alerting the community, and we organized.

Who were they?

Father Manuel Román and Sister Gregoria. If you look in the papers, you'll see that one day we even dressed the church in mourning; we draped it in black, and we announced that the day the national park took over was the beginning of the end of the San Antonio missions as communities. We felt that the archdiocese had handed us over, lambs to the slaughter.

So from your point of view, the ultimate results have been different at Espada than here at San Juan?

Yes, people at Espada have managed to hold on to their community. They have even managed to hold on to their parking lot! It's the only mission where the parishioners can still drive into their own compound to park for church services, and that means a lot to elderly people who can't walk long distances. I can't say that I am aware of major changes at Espada since I've lived there. But that was because they stood up and they organized, they were aware of what was going on.

NOTE

1. Tufa is a porous rock prevalent in the San Antonio area.

Josefina Flores

Josefina Flores, *eighty-one, is a quiet, unassuming woman who insisted throughout that she was not worth interviewing. There is no denying, however, that she is probably representative of a lot of the humble people who have been neighbors of missions Espada and San Juan for generations. Mrs. Flores is the sister-in-law of Emilio Guerra through his first wife, who died at twenty-one of complications following childbirth. The interview, conducted in Spanish, took place on July 31, 1995 at Mrs. Olga Zamora's residence and beauty salon on South Presa Street. Mrs. Zamora is Mr. Guerra's daughter and Mrs. Flores's niece and godchild.*

What is your maiden name, Mrs. Flores?

Jiménez; my full name is Josefina Jiménez Flores.

And what was your husband's name?

He was Enrique Flores.

Where were you born?

I was born March 19, 1914, on a ranch near Elmendorf, Texas. I was born in my grandmother's house, my mother's mother.

Were you raised there also?

We grew up on a ranch near the river. Then we lived in Elmendorf for ten years. We came to the mission neighborhood in 1930.

Why did you move here?

Because my father worked in agriculture, and he started having difficulty finding work to do. He also wanted us kids to have access to schools; that's why he found the house near the mission.

What kind of work did he do when you moved here?

My dad was a laborer, and he did various things. For a time, he worked with the WPA, where they gave work to people who didn't have jobs.

So you were about fifteen or sixteen when you came to this neighborhood?

About that. I went to school here at the mission, but my school has been torn down. I only got to the sixth *libro* ["book," meaning year or grade]. We were *picadores de algodón* [cotton choppers or pickers], the whole family. There were six of us. That's why I never got much education. We were laborers. We used to work out towards Corpus Christi and north from there, and we moved where there was work.

Did you continue working cotton when you came here?

Oh, no, there was no cotton around here. We had a little truck, and we would go north to find work, from September on until it got cold. That's why I didn't get to go to school much. The whole family went along. That went on until my sisters started to get married. It was a sad life, because it was all work.

And when I grew up, I did housework for people.

And your house was near which of the missions?

It was very close to Mission San Juan.

But was the school you went to a church school?

No, it was a public school, right there on Corpus Christi Road. I can't even remember the name of the school now. But they've torn it down; there's only an empty lot where the school was. That was years ago.

Then I got married and was married for fourteen years. We lived on White Avenue. There was a dairy there, and my husband worked for the dairy. But he died just before the fifteenth year of our marriage. He had a heart attack, and he was only thirty-nine years old. He had worked at the dairy for some time, and during that time he got pneumonia. Then he later worked for the county. It was very hard work, and he did not last long.

He left me with two children, one seven and the other fourteen years old. I raised them alone. They went to the Catholic school at Espada. The older one retired from the Army, and the younger one is about to retire from the Navy. But until they grew up, they did yard work to help me out. We also had to go on welfare for a time, and got twenty-four dollars a month to live on. With ten dollars rent on the little house we lived in, there wasn't much left.

After the boys married and left, I went back to live with my parents, but first my father died, and then my mother, so now I live alone.

Are you active in the San Juan congregation?

Not too much, but I help with sweeping out the church, seeing after the candles, and such. We take turns doing it. I do what I can to help the priest. And I help when we have parish festivals or other activities.

What condition was the mission in when you came to the neighborhood?

Oh, it was in very poor condition. It wasn't until '69, the year my mother died, that they started doing repair work on it. They put in a stone floor, repaired the roof, and fixed everything up nicely. And that's the way it has stayed. The current priest, Father Jorge Baistra, is from Mexico, and he keeps it very nice. The parish is very active.

The trouble before was that the priests were here just for a couple of years and then left, three or four years at most, and they didn't even live here. Once, they lived over at Espada. But now they have a house here on the mission and live right here.

Also, when the park came—I don't remember exactly when that was—things changed. There used to be houses there at the mission, but they got swept away.

Were the houses within the mission compound?

Oh, no, but all around it. There were families living around the compound. The interior of the compound always belonged to the church. First it was something with the river that caused many homes to be torn down, then it was the park. That's why there are hardly any left around. We have few people left here at the mission. People went into town to find a place to live.

And there were also a lot of trees, but they also disappeared.

What kind of trees were they?

Palo blanco, mesquites, and anaquas, I think. We used to have our parish feasts under the trees. But many of them came down in a storm; I think it was in '42.

It wasn't that the trees were cut down?

No. We had strong winds and rain, and they were torn down.

Didn't people protest when they were forced to leave?

Not much, because they were poor folks. The government paid people, and they had to leave.

Now it's the park that gives the orders. Any time the congregation wants to have a festival, they have to ask the park people permission to use the plaza at the mission. All the priest controls is his own house and the church. This coming Saturday, for example, we're going to have an activity, but we're going to have it by the river. Without trees there's no shade, and it's too hot in the mission compound to have any activity there.

When they have a *jamaica* [a parish feast to collect funds] like we're going to have on Saturday, it's a lot of work. Because there's no shade, they need to set up tents, and each person who is going to sell something has to set up their own booth—for food, drinks, things for children, and so on.

So when you first came the priest's house was not there?

Yes, it was there, but it wasn't being used for that. There was a caretaker who lived there, but no priest. The house was stone, but it was kind of dilapidated.

If I remember correctly, there was a little store at the mission where they sold souvenirs for visitors. I think the store belonged to the church, but I'm not sure. That was before the park.

I wasn't too active in the church, because I had to work very hard to make a living for me and my boys. Even before I got married, I used to have to go on foot to work from here to Hot Wells. There were two or three women from the neighborhood who went together. There were a lot of houses around Hot Wells where schoolteachers lived, and we worked for them. But it was very tiring to have to walk there, work all day, and then walk back home.

And now you live alone?

Yes, all by myself.

In a house or in an apartment?

Oh, not in an apartment! I couldn't live in an apartment. It's a little house on Corpus Christi Road; I'd rather die there than go to an apartment. You couldn't pay me enough to do it. I know all my neighbors, and I'd rather live among them than among strangers.

Betty Beuché

Betty Beuché has packed a lot of experience into her forty-six years and seems ready for even more adventure as she prepares for a new career. Born and raised in San Antonio, she was the first female superintendent hired by the Texas Parks and Wildlife department at the beginning of a varied and interesting professional life. She talks about her experiences with grace and humor, and her sharp mind provides all sorts of interesting details, connections, and insights. After a divorce and raising two children, Betty is currently at the University of Texas in Austin, studying to become an architect. She was interviewed on July 15, 1995.

Is Beuché your married name or your family name?

It's my family name. When I was working at San José, I was using my married name, which was Calzoncit.

What kind of name is Calzoncit?

It's Tarascan, Mexican Indian.

Are you a native San Antonian?

I was born in San Antonio. My father was in the Air Force. We lived in
Europe for a while and in other parts of the Southwest, and then we
came back to San Antonio when I was twelve. I've lived here from that
time on.

    I'd always been a "southsider." We lived on the south side of town,
and I grew up about eight blocks from Mission San José. My father grew
up just a few blocks from Mission Concepción; he lived on LeCompte
Place, and he and his family were members of St. Leo's parish. We also
were in St. Leo's where I grew up, by the southside Sears, but we
preferred to go to St. Lawrence Church on Petaluma. However, frequently on Sundays we would go to Mass at one or another of the
missions. That was just a part of our routine.

So you grew up with the missions and in constant contact with them?

Oh, yes, always. And from my parents on, even my kids grew up with the
missions. When I was working at San José and they were off from school
in the summer, they would come with me to work. They literally grew
up on the grounds. Both of my children were baptized at Mission
Espada; I was married there also, as were two of my brothers, and also
my in-laws. We're all in the historical records there now! [Laughs.]

**Obviously there is a family affinity with or attraction towards the mis-
sions, but where does it come from?**

I think it was just a matter of our living in the area and finding them
beautiful, wonderful, mysterious places. My father is seventy-three,
and he still talks about playing around Mission Concepción as a boy,
of playing along the San Antonio River and digging clay and fishing.
That was before they did the channelization. I also have all kinds of
memories around San José from before the channelization of the river:
spooky stories, and funny stories, and good stories. I can't really tell
you that there was a conscious decision on our part that we were going
to become connected to the missions. They were just there, and it just
happened.

It was not because your father had any particular interest in the history of the missions, or anything like that?

Well, I think that we all have an interest in their history, particularly since he was in Europe during World War II and was exposed to all the cathedrals and historical monuments and so forth; he brought that back with him. After those experiences, the missions became more important, but I think that the connection was mainly that they were just *there* and that they were so intriguing. The nature of those places and those structures drew us to them.

My father retired from the military in '67 and went into business. In fact, he still is in business today. We continued to live on Dixon Avenue. He started a trophy shop on Military Drive. I was a senior in high school then. When I got married a couple of years later, Espada didn't have its own priest. Father Smith was at St. Lawrence, which was our church, and we asked him to perform the ceremony, but to do it at Espada.

The other interesting thing is that my father is not Hispanic, and what I think is important for people to understand is that there was a host of other people from that area who found a connection to the missions. His heritage is mainly German and French; in fact, his family came here in the 1800s through the port of New Orleans—they didn't come through Ellis Island— and they had land in what is today Windcrest.

In fact, our family cemetery, the Bueché family cemetery, is still there, on a street called Crestwood, which once was called Bueché Road. A lot of the Buechés who came here spoke German, and *they* were living in the area also. And that was in the time period when Germans had to go to the back door of the restaurants, which is probably why we wound up on the south side! We were sod busters and sausage makers, not people born with silver spoons in their mouths.

What is your professional history?

I went to Incarnate Word, both the high school and the college, and got a double degree in art and biology, and then I went to UTSA, where I was working on a master's degree in anthropology when I saw a notice for a job as park superintendent. It said to apply at San José Mission.

I thought it was the job of superintendent at the mission, so I applied but found out that the superintendent at San José was merely interviewing applicants for a superintendent's job somewhere else, namely the

Navarro House downtown. Coincidentally, the Texas Parks and Wildlife department had been placed under court order at that time to hire women and minorities.

Now, I didn't know any of this. I just happened to knock on the door and they went, "Oh my God, it's a *woman*! And she's got a *degree*!" So I became the first woman park superintendent with Texas Parks and Wildlife. I was hired in 1975. I spent about two and a half years at the Navarro House, and when Pete DeVries, who was the person who interviewed me, left San José to work for the archdiocese running the other missions, I was promoted and became superintendent at San José. So Pete was running the other three missions, and I was running San José, until the Park Service entered at that point, and all that uncertainty . . . .

Somehow your degrees don't seem to me particularly related to becoming superintendent of the Navarro House. Did Texas Parks and Wildlife provide any special training for you?

Yes, as a matter of fact; I was hired in December, and in January they had two training programs right away, which were the first that Parks and Wildlife had ever had. They had always been in the recreational park and the wildlife business and, frankly, they didn't know quite what to do with historic sites. But, at LBJ National Historic Site and Johnson City, they had a collaborative training program with A&M's Parks and Rec. department and the National Park Service (NPS), and we had several weeks of training in historic sites management and preservation.

Then, that was followed by a week of training at Bastrop State Park on interpretation of parks. So I was very fortunate that at just that moment in time they also decided to do some training. But a lot of the work that I had been doing prior to that in my artwork involved interpretation, and I had done a great deal of work in the area of North American Indian arts. Thus, I had quite a bit of information and expertise and had been hanging around museums and that sort of thing for a long time prior.

So you weren't exactly a babe in the woods; you had a background you could build on.

Yes, but in the position of park superintendent, you're basically the janitor for the site [laughs], so *that* part wasn't hard! I knew how to keep the restrooms clean and mow the grass and that kind of stuff. Supervision is a whole lot like being a mother, and I'd done that already. And I could balance a checkbook, so budgeting was easy. In general, there was a relatively easy transference of skills!

Any particular problems you encountered as the superintendent of the Navarro House?

I had a blast! Quite frankly, my experience was so wonderful that those five years at Texas Parks and Wildlife were the best five years of my professional life. I think that they didn't quite know what to do with a woman, and they didn't know quite what to do with a historic site, so basically they let me do anything I wanted to do.

There were humorous things, like: when it was time for me to get uniforms, they only had uniforms for men, and they finally told me that they would buy me some yard goods, if I was willing to make something myself [laughs], which I did. But it was all a lot of fun.

At another point, they had what they called EEO [Equal Employment Opportunity] sensitivity training. I remember I went to Austin for that. There were about eighty game wardens in this room, and they were all like six-foot seven, all looking even taller because they were wearing high-heeled cowboy boots and big cowboy hats. Of course, I'm five-foot four, so it was like walking around in a forest! [Laughs.] And all these big old burly guys who were chewing tobacco and snuff and stuff were sitting around talking about EEO sensitivity . . . I just thought it was a hoot!

And they were trying so hard! Those poor guys were just fumbling all over themselves trying to figure out how to be sensitive to women. They hadn't a clue back in the '70s, when this was all first happening, but they were very sincere. I was trying to make light of it, because it was obvious to me that they *were* sincere, and really were trying hard, and they wanted to do better, but they really couldn't figure out how to do it.

I was the only woman park superintendent for about three years. Then, when they did hire more women superintendents, they usually started in a small historic site, like I was. When I left Parks and Wildlife five years later I was still the ranking female in the field, but a few years after that there was a woman who became a regional director.

When you became park superintendent, didn't they have any other women: not in interpretation, not as rangers, etc.?

Oh, yes, they had a few women, and frankly, it was because of Pete DeVries. He had hired a number of women at San José as park rangers, and they were doing both interpretation and maintenance. That was a sort of real revolutionary thing to do! From the way you smile, you must know Pete DeVries!

No, I've never met him, but I have heard a lot about him, and I have a certain mental picture of what sort of person he must be. But I was just thinking about the current headlines regarding the Texas Rangers and the problems they've had with the few women they've hired.

Yes, I know; they were too "ladylike!" Well, women just have a different way of doing things. If they hired women expecting them to accomplish things in the same way that men do them, then they hired them for the wrong reasons. Women will get the job done, but they will do it in a different way.

It sounds like you encountered a positive atmosphere, whereas these poor women seem to have had a hell of a time with the Texas Rangers.

I think those situations work both ways. First of all, if you've got upper-level management that really doesn't want this, and they're set to be hardnosed about it, it will never happen. Then, you can have a situation where you have upper-level management that kind of wants to do it but isn't quite sure. There, if you have someone in position who can make the best of it and say, "Well, I'm not quite sure what I'm doing either, but we're all going to figure it out," you can make it work.

I will say this: I'm confident that not just any woman could have been the first woman park superintendent in Texas Parks and Wildlife and made a success out of it. I think that some of them would've gotten their nose out of joint or have been grossed out and left.

We had an annual park superintendents' meeting in Austin, and everybody had a pickup truck with the state seal. Well, the local prostitutes always knew when these meetings happened, and there were a hundred or more of us, and they would leaflet the trucks, and I would get on my windshield these handbills: "Call Susie for a good time" or "Get 20% discount with Linda." [Laughs.] I mean, if you didn't laugh at it, you'd have to cry or get real upset!

And there were always things like that. But you just have to decide what's important to you and fit it into the right spot and go on. And I can't tell you that all of them liked me; but I can tell you that all of them felt that I did a good job, and also that I made a lot of changes, because of being how I was. They were all astounded, I think, that they could have a woman among their group, and it would be okay. They were shocked to find that that was all right.

A revelation! Now, you credit Pete DeVries with being very forward-looking in this area. Where did that come from? Why was Pete different from the rest of them?

Pete was just different anyway. Pete's background was that he had worked on—though, I think, never finished—a degree in theater arts at Baylor, and theater people and art people just view things a little differently, number one; and they're creative problem-solvers, number two. What Pete told me was that after Texas Parks and Wildlife had been taken to court a couple of times, he just got to the point where he said, "What is the matter with you guys? Can't you figure this out? You're supposed to hire women and minorities, so let's just get on with it and do it!" So he did.

However, I think Pete was a little bit out of the loop of the good ol' boys in the department because he was willing to do things like this. But nevertheless, he really was the one who broke the ice and led the way.

So you were at the Navarro House for two and a half years, then Pete moved on to the job of being diocesan caretaker of the other missions, and you moved into the position at San José.

Correct, and this was still with Texas Parks and Wildlife.

What can you tell me about the background of San José as a state park?

When San José was designated a National Historic Site [1941], people didn't know what to do with it, so it was also designated a Texas state park. There hadn't been any state parks like that before, and it was the first National Historic Site to be designated west of the Mississippi. Everyone was at a loss as to how to administer it. They let the San Antonio Conservation Society, which had just gotten organized, handle it, and a woman named Ethel Wilson Harris moved into the grounds and actually lived and raised her family in part of the Indian quarters.

If the place had been designated a state park, how could she get to live on the grounds?

Well, the state park system was run rather informally in those days, and everybody knew in San Antonio that the Conservation Society people were really the ones who were interested and wanted to take care of the place. Ethel owned a piece of property out there, which she had bought next to the mission, and she just sort of stepped forward and took on the care of it. She was a single parent back in the '40s and had to raise her kids, so this was how she did it. She also was a contractor; she built her own home and others. The Harris house at San José was built by Ethel herself.

She supported the place, maintained, did repointing and so on, by running an arts and crafts gift shop on the grounds and later by having outdoor theater productions. There was something like a gravel pit behind San José where the amphitheater is now, and she created that outdoor theater, which is why Pete DeVries first went there. He began working there as a student doing maintenance work and worked there for a long time. He had been a theater arts student. And every summer she would have these productions at what was later designated the Texas State Historic Outdoor Theater, and the students who participated also lived in the Indian quarters, dirt floors and all. Pete would help her with this, and when she was ready to stop running San José and retire, Pete was hired as superintendent.

It was a real seat-of-the-pants, bootstrap kind of effort. She was a very strong personality and chafed a lot of people—there were a whole lot of people who disliked Ethel Wilson Harris—but if she hadn't been the kind of person that she was, San José wouldn't be there today! I consider her to be the real pioneer in historical preservation of the missions. San José was way out in the "boonies" in those days, a long way to go from downtown, and she was able to attract people to come out there. She was actually the one who started the San José Indian Festival, which later became NIOSA—A Night in Old San Antonio—one of the most popular attractions of the San Antonio Fiesta today. That's how she supported San José.

What years are we talking about now?

Well, from the '40s until Pete was hired. Ethel Wilson Harris ran San José, and she had a special deal with Texas Parks and Wildlife that she could keep half of the admission fees. She would make trips to Mexico: Chiapas, Oaxaca, and so on, to visit villages and ranches and bring back gates and potter's wheels, and she would bring Mexicans from Mexico

Ethel Harris, right, at Mission San José, with Dorothy Pouquet, who assisted her with bookkeeping and office work, and Angel Rendón, who worked in the tile and pottery production at the mission workshops and was also an excellent palm and cane weaver. Courtesy of Donald and Trudy Harris.

to demonstrate crafts, and that sort of thing. She had an entire pottery production plant in the Indian quarters, with kilns and all the rest.

In fact, when I got there, the vigas and *sabiños* [roof crossbeams and ceiling lattice work made out of branches] were still scorched where the kilns had been, and I replaced them. I also found all of her ceramic production equipment still there. She was in a nursing home at that point, so I notified the state archaeologist about this material. He was her contemporary and knew her, so he visited her and asked her to sign over to the state all of those things so that they could be used for research and as part of exhibits and so on. But, lying in bed in a nursing home, she replied, "Well, I am just not ready to do that." And she never did. But it's because of people like her that the missions are still here.

What happened to all that material?

When I left the Park Service it was still in storage, and ownership of it was still in limbo. The family was told that it was there, but I don't think the family knew what to do with it. When you looked at it, it looked like a pile of junk, but if you knew what you were looking at, there was some pretty interesting stuff there: her molds, jiggers for the wheels, and that kind of thing.

I've heard of the Conservation Society's efforts in regard to the granary at San José. Was this before Ethel Harris, or what?

I'll recount to you what Wanda Ford, O'Neil Ford's wife, has told me about that on a number of occasions. Wanda and Ethel were both very handsome young women, and the guy who was either the director of the Park Service or the Secretary of the Interior back in '33 was kind of sweet on both of them, and they knew it. Ethel was then a widow, and Wanda was married to O'Neil, but they decided to play that for all it was worth to get San José designated as a National Historic Site.

The man came to San Antonio over and over again on inspection tours to "see the site," and they just flirted with him, and wined and dined him, and so on. I think in those days that was what you would call a flirtation. Today, I guess, they wouldn't stop with flirting, but in those days it was different. Wanda told me that she and Ethel used to tease each other about which one of them he liked best. Wanda was a very striking woman who drove a red convertible, and Ethel was pretty spiffy, too. Anyway, these ladies were the ones who got San José designated a National Historic Site. There are photographs of the signing ceremony in the granary, and you can almost see the twinkle in the guy's eyes! [Laughs.][1]

Once it was so designated, then it became eligible for WPA funds, and after that work was done, the question was what to do with the site. And that was when Ethel stepped forward. Given Ethel's "special position" in the process, it all quickly and easily fell into place.[2] The WPA work was directed by Harvey P. Smith, the architect, who told me before he died that his work was inspired by the missions in New Mexico.

There were a lot of people who didn't like Ethel Wilson Harris, but if she hadn't been willing to do what she did—nobody else was willing—San José would be something quite different today. I think she is a hero. I met her and talked to her, and admittedly, she was pretty ornery, but she was a hero nonetheless! [Laughs.] It takes being ornery sometimes to accomplish something like that!

Tell me about your move from the Navarro House to San José. What did you encounter when you got to San José? What kinds of things happened to you in your tenure?

The issue of whether San José should become part of the national park was already on the table. There had been a couple of studies done: one done in the '60s, and the Park Service finally did what they called their feasibility study in 1975. I went to San José in '77, and it was pretty much a unanimous feeling within the Park Service that they absolutely did not want these missions in the park system.

No question about it: the site was not pristine enough, the urban area had encroached too much, there wasn't enough original fabric, the proposal that the city wanted included too many things besides the missions, etc. There was just too long a laundry list of negatives. All of the representatives of the Park Service that I talked to told me there was no way this was going to happen. They were recommending against it.

But San Antonians rallied and lobbied in favor. The Department of the Interior had its Subcommittee on Insular Affairs hold meetings in San Antonio. Henry Cisneros, who was a city councilman at that time, was mayor pro tem, and he went to the meeting and told the subcommittee, "We'll pass a zoning law to protect the mission area. We'll acquire land that you don't want to acquire but is needed."[3] Basically, he promised to do anything that the Park Service felt it needed, and there was a lot of behind-the-scenes lobbying by the Conservation Society and by the congressman from Laredo, Chick Kazen, who later was designated an "honorary park ranger" for his part in making the park possible. In fact, when Chick went out of office, he turned over all of his files on the park to the Park Service, and I was put in charge of sorting through these files. In his files there were letters from virtually everyone saying, "We want this park, and we promise we'll do whatever the Park Service says we need to do in order to get this approved."

So, that was happening on one side. On the other side, I was talking to Park Service representatives, who were still saying, "Look, this is a bad deal for us. We never take a park that's so trashed out. We don't want parks that have hot dog stands right in front of the door, etc." And the historical architect from the regional office also had some very strong opinions about how the architecture had been compromised too many times, and there was not enough original fabric, and so on and so forth.

Nobody knew exactly what would happen, whether this would get passed or not. President Carter then was elected, and he was a real progressive thinker in the area of parks and open spaces. He created what came to be affectionately known as "Hookers": HCRS, the Heritage/Conservation/Recreation Service. The "Hookers" were real interesting people. They believed in open space, but they were not the regimented, Army-like folks from the NPS, and they wanted to find ways to do things cooperatively and with public involvement to raise funds, etc.

The NPS heritage is literally from the Army. When Yellowstone was created, they dispatched a number of Army folks to go protect it, literally, and their uniforms come down from the Army green, and campaign hats, etc. Its not a "Smoky the Bear hat," it's an Army campaign hat, and they had a very rigid view of how a park should be acquired and operated, and how it should function. They felt they needed to have total control over it, and that sort of thing.

The "Hookers," on the other hand, would say, "Hey, let's get everybody involved; the more the merrier. You want to pick up the trash and have volunteers, great!" Anyway, these two outlooks were like night and day, and it was during that time also that there were many parks that were being acquired. They referred to this phenomenon as "the Park-of-the-Month club." And our park came in under that, when all of that was going on.

It was held up for implementation, though, because the Department of Justice had said to President Carter, "We have problems with the church/state issue and First Amendment issues in reference to this proposed park." So the president did not implement it. Fortunately, Congressman Kazen had attached this park to a bill that authorized funds for the improvement of Pennsylvania Avenue in Washington, in front of the White House! [Laughs.] So anyway, the thing got done. But not until we had literally an army of First Amendment attorneys—I didn't even know before then that there are attorneys who spend their entire lives studying just the First Amendment—traipsing through San Antonio and leaving no stone unturned over the issue of separation of church and state. I thought they were very hypersensitive. Here I was, having grown up in the neighborhood and working at the park; dealing with the missions was like walking and chewing gum at the same time—you just did it! It was not a big deal.

I did hear stories about when San José was designated as a National Historic Site. Apparently, at that time, and I've seen old photographs of this, they actually built a chain-link fence around the church, so as to say, "Okay, that's the church part, and over here's the part where we can spend funds." Despite that hypersensitivity in the '40s, eventually that fence came down, and everybody relaxed again.

So when the NPS people were basically told, "You will operate this park," which was against their better judgment, they too had this sensitivity, and they had to run the gauntlet on all of that.

You say that the failure of Carter to implement this project came from First Amendment questions in Washington, but I've heard it said that there was a Baptist preacher[4] here in San Antonio who raised a fuss about money being spent on Catholic Church property.

There was a Baptist preacher in San Antonio who had been raising that question for many years. You have to understand that this national park was first proposed in 1932. I had documents in my files which discussed the same question from that time until the law was passed in 1978. So exactly who initiated concerns about separation of church and state, I think, is open for a great deal of discussion.

The fact was that when the park was authorized by Congress, it was the Department of Justice who raised the question; whether it trickled up from the people who were alive in '32 or not, it was Justice who advised Carter that he really needed to be careful about this. You also have to remember that about the same time, the Martin Luther King site was acquired, and the Ebenezer Baptist Church was a part of that site, so the issue didn't apply just to San Antonio.

And actually, when they looked around, they found out that there was a whole bunch of churches in the NPS. There were other missions in New Mexico that had had churches, even if they were not active parishes; there was the Old North Church in Boston; there were several churches in Philadelphia at Independence Hall National Historic Monument; and a number of others. Ebenezer Baptist Church and the missions of San Antonio were only the ones that were still active as churches, so, really, that was the only new set of issues they were looking at.

The other reason I thought that those issues were a bit ridiculous was that I was a military brat, and the government has military chaplains on its payroll, for Pete's sake!

Of course! They even have one in Congress, for that matter.

Yeah! They were worried about teaching religion at the missions or at Ebenezer, and I had just come from catechism classes taught by a military chaplain in a military chapel at a base in England! So, I really didn't understand the concerns.

On a more academic level I didn't understand it either, because I come from an academic background, and I knew that historically, in our area, there was no separation of church and state. In Spanish colonial times, the church and the state went hand in hand, and if you wanted to recognize the cultural diversity of our country and acknowledge the history of this part of it, you couldn't obscure that fact. In fact, all of that happened here before the English tradition got established on the Eastern seaboard.

When they finally agreed that, okay, they could run the park, and the interpreters could go up to the church door, but they can't go into the church—then they have to run around the side and meet visitors as they come out the back, and all this nonsense—I thought that was pretty stupid. I think it is entirely possible—in fact, I've done it—to interpret the history of the missions and how they functioned as an arm of the state as a religious institution, and not be teaching religion! That's a no-brainer for me!

And that's how I was running the park. I remember specifically one day, when there was a terrible windstorm, and the pastor at San José came to my office to tell me that the doors had been blown off the front of the church; you know, those huge wooden doors that weigh a ton. He said he did not have the people to put them back up—at that time, they were all older brothers and priests around the mission, except for one of them—so he needed some help. So I just went to the rangers and told them, "Look, you guys, after work, anyone who wants to volunteer to help put the doors back up, show up at six o'clock, and Father will direct you." That was the end of it. Some of them showed up, and some of them didn't, but it was no big deal, and the doors were put back up. What were we going to do otherwise, leave the doors off the church?

We've been talking a little bit ahead of the game. Tell me what kind of problems you faced as superintendent of the San José Mission State Park.

At San José, because there was uncertainty about whether the NPS was going to be taking it over or not, there was always uncertainty about our funding. We had certain projects underway . . . one of them was repointing the mortar in the walls . . . and one day, in the middle of the project, I was told, "We're not spending any more money; send everybody home!" And I had to do exactly that in the middle of the afternoon.

They also didn't want us to fill vacant positions. And a lot of that was understandable. But the problem came in the area of personnel. You've got ten permanent employees, and you have half a dozen part-timers and volunteers and some Youth Conservation Corps workers, and there was no way for me to reassure them that they were going to have a job either with the NPS or with Parks and Wildlife when this was all over.

As a result, morale really plummeted at that point. These people had to feed their kids, go to the doctor, and meet their obligations; wages were not that good, and they were living from paycheck to paycheck. So a lot of them started looking for other jobs, and by the time it became clear that the Park Service was going to take over, we were short-staffed, and it was difficult to get even basic things done, like mowing the grass, picking up litter, and that sort of thing.

Part of that also was that the NPS feels that they are the premier conservation organization in the world . . . and that is partly justified. But the Park Service representatives had this air of superiority that rather chafed Parks and Wildlife people. In effect, as Parks and Wildlife saw it, they were saying, "Now we're going to take over and do the job right. You guys have fooled around here since the 1930s and never did it quite right. We're not real happy to have it, because you've messed it up all these years, but we're going to come in and fix it!"

Naturally, Texas Parks and Wildlife was very offended by that, and a conflict between the two agencies really bubbled to the surface. In fact, when it came right down to it, Texas Parks and Wildlife could have signed over the management of San José to the NPS much earlier, but they decided to rebel and get stubborn. They claimed they had to go to the legislature and get a new law passed authorizing them to have a cooperative agreement to sign over operations to the Park Service. They really didn't have to do that, but that's what they chose to do.

The governor of Texas at that time was Governor Clements, and he was a good friend of the Texas Parks and Wildlife department's director of parks, Mr. Bell, who took a really serious disliking to the NPS. Because of that friendship, the necessary legislation was dragged out for a long, long time, until finally they just couldn't say no anymore, and they passed it.

When it was time for the governor to sign the bill, we all went up to Austin to watch the signing, and as the governor leaned over his desk to sign the bill, he took one look at all the Park Service uniforms around the room and said, "Ah shore do hate to see this park leave the state!"

One of the rangers rather idiotically pointed out, "Well, it's not going anywhere; it's going to stay right here!" It was an obvious thing that would have better been left unremarked! [Laughs.] But right down to the signing of the agreement, there was this kind of thing going on.

It was a lot of unnecessary conflict that didn't need to happen. I actually joined the NPS in 1980, and they still hadn't acquired the operation of the mission at that time. The superintendent of the new national park had come to town and set up an office. He started hiring people, and I didn't want to get left behind, so I applied for a job and was hired. I thought the transfer was imminent and would happen, but when the conflict bubbled up and Parks and Wildlife decided they were going to dig in, they hired another superintendent. They "camped out" and were ready to stay. They started to put funds back in for projects, to hire employees, and to restore all the allocations that had been taken away. They were not going to give up easily.

So they were, in effect, mounting a sort of rear-guard action.

Yeah, that was a very amusing time.

Well, where did you go in the meantime?

I worked for the NPS.

But where?

There was an office in the Federal Building downtown, so it was very different situation from having daily contact with the site to going into an office building in the city. We had our office down there for five years, until a building was built closer to the missions, the one the

NPS is in now on Roosevelt Road. But before they moved in, I left the Park Service.

I had started the Los Compadres organization [a secular support organization for the missions; see description p. 110] and went to work for the organization as its executive director. So my office then was back out at San José mission, where I wanted to be to begin with, in the Harris house.

What did the NPS people do in those five years when they didn't have access to the site, but were here in San Antonio?

Well, I'll tell you what: we read a lot of memos and wrote a lot of memos! [Laughs.] But the main thing that we produced was called the General Management Plan or the concept plan. The team leader was David Gaines, who was in Santa Fe; he is a landscape architect. Then there was a team of around ten people. I was not initially on the team, but since I knew San Antonio so well, and I knew everybody in town, I wound up basically coordinating the whole plan in San Antonio. When it came down to it, David said, "Well, your name needs to be added to the team."

I was dealing with VIA to come up with a plan for a bus line; I was dealing with the San Antonio Police department drafting the cooperative agreement between the rangers and the police department; I worked on the zoning task force to rezone the whole area, etc. So I was listed as a core team member. That was not originally what I was hired to do, but since we weren't running a park, that's what I did.

Recently I've become aware of opposition from the local community to the establishment of a national park at the missions. Did you have any experience in dealing with that?

Sure. First of all, I should say that there's always been opposition to the establishment of a national park, or it would've happened in 1932. It took forty-five years to get it done. It took every politician in the state of Texas making promises to the Department of the Interior that we would be good and do the right thing if they would just make this a park. There was lots of opposition to it.

On church/state grounds was one source of opposition. The other thing was a feeling that the NPS was going to be intruding in the neighborhoods, in the communities, in the parish functions, that sort of thing. There was a lot of concern. We held a series of public meetings on our Land Acquisition Plan, which was part of the general management planning process.

The meetings were held at all the missions and at different locations around town, and there were people who showed up at these meetings who were very concerned about not just what was going to happen to their land but about what would happen if a landowner stayed and the NPS bought a scenic easement: "Are tourists going to come and look at us as if we were curiosities?" I remember someone specifically asking whether the tourists were going to be expecting the locals to dress up in Mexican dresses and put a rose between their teeth and dance for them. People were very concerned about being "put on display," and I think that that was a very valid concern.

The people of Espada Mission were particularly opposed. They have never, never been in favor of the creation of a national park. Father Manuel Román was the pastor there at the time, and he was often a spokesperson for his parishioners. Father Manuel, I think, saw both sides of the question. He saw that there would be advantages, because that was the poorest of the poor parishes, and they would benefit, if from nothing else, from someone taking over the maintenance of the site, or the maintenance of the local roads.

There was also a water problem in the area: everyone was using well water, and when the city of San Antonio tested the wells, it was found that they had a very high coliform bacteria content. The people using this water obviously had some natural resistance that they had built up over the years, but if there was to be a national park there, it would be necessary to have good water provided by the city. That's another aquifer out there, not the Edwards Aquifer. It's a very shallow aquifer, and all those wells were in that shallow aquifer where the pollutants could get to the water very easily.

So he could see that the community would get water, sewers, better services all the way around, but with all of those good things comes the impact of change, and these people wanted to keep their traditions, they wanted to keep their land, and they did not want to feel like they were being shoved around. On the day when the NPS took over, there was a ceremony with the regional director, various dignitaries, and, of course, the newspapers and television. For that same day, Father Manuel proclaimed a "Day of Mourning for the Missions" at Espada and called his own press conference for shortly after the NPS ceremony would be over, so the papers and TV had time to go from one event to the other.

I was perfectly in my element in this controversy, because that was what I focused on when I was working on my master's in social anthropology: what happens when a group is put under pressure to change, and what is the best thing to do in such a situation. I think the Park Service at that time didn't have the skills to handle that. They may have improved since then, but at that time that was not their forte, and I don't think that they answered the questions of these people, that they allayed their fears. I think that that still exists.

In connection specifically with San Juan, someone mentioned "the River Corridor." What was all that about?

The River Corridor has nothing to do with the NPS officially. It is a boundary that was designated by the San Antonio River Authority (SARA), which is a state agency. The state has created such river authorities all over Texas; ours is the SARA. Those river authorities get funds from the state and the Army Corps of Engineers to do flood control projects and other things.

The River Authority activities and the channelization of the river were occurring in the '50s and '60s, and the people carrying them out were very insensitive They were engineers, and engineers don't even know how to communicate with each other, much less with the public. [Laughs.] They just don't have people skills. I think today they are taught such skills, but in those days they were not. And the result was like this: "What do you mean you don't want to move out of your house? The water's going to come right through here!"

The Army Corps of Engineers displaced a lot of people to do the channelization, and in the minds of the people affected, all the authorities that came in after that were regarded with suspicion, whether the city, the Corps, or the National Parks Service. Some of the anger toward the River Authority and the River Corridor was transferred over to the NPS and the new park proposal. The NPS was, of course, innocent of all that, but they got hit nonetheless.

Someone compared the two communities, Espada and San Juan, and said that, as you mentioned, there was concerted opposition at Espada, so they were able to better take care of their own interests, whereas at San Juan, the community didn't have that capacity or didn't have the leaders for it. Consequently, the San Juan community

was virtually wiped out between the River Corridor and the Park Service. Do you think that is a fair assessment of it?

The community at San Juan did have leaders. However, their leadership was more in favor of the NPS. Many of them either were or had been employees of the federal government themselves, or their wives or relatives had been, or they had been in the military. So they had more trust in the federal government. Anyway, their feelings about government were quite different than the strong alienation that was felt by the community at Espada. They more easily saw the good things that the government might be able to do for them through the NPS. That is not to say that there wasn't some opposition at San Juan, because there was.

The other thing to understand is that San Juan has a number of different churches that that parish takes care of. As a matter of fact, I think that at one time Espada was a *visita* [a small, subsidiary congregation of the main parish] of San Juan, and Mother Cabrini Church was a *visita* of Espada. And when you get farther and farther away from where the headquarters are, then you have enclaves or groups who think differently. So San Juan was the leading church of this community, but each one of its subsidiary centers wanted some independence. I think Espada resented not having its own parish designation.

Espada is also much poorer than San Juan, and I don't know within the Catholic Church how they measure who gets a priest and who doesn't—whether it's based on population or money or both. But whatever the reasons were, Espada for a long time didn't have its own priest. They finally got Father Manuel, but it remained a visita of San Juan. So that's part of it, too.

The other thing has to do with the acequia organization. Missions San Juan and Espada both have their full acequia systems existing. Espada, however, was the only one that continued to operate, the Espada Ditch Corporation. It is an organization of the people who live along the ditch, who continue to maintain it. The water still flowed, and the people would have their *suertes* [irrigation period assignments], and they grew their crops.

The ditch company at San Juan still existed, but the Corps of Engineers and the River Authority had destroyed the San Juan dam during the channelization of the river. The Corps looked at the dam and thought, "Oh, this is just a pile of rocks; we'll just bulldoze it," and they did.

The Espada aqueduct over Piedras Creek was finished in 1740 and is still in operation as part of the acequia system that has continued to be an important part of the life of the two southernmost missions. Courtesy of the National Park Service, San Antonio Missions National Historical Park.

On purpose, or without realizing what they were doing?

No, they had no idea what they were doing. I mean, it just looked like a pile of rocks. I think somebody did tell them, "Hey, that's really a dam." But their reaction was apparently, "No way!" I think there was just no understanding at all, no sensitivity, no realization of significance. So the San Juan Ditch Corporation had their water cut off when the dam was destroyed.

They were, of course, very angry; after all, they had Spanish colonial water rights, which had been upheld in the Texas Supreme Court. There had been a case in the 1950s and '60s, just before that, that had gone all the way through the courts, and they had upheld that colonial water rights were enforceable. The Corps of Engineers and the River Authority then said, "Look, it's too expensive for us to rebuild the dam. We've already planned our channel, and you can't expect us to build a dam just to supply this little ditch. So we'll tell you what: we'll build a pump; we'll pump water for you."

The San Juan ditch people wanted their dam back, but the courts decided that they didn't have the right to a dam; they only had a right to the water, and if the River Authority could give them water by pumping it into the ditch, that was all they had to do. However, it took so many years to get that settlement agreement that part of the ditch eroded, and when they went to pump water into it, it started flowing out all over the place. So the Ditch Corporation was told that they had to repair their ditch before the Authority would start pumping water again.

The ditch had not only been a means of irrigating the land, it had also been a means of holding the community together, a real connecting thing, a unifying force. With the acequia out of commission, I think there was also less unity in the San Juan community than there was at Espada, where the people were still connected by their stream of water that flowed for nine miles and came directly out of the San Antonio River.

That dam, I want you to know, would not be in existence either except that after the Corps had destroyed the San Juan dam, they were forced to leave the Espada dam alone. This happened partly because of the fuss over the San Juan dam, but also because of the people who own Mission Cemetery, a family-owned business. They, too, have Spanish colonial water rights, which they use to water the cemetery.

This was a very important business in the community, so they also entered the fray, and all of those forces together helped save the Espada dam. One time I visited the office of Mission Cemetery, and they had pictures on the wall of a time when they had themselves repaired the dam. I don't know if the people at Espada realize that they wouldn't have their water today if it wasn't for this family and their efforts both to repair the dam and to protect it legally.

I think that the acequia system is a real unifying force, and when that water ceased to flow at San Juan, some of the community's unity fell apart.

So San Juan was left without water until this whole question was resolved?
That's right!

Then it makes perfect sense that the one community would benefit from the fact that its water continues to flow uninterruptedly, while the

other is destroyed by the fact that water ceases to flow to it for a period of several years.

Water is the basis for our whole city and all of our heritage in San Antonio. The reason the city is here, and there are missions here, is that there was water available. And when the King of Spain would grant land, he would grant the water to go with it; otherwise the land would be worthless. You take that factor away and you don't have a community.

Tell me about Los Compadres.

When President Reagan was elected after Jimmy Carter, it became clear that funding for a lot of things would dry up. In fact, Carter's "Hookers"were deactivated and had to be absorbed by the NPS. But along with Reaganomics came a whole new Park Advisory Board. The law that created this particular national park included the provision that the park would have an advisory board and specified who would be on the board. All were political appointees, but some had to be from the church, a conservation organization, etc., but, in the end, the board had to have the approval of the political party in power.

Well, we got a whole new advisory board, mostly Republicans, and they had their marching orders from the Republican party that they were to reduce the budgetary needs of things, and one of the ways to do that was to establish a "friends" organization for this particular national park. And there was a precedent for that.

In Philadelphia, the Friends of Independence Hall had been in existence for ten years already. Their purpose was very limited in scope. They had been created to raise large sums of money to do "opportunity purchases," like the original chair that Benjamin Franklin sat in, etc., to act quickly on things that the Park Service could not do. They were also to foster general political support in that community.

So it was decided that we would do a similar thing in San Antonio, but it wouldn't be just for such purchases but of a broader scope, partly because of the church-and-state problem, partly because of Reaganomics. It was to do anything which the government either couldn't fund or wouldn't fund. That core of Los Compadres started from the members of the advisory board, and I was assigned to be the one to get it started.

There were several of us who went to Philadelphia to meet with the Friends of Independence Hall. I was doing this as a Park Service employee. I then traveled to some other national parks: Channel

Islands, Golden Gate, etc., to look at their initiatives and what they were doing with fund-raising and volunteers and so on.

The group [Los Compadres] in San Antonio was very ambitious, and they wanted to really be an outstanding group that raised a lot of funds, so we put together a very influential, high-powered board that could do so. Simultaneously with this happening, the Statue of Liberty/Ellis Island Foundation was established, with Lee Iacocca at its head. Such an unbelievable amount of money was needed to restore the statue that they needed to get a Lee Iacocca to do it. So these kinds of efforts began to spring up throughout the Park Service.

Within the NPS there was lots of resistance to it, because they were feeling a great deal of loss of control. They felt that if the Park Service took money from outside people, then those donors would want to control what the NPS did. As it turned out, those "Hookers," who had been absorbed into the NPS, knew how to do all this stuff, which was exactly what they had been doing, and Park Service-wide they were assigned to coordinate and lead these kinds of efforts. And it turned out that they were very handy at doing that.

I knew a lot of people in San Antonio already. I grew up here, and, in fact, the woman who was appointed chairwoman of our advisory board at that time, Patsy Light, and I had met at Incarnate Word College, where we were in some classes together. Even though I was a southsider, I knew a lot of these people already, because I had gotten around all over town.

With that advisory board, we put together a really strong board of directors for Los Compadres. We had an attorney who offered the services of one of the attorneys in his office to write all of our legal documents; we established ourselves as a nonprofit corporation; we got our designation from the IRS and started raising funds.

Shortly after we kicked all that off, we were contacted by the Meadows Foundation from Dallas, which wanted to do something with us. We talked to them quite a bit, and eventually they gave us a grant of $400,000. It was the largest grant that they had given to anyone in San Antonio at that time, and the tenth largest that they had ever given. Of that, $375,000 was to be spent at Mission Concepción, and the other $25,000 was to be used to start a volunteer program for the park.

The Meadows Foundation is a foundation that has a lot of money. It was established by Alger Meadows, who was an oilman and multi-millionaire. He set up the foundation, which his children have operated for many years. They are on the board, and so are his grandchildren, and they make the decisions about things that they are going to fund. So it's a very personal thing for them to make these decisions using Dad's money and Grandpa's money, and they want to do it within the spirit of what he intended. One of the things that he said had to happen was that the money could only be spent in Texas. [Laughs.] So the Meadows Foundation hired some really sharp young people who had a lot of experience working with groups, and they beat the bushes looking for projects in Texas, because, frankly, they have so much money that spending it becomes a problem. And they have to worry about their own tax-exempt status: they have to give grants in order to keep it.

They were very impressed with Los Compadres, and what we were doing, and the nature of our activity, and that's why they gave us this big grant. Well, that gave us a huge boost, and very quickly Los Compadres became—next to the Statue of Liberty and Ellis Island Foundation—the third most successful "friends" organization in the Park Service.

Subsequent to that, the older parks like Yellowstone and Yosemite also established fund-raising groups, and they have raised more money than Los Compadres, but they have a bigger need, and they have a bigger audience. Los Compadres has funded things that run from minor maintenance problems to major restoration of the wall paintings at Concepción and the arches and the convento area behind San José. They fund volunteer activities to support tours—they have bus tours occasionally, every year they have a bicycle tour—and a lot of other things.

You said that you started organizing Los Compadres as a Park Service employee, and yet this kind of organization was supposed to be outside the realm of the NPS. How was that conflict resolved?

Well, these people I mentioned before from the "Hookers" that came into the Park Service understood that you could provide staff support to a community effort that was supporting your park. That was kind of a new concept in the NPS, but it became an accepted practice because of the infusion of these people in the Park Service staff. Although I think that even today the Park Service would still prefer to have its own government-allocated funds rather than take money that is raised from the community, because they feel that compromises their control over what goes on within a park.

The other part of this is that anyone who contributes money to your efforts is one of your constituents and supporters. If you need help, they're going to be there, because they've already reached in their pocket and proved they are with you. That helps, too, and I think that Los Compadres has been able to influence allocations of federal funds subsequently as well, to make sure that the park did get additional funds when it needed them.

Now, the missions have been around for a couple of centuries, and for the longest time they had been pretty much ignored. Why the change of heart? Why, apparently all of a sudden, should we find people willing to dig into their pockets to help them and preserve them?

I guess I don't agree that people hadn't paid much attention to them. They had paid a different kind of attention to them. I think that everyone in San Antonio has always loved the missions, and the people who have lived at Espada, for example, who have been born and raised there, certainly have a right to feel possessive about it. They may be surprised, however, to find that people from all over San Antonio, even those not born and raised there, feel very affectionate and possessive toward it as well.

There had never been any kind of organized mechanism for these people to participate in support of the missions prior to the establishment of the park and of Los Compadres. But when there was that mechanism, they all jumped on board. It was like fishing in a barrel to enlist support and to get help for members of Los Compadres. It was the ultimate "feel-good thing" about San Antonio. So I guess I disagree with a statement that people hadn't paid attention to the missions.

So, ultimately you left the Park Service to work for Los Compadres full time.

Yes, I became their executive director. And that was in '85.

And you held that position for how long?

For two years. I left Los Compadres in '87 and went to work for my father because I didn't want to leave San Antonio. In fact, I still would be doing that [working with Los Compadres], probably, but I had gotten a divorce, and my kids were about to go into college, and I just had to give up my "nonprofit" way of life. [Laughs.]

Yes, I guess financial reality does have a way of intruding into our preferred mode of life sometimes!

[Laughs.] I have a daughter who first went to Brown University and then to Harvard for a master's degree, and there was no way that was going to happen on my salary at Los Compadres, so I got a private-sector job.

Are the children through with college now?

Yes, my kids are on their own now. My daughter is twenty-four; my son is twenty-six. She works in Washington for the Healthcare Finance Administration; he works here in San Antonio. So I decided to go back to college myself and get a master's in architecture!

Why in architecture?

Actually, I was interested in getting a degree in architecture at around age thirteen or fourteen, when I was in junior high school. We were assigned to write a paper on what we wanted to be, so that's what I wrote it on. My teacher told me to go visit an architect, and I had been a babysitter for one in my neighborhood, so I interviewed him. This was in the early '60s, and he just flat-out told me, "You know, women can't be architects! There's no architecture school in this country that would ever accept you, and if by some chance you were accepted, nobody would hire you. So my advice to you is to give up this idea."

At the time I accepted that, but in the back of my mind I always still wanted to do that, so I did things around the periphery of architecture, working at historic sites and working on art. Also, in anthropology you have to look at a lot of architecture; also in archaeology. So finally, since I had the opportunity, the time, and the money, and the good health, and the intelligence—thirty-three years later!—I decided to go to architecture school! [Laughs.]

How far along are you now?

It's a three-and-a-half-year program, and I've finished a year and a half, so I have two years to go. But then there's a three-year apprenticeship after that, so it's somewhat like becoming a doctor! [Laughs.] But I'm having a wonderful time. I'm surrounded by people who are the age of my children, and it's really, really interesting to have that kind of an exposure, to be a peer of people of the generation coming up behind you.

Well, are you a "buddy" or a "mom?"

A little bit of both, I guess. I don't try to be either one. I'm just me. What's interesting about these kids is that they don't have that kind of stereotyping hangup that I remember our having in my generation. Age does not really make a lot of difference to them, nor does the color of your skin, nor does your sexual orientation, nor does anything!

Nor the fact that you are a woman!

Right! Exactly. It's a very different world.

What other thoughts have you about the park and the missions?

There's a concept that came into existence in the early 1980s during the period of the "Park-of-the-Month club." It grew out of the NPS, and I wish they had picked up that concept and more fully examined and defined it. It was called the "cultural continuum concept" and first came out of the Cuyahoga Valley in the East. That was a park that was designated all along the Cuyahoga River—the river had ultimately caught fire because it was so polluted, so they finally decided that they needed to protect it—and the park area included urbanized areas and lots of different kinds of communities. They couldn't quite get a handle on this new animal. It was not an ordinary national park, so they came up with this concept, but I think that the way they developed was to look at the different "cultures" that existed as you went down the river.

In my mind, with my social anthropology background, I saw the concept of cultural continuum as having at its base the historical and anthropological development of an area. And in San Antonio, if you could take that and develop and define such a concept, it would really be a handy tool for helping the NPS and its audience to understand what has happened here and how to best manage it, because it's not just Hispanics and Indians who have been out at the missions, even though they were the first ones there. Very early on there were others who came in, and in reality the mission communities are a large mixture of people from different backgrounds who were equally affected by the missions and by their living in the proximity of the missions.

My mother is Hispanic; my father is not. Yet if you look into their background, they have been equally affected by the environment of the missions and by the river. Exactly what one would choose to interpret would have to be decided.

It may be true, as the NPS said when they were asked to take over, that the missions are not pristine enough and have been too encroached upon, and there is not enough original fabric, but that does not mean that that is not good or that it does not have its own validity. You don't necessarily have to say, "These are the San Antonio missions as of 1758," and anything later than that has to be ignored, or devalued, or rooted out from the site. If you did that, you'd have to start by demolishing all the Indian quarters at San José, because they were reconstructed by the WPA.

You need to set up some way of understanding how the site evolved and explaining how it happened. The missions are so important to everyone that you have to include both the Janie Garzas and the Patsy Lights! They can't belong to just one group, or even to just the United States. They belong to the whole world. At some point, Father Antonio Margil de Jesús[5] is going to be designated a saint by the Vatican, and Mission San José is going to become an international pilgrimage site. God help us when we have to look at church/state issues then! [Laughs.]

Everybody has to stop being selfish; they can be possessive, they can be protective of these missions that they grew up with and that they love dearly, but you cannot be unwilling to share them. When you have one hundred thousand pilgrims at your front door, you cannot possibly ignore them! I am convinced that Margil is going to become a saint and that we're going to become a pilgrimage site because of it, so we just have to get ready!

Have you followed the recent proposals to destroy the nineteenth-century buildings on Alamo Plaza and reconstruct the compound walls?

Yes, I have. The word has even reached Austin! [Laughs.]

The whole thing seems so unrealistic: you don't have any definite information as to the shape of the compound to begin with, or where the walls went, or how they looked at any particular point. Then, what year are you going to chose as your reconstruction point?

Beyond that, do you deny the validity of *everything* since the 1700s?

Of course! The nineteenth-century buildings are just as genuine as the compound! The compound didn't stay encased in glass. It evolved through the years.

Exactly. There's an example of the kind of silliness that can result in Philadelphia. They discovered archaeologically the site of the house of Benjamin Franklin, or one of the other Founding Fathers. They had descriptions of it, and they knew a lot of details about it. But since they couldn't make it the way it had been made back at its time of construction, instead they decided to have in space this configuration of steel I-beams that would show the space that the house would have occupied! And the effect is really bizarre and ridiculous! The whole thing looks peculiar and doesn't communicate anything to the spectator. I'd rather have the vacant lot with just a marker on it.

At a place like Alamo Plaza, you built there because business was booming, the merchants came, and it was one of the centers of the city. That's a genuine thing. The same thing happens at the missions. There's stuff on the sites that one perhaps doesn't like, but it certainly is genuine!

NOTES

1. When asked to review this passage, Wanda Ford had no recollection of the incident. She believes that, in fact, if anyone in her family worked with Ethel Harris towards getting San José declared a National Historic Site, it would have been her mother, Elizabeth Graham (see the interview with Mary Ann Noonan Guerra), who was Ethel Harris's contemporary. Wanda Ford, at age 22, had just married O'Neil Ford in 1940, the year before the National Historic Site designation, and, as she puts it, she "had other concerns at the time." Ford also speculates that the woman with Ethel Harris in the photo of the signing ceremony was probably the current president of the San Antonio Conservation Society, either Lane Taylor, who was president from 1939 to 1941, or Mrs. John F. Camp, who held the office from 1941 to 1947.
2. The chronology in Betty Beuché's account and the motives she sees in the events are in error. San José was declared a National Historic Site in 1941, and by then the WPA work, which took place in the early '30s, had already been completed, thus the point of getting the designation was not to secure funds for the reconstruction. In his interview contained in this volume, Fr. Balthasar Janacek asserts that Ethel Harris's purpose in seeking the designation was to get the National Park Service involved with the mission, even if it was only in an advisory capacity.
3. The NPS was interested in securing "buffer zones" to protect a future park, and if possible, its future development, and wanted this done through arrangements *other* than direct ownership: cooperative agreements, land trades or donations, scenic easements, local governmental protection through zoning, etc.
4. Jimmy Allan; see p. 174.
5. Father Antonio Margil de Jesús, a Franciscan missionary, was active in East Texas missions established by the College of Zacatecas. When those missions had to be given up, he persuaded religious and civil authorities to authorize the founding of a second mission in the neighborhood of the earlier established Mission San Antonio de Béxar. The dedication ceremony for Mission San José took place February 23, 1720.

Cliff Bueché, *seventy-three, is Betty Bueché's father. He went into the Air Force in 1942 during World War II and after being recalled during the Korean conflict decided to make the military his career. He finally retired in 1967 and has been in business in San Antonio ever since. In this interview, conducted at his home in north San Antonio on July 20, 1995, he talks about growing up close to the San Antonio River and to missions Concepción and San José. The picture he draws has both light and darkness in it, and a comparison of his interview with that of his daughter shows us clearly how much San Antonio has changed in the relatively short span of a generation.*

Tell me about your family background, Mr. Bueché.

My mother was born in Moulton, Texas; that's halfway to Houston from San Antonio. My father was born, I believe, in Beeville. He had a meat market there, and my grandmother arranged for the marriage between my mother and my father.

Mother had eight children, two of whom died early on. One died at a year and a half; the other died in 1917 from pneumonia. He had been called into the Navy for World War I, and they had sent him off to training camp up north somewhere, where it was cold. He slept out in a tent, got pneumonia, and died. My oldest sister died about twelve years ago. Brother Ed died about five or six years ago. There's still a brother, Clem; two sisters, Mary and Emily; and myself, so there's four of us left.

And you were the youngest?

Yes, I was the baby. I was born in 1922 on West Hafer Avenue, over by St. Leo's Church. After about six months, the family moved to LeCompte Place, which is just a few blocks away down there in the south part of town. That's where I grew up.

We had two large screened-in sleeping porches, and I grew up in one of them. I was attending school at St. Leo's, and we had Mass every morning before they started classes. We all had to line up outside and march into church, but when I heard the church bells, I'd still be in bed. I'd jump out, slip into my clothes, and run to St. Leo's just in time to be the last one in line. But I never bothered to comb my hair or brush my teeth, because nobody told me to do that. That's the way I went to school every day.

What is the ethnic background of the name Bueché?

They tell me that it had a "t" on the end originally, but they dropped it when they came over. On my grandmother's side, the family was from Czechoslovakia and Alsace-Lorraine, the pocket of land between Germany and France.

Even though the name sounds French, I think my father was more German than French. One thing is for sure: nobody can pronounce our name properly the first time. I think in all my seventy-three years, I've only met two people who were able to do it right off.

Were the grandparents born abroad, or were they born in America?

Abraham Bueché was the first to come over in 1886. We have a family cemetery over in the Windcrest area, about a two- or three-acre plot, perhaps bigger, but Windcrest has been built all around three sides of it. So there is only one entrance on Crestway. That street used to be called Bueché Road for many years until they developed Windsor Park there. Then they renamed it, but no member of the family realized that they were doing that, or we probably would have objected. In that cemetery there's a lot of Buechés, a lot of Becks, a lot of Ackermanns; I imagine there's about 150 or 200 tombstones there.

My father is buried there. My mother is buried in San Fernando Cemetery. Baba, my grandmother on my mother's side, was also born in Beeville. She was married four times and outlived all four husbands. She must have been a tough old bird! [Laughs.]

I didn't know my father well. He was a butcher here in town and had the best barbecue of anyone here in San Antonio. He had a meat market on South Flores Street with a big vacant lot behind it, and the farmers used to come in on their wagons to buy their weekly supplies, and they would park behind the market and build a little campfire in the vacant lot and cook the meat they bought. The next day, they would load up their wagons and go home.

As far as his barbecue was concerned, he was making a Bohemian barbecue, and everyone in San Antonio knew about it. But he would go to work in the morning before I'd get up and come home at night after I was in bed, so the only time I'd see him—and that would be for only fifteen minutes or so—would be on Sunday, when he would bring us a bottle of Hippo Soda Pop.

He finally left my mother when I was ten years old, and after that I may have seen him one time a year, but that was all. Until he died, I'd go by and see him maybe at Christmas and times like that, but I really never knew him. I actually knew him better in his later years than in his younger ones, because as I got older I realized that he was a specific personality type and he couldn't help the way he had treated his family.

He finally died out here on a farm. My brother had a farm, and he sold my father a few acres, where he lived until his death. He just dried up, and by the time my brother called me and I got the doctor to come out, he had died. In those days, there were no emergency crews like we have now.

But that's pretty much where we came from.

How far was your home from any of the missions?

Well, we lived on LeCompte Place, so Mission Concepción would have been about a mile and a half away by direct route, which is the way we would go as kids. I spent a lot of my time on the San Antonio River, from the time I was ten or eleven years old. Our parents then didn't have the fears of the parents of today, so we'd take off during vacation time at eight o'clock in the morning, go home late for dinner, and then, as soon as we had eaten dinner, take off again. Our parents would get angry with us only if we were late for the meals.

We used to hike to Concepción Park. The river in those days was nice and clean, and I remember that when I was a Boy Scout at age eleven, going on twelve, they taught us that the river cleans itself every fifty feet, so we had no fear of drinking the water anywhere in the San Antonio River!

However, our favorite place was about halfway to Concepción, where there was a very nice spring, and it was so cool there, even in the hottest days, that we'd just go down there to drink the cold water. There were always crawfish there, so we'd lift up rocks and look for them. We seemed to know every rock for miles around, I guess, and we knew where to step and where not to step, where the snakes were, and where the turtles were. The river was always full of fish, and there wasn't any time when, if I wanted frogs for supper, or if I wanted perch, I couldn't go down to the San Antonio River and catch any number of them in a short period of time. I've also caught bass and catfish in the river. We also could go down to the river and seine and catch all the minnows that we would need for fishing at Medina Lake.

The biggest bullfrog I ever got, the pair of legs weighed a pound and a half! We never thought twice about eating anything we caught in the river, and it made you feel good that you had provided something for yourself, without going to the store. We stepped on glass occasionally, because we never ever wore shoes, but everyone went barefoot anyway.

I can say that I had as happy a boyhood as any boy could have because of the freedom that I had. I know that parents worry about you when they don't know what you're doing, but we really never did have any kind of problem, nor did we get in any kind of trouble. I guess the Boy Scouts were a big influence on us; we took seriously those twelve Scout Laws.

We didn't have many neighborhood fights, but of course in those days if you had a disagreement you could fight it out and didn't worry about somebody killing you or cutting you! You just had a fight and found out where you fit in the pecking order, and that was it! Same way in school: a fight would break out every once in a while, but these were fistfights, and that was it.

I guess San José was the next closest mission, and that would have been maybe two miles away. I didn't have very much to do with the missions for my first ten or eleven years, but after I began roaming around on my own, we would go to these places. At that time, they were mostly rubble. There was at least as much rock on the ground as there was on walls, and nobody cared for them. If you wanted to pick up a rock and throw it or carry it away, that was fine.

Nobody realized they were doing any damage or harm. These old buildings weren't any good anyhow! So as kids, we didn't have any special respect for them from that point of view; not that we wanted to destroy something, but we just thought of them as something that was decaying and soon would be gone anyhow. We never heard the idea that this was something that should be restored or preserved or revered, and consequently I'm sure they deteriorated all that much faster. I'm talking about the early '30s, now, maybe '33-'34; that's when I got my first bicycle and got a paper route at age twelve.

One time, we went to San José and after fooling around there for a while, we decided to go swimming in the river. We stripped down to our shorts, left our clothes on the bank, and went in the river searching for mussels. We were breaking them open, because sometimes you could get these little pearls out of them, and right in that area the mussels were real thick. And while we were so busy cracking open the mussels, these two guys came by in an old car, grabbed our clothes, and drove off laughing! There was a house fairly close by, and we went over and shyly asked the lady if we could use her phone, because we were embarrassed to try to make our way home in our undershorts. She let us, and we called my friend's dad, and he came and got us. But whoever did that, they did it for fun.

We'd get involved in all sorts of pranks, but they were just aggravating, just for fun. For example, we would bend a straight pin, tie a long thread to it, and hook it on a door or window screen. Then you could go fifty feet away and set the thread vibrating and the screen to making a terrible noise. The people would come to see what was causing the noise, and they couldn't see anything! In the meantime, we'd be in the bushes giggling.

I guess there were knife fights. We heard of some, but I certainly never saw one. We'd make what we called "nigger-shooters," you know, you'd take a forked branch ... and we got pretty good at shooting stones with them. We didn't kill a lot of birds, but we killed a few. We had heard that there was a state law about harming mockingbirds, so we left them alone, but sparrows were good for target practice. Nobody taught us that there was anything wrong with it. We'd also make slingshots, but I never got to be good with them.

What's the difference between a slingshot and a "nigger-shooter"?

A slingshot was a piece of cord with a little leather pocket in the middle. You'd put a stone in it, sling it around a few times, and then let go of one end to release it. It would throw at a much higher speed than a "nigger-shooter," but it was tough to learn accuracy with it, cause you had to let it loose at exactly the right moment. But some of the boys got pretty good with them.

I realize that nowadays you don't use names like that, but in our days the word *ethnic* was probably not even invented yet, I don't think. The only thing I remember in those days is that we knew Terrell Wells was a discriminatory pool—although we probably didn't know that word either—because they would not allow Mexicans to swim there. And again, we thought nothing of it. It never entered our minds that this was right or wrong, nor did we ever hear it discussed. That was just the way it was.

Was your neighborhood all-Anglo?

It was all-Anglo, and there were probably restrictions about it. In all of the Harlandale High School, there were only two Mexicans that I knew of. Mexicans were not allowed to buy property in that area. And again, we were totally oblivious of this situation, nor did we think anything of the fact that colored people had to sit in the rear of the bus. I was born when I was, and we grew up thinking that was the way things were supposed to be. You weren't taught any better, and you certainly did not hear anyone question it. Same thing when you went to the Majestic Theater: colored people had to sit in the balcony. They weren't allowed to sit downstairs, and they couldn't sit in the front of the balcony, either; they had to go to the extreme top area. We've come a long, long way.

What were the neighborhoods like around the missions ?

Well, they were mostly empty, not populated. Very few houses existed around the missions, and those that were there were very small houses. The area has become populated since, and there are some nice houses there now.

Your daughter Betty tells me that although her heritage from your side is mostly German, there is some Hispanic blood on your wife's side. Can you tell me more about her? What's her name, and what is her background?

My wife's name is Mary Elizabeth, and she was born in Phoenix, Arizona. Her maiden name was Midkiff. Her father was of "mixed American" background, mostly Scotch/Irish, but her mother had been born in Mexico, so I guess you'd call her a Mexican-American these days. The father had "read for the law," which you could do in those days, and eventually became a lawyer for one of the railroads in Arizona.

Did you meet her in Arizona?

No. She grew up here in San Antonio. When she was about ten years old, her mother died as a result of blood poisoning which developed when she underwent an operation, so Mary Elizabeth came to San Antonio in 1942 or '43, and was raised by a married half-sister who lived here. Her husband was an engineer involved in large construction—dams, bridges, and the like—although later on he also built homes.

How did the two of you meet?

We met through a friend of mine. I had a 1940 Willy coupe, and I had taken the lid off the back of it and made it into a sort of rumble seat with a cushion to sit on and a little picket fence painted red, white, and blue to lean on—and keep you in! My friend wanted to go to Austin to a UT football game, and talked me into driving there. Mary Elizabeth was his date, so I pretty much ignored her that time. In any case, she rode in the rumble seat, so there was no way of holding a conversation while we were driving! [Laughs.]

A year later, I went to a school play at Harlandale High School, and there she was on stage, with her hair pulled up, singing about "The Man on the Flying Trapeze," if I remember correctly. I was terribly impressed, and thought to myself: "Now, *that's* quite a gal!" So I made it a point to go backstage after the play and meet her, which was easy to do, because I knew some of the other young people in the cast.

I was having a party for my birthday a couple of days later, so I talked her into coming to the party . . . and that was that! I was in the Army Air Force at the time, and we got married in 1944, just before I went overseas.

Can you put into words what it is that attracts you to the missions?

I love to go to Espada and San Juan Capistrano, because you don't even realize that you're in San Antonio when you're out there. You're in a different world; you're somewhere else. We love Espada so much that many family members have married out there.

When my son Cliff, who is around forty-eight now, was only about ten months old, I remember taking him into the church at San Juan. And we were standing in front of the altar, me holding him, when he began to laugh out loud, like that was the happiest moment of his life. There was nothing obvious that should strike him funny, but it just seemed like he was very, very happy. I left there wondering whether he had seen Jesus or the Blessed Virgin Mary. *I* certainly hadn't, but maybe he had!

Margaret Benavides

Margaret Benavides, forty-seven, was a leader, with her first husband, Edmon, of the small but active congregation at Mission Concepción. A change in pastors resulted in a complete change in atmosphere at the mission, from one of cooperation and encouragement of the congregation's initiatives on the part of the pastor to one in which the congregation was forced to submit to autocratic control and to what appeared to be blatant abuses of pastoral prerogatives. The diocesan authorities, while recognizing the wrongs of the situation, proved either unwilling or unable to step in and correct them. The result was that the congregation withered and eventually disappeared, giving Mission Concepción the sad distinction of being the only one of the four missions where no active congregation exists today. Margaret and her second husband, Louis, live in the heart of the city, just south of the downtown area. She was interviewed on July 18, 1995. The interview was conducted in both English and Spanish.

What is your family name, Margaret?

My maiden name is Garzés.

And your husband was?

My first husband was Edmon H. Benavides.

You have a daughter from your first marriage and a son from your second?

Yes.

You've told me your first husband's name was Benavides, but how come you're still Benavides?

[Laughs.] Oh, I see that you're confused. In my second marriage, I married my first husband's older brother, so that's why I'm still Benavides!

Now I understand! That's very biblical! You are a born-and-raised San Antonian?

Yes.

Born where?

Before I married, I lived *en la Calle Huerta* [on Huerta Street], between Zarzamora and Frio City Road; that's where I grew up. My husband Edmon lived on the adjoining street, which was Obregón, and after we married we moved over to Rockwood Court. We started going to Mass at St. Cecilia's parish. We didn't like it too much, and we were kind of looking around for a congregation where we felt more at home, and we ended up at Concepción. My husband went there one Sunday and liked it very much, so we started going there.

What year are we talking about?

It was 1975.

What was happening around that time, as far as Mission Concepción was concerned?

Not much, really. They only had one small festival annually. Of course, they had their Posadas, the Christmas Eve Mass during the holidays, and the feast of la Virgen de Guadalupe. The main holiday was Easter Sunday, but otherwise that was it. It wasn't until after we joined that we started really getting together and being more active as a congregation.

How big a congregation was it when you joined?

I'd say maybe fifteen, twenty families, tops.

I've been told that today Mission Concepción is officially classed as a "chapel of ease" for members of St. Cecilia. In other words, if you can't get to the main church, you can go to Mass there. But is there Mass being said at Concepción now?

No, there's no Mass there on a regular basis.

Who was the pastor when you joined?

When we joined, it was Father Peter Meller.

And he was there for how long?

Oh gosh, I can't tell you exactly how long, but he'd already been there a while, and he was there for about another maybe eight years after I joined. See, the way it was at that time, the head church or the mother church was St. Cecilia's. Concepción was like a satellite mission. So all the congregational organizations—Knights of Columbus, Guadalupanas, children's CCD programs—all would take place at St. Cecilia's. Main church services also took place at St. Cecilia's, except for a few major holidays during the year. So nothing was held at Concepción except for your basic Sunday ten o'clock Mass. That was it. We had the feast of Guadalupe, and I think the Christmas Eve midnight Mass, but everything else was at St. Cecilia's.

If we had a special function where we needed chairs or booths or anything like that, everything had to be borrowed from St. Cecilia's, because as a congregation we had nothing. That's where we came in. And we started asking, "Why can't we have our own chairs? It'd be nice to have them and not have to truck them over from the other church every time we needed them."

The only income that the little congregation had was from this one little festival they had. It was Mrs. Trujillo and a few of the other ladies, who would set up some tables and sell chalupas or tacos and maybe some lemonade or punch. Whatever income came from that was it; that was the income that we were allowed to keep.

One thing led to another. At the time, the street, Mission Road, ran right in front of the church, not where it is today. Then across that street there was a little parking area, which was always overgrown and full of trash. One day we parked there, and I stumbled over something.

We discovered that it was actually one of those bumps they use to divide up a parking lot. The lot was divided, but the divisions were hidden by the weeds!

After Mass, we'd always have coffee and cookies, a little get-together. And we got to talking: "Wouldn't it be nice if we could clear up that parking lot?" People couldn't use it as it was, however, because it was so overgrown. If we could get it cleaned up, we could have more parking space for the congregation. So the congregation decided to go ahead and clean it up. We came back on Sunday afternoon, brought our rakes and our hoes, trash bags, and everything, and we did the work. Lo and behold, we had parking spaces!

And the people liked that. It was really nice. Then we started looking around. There was an area in front of the mission that was also overgrown and full of trash, and we decided to tackle that next. We started cleaning up the area little by little, back behind the mission and everywhere around it. We did this over several weekends.

Then one day either Father Balty [Fr. Balthasar Janacek; see p. 160] or Pete DeVries, who had just come in with the diocesan OSM [Old Spanish Missions] organization, came to us, and we asked, "Who does the maintenance work at the missions?" We had noticed that the bathrooms were often dirty and so on. And we were told that all the other missions had a contract with a particular company or with someone to do the work. Concepción didn't; they had hired someone who was supposed to come around and do that, but they did a lousy job.

So Pete came up with the idea that, as a way for the congregation to earn money for chairs or whatever, if we agreed to do the yard work and whatever other cleaning was necessary—which we were doing already— he would talk to the archbishop and see if he could pay the congregation for the work instead of paying an outsider. A separate little account was set under the mission's name, and the money would go in there for our own needs. So that's the way we agreed to proceed.

We started to get paid and to put money in the account. My name was on the account, and so was Father Balty's, as well as whoever was the head pastor of St. Cecilia's, which at the time was Father Peter. So we started collecting the money and putting it in the account, and every three months we'd have a meeting and give an accounting to the people of the congregation. And that's how we started getting the things that we needed at the mission as a congregation: fans, the altar that's still there, which cost us about three thousand dollars. We'd have a dance to raise money, and we'd have chalupa sales. Everything that is at the church now the people paid for by themselves; they really worked.

Are you referring to the pews also?

No, the pews were there, but they were refinished. I'm talking about the lecterns that are there now, the altar, the new cabinets in the sacristy and the display case, the cross and all the matching adornments. The altar was done by a parishioner at St. Cecilia's, and my husband got the cabinetmaker who made all the other things. And we continued doing that until the Park Service came and took over doing the maintenance work on the grounds. The rangers came by one day shortly after they had taken over and saw us working. They said, "Golly, you all do such a good job that we should hire you for this work!"

The little festival that we had, we enlarged so that we could make more money. Father Balty and Pete DeVries had come up with the idea of having a Semana de las Misiones [Old Spanish Missions Week], so that on one particular week all the missions would have special activities, and the culmination would be our festival on Sunday, the last day of that week.

Eventually, all the other missions dropped out, and we were the only ones that continued with our event, and we had to stay with it because it was the only source of income for the congregation. The other missions had other sources of income. So that's how we acquired our things, little by little over the years.

This festival, when you had it, did it occur on a specific day, a saint's day or something like that, or did you just choose a day when to have it?

No, it did not fall on a special day; we just chose the date. Later, when we participated in the Semana de las Misiones, that was in August. Usually our festivals were in the summertime, in the hopes that we could get some tourists to visit.

So the Park Service was taking over and the national park was being created. Tell me about that transition.

Before the park came to be, we were told that it was coming and that an advisory board for the Park Service was being created. The priest at that time, Father Bob Markunis, approached me and asked if I would serve in it. Eventually I became a member, and so did a representative for each of the other missions. We were made aware of what was coming, what the plans were, short-term and long-term goals, funding, and things like that. We, in turn, were able to go to the advisory board and tell them what the concerns of the parishioners were. That worked out real well.

Then our terms expired, and eventually the representation of the mission congregations on the advisory board was dropped, so we lost that communication. But my husband and I were still involved with the Old Spanish Missions group; we were on the board there. That was something we were supposed to continue regardless of what developed with the park, but we usually had a representative from the Park Service at our meetings, and he would fill us in about what was happening. We, in turn, would go back to our missions and inform the people.

The Park Service came in, the dedications were held, and the parishioners were really looking forward to working with the rangers. All we were concerned about was that they did not interfere with our church services and the activities that we had there. Our congregation made more use of the grounds than the other missions did. Because of the way the mission was fenced in at the time, it was easier for us to hold activities there. For example, on Easter Sunday we would all get together and have a cookout. We locked the gates, and no one was allowed in except for parishioners. This became an annual thing, and when the Park Service came in, we were still allowed to do it. We actually had people from out of town, who came back three, four years in a row, because they knew that on that Sunday we would be there. The rangers were always invited to join in.

What was the people's reaction at Concepción to the park coming in? From what you tell me, it sounds like everyone welcomed the idea. Why?

Because they felt that finally the buildings would be properly maintained. We couldn't do it ourselves, and we wanted that. We also felt that the mission would be better protected.

Were any of the rooms that are now available in the convento used by the congregation?

Oh, yes, we used all the rooms. The room where the loft is, that was our storage room; we kept everything in there: our lawnmowers, our decorations, coffeepot, everything. The two adjoining rooms were also used. The middle room was where we usually set up in the winter for our congregational coffee and cake after Mass. In the springtime we had our

The pastor, the honored fathers, and members of the congregation are serenaded by a mariachi group after a Father's Day Mass. Courtesy of Margaret Benavides.

During Lent, the congregation celebrated the Stations of the Cross once a week. In this photo from 1982, Father Peter Meller, assisted by Tony Garza, leads the congregation in prayer at each station. Courtesy of Margaret Benavides.

In 1982, at the only large Confirmation and First Communion held by the Concepción congregation, each of the first communicants comes to the lectern for a reading before the congregation. The chancel has been decorated for the occasion with helium-filled balloons. Courtesy of Margaret Benavides.

After the ceremony, while Father Peter Meller greets departing parishioners, Candelario Rendón and Juanita Castañeda perform an impromptu *jarabe*, a Mexican folk dance. Courtesy of Margaret Benavides.

Christmas 1982: Parish choir members help the pastor decorate the church for the holidays. From left to right: Daniel Garzés (Margaret Benavides's brother), Father Byron Haaland, María Salinas (today Mrs. Daniel Garzés), and Brother Tom Bridges; in front, Rosemary Salinas (now Jiménez). Courtesy of Margaret Benavides.

Christmas 1984: Preparing to consecrate the elements for the Eucharist, Father Jim Walters presents the bread to the congregation, one of the loaves that Margaret Benavides regularly baked for the sacramental use of the Concepción parish. Courtesy of Margaret Benavides.

Stations of the Cross, and every Friday we would have our parish meal in those two rooms. We would set our tables up and eat in there. So they were always in use.

And there was another little room in the back. I don't know what you would call it, but we called it the kitchen, and that was also a storage area. When we were told by the Park Service that we had to vacate it and only use one locked room, we crammed everything in that one room. Then they told us that they needed that room, too, so we told them, "Okay, we'll move, but get us someplace else for storage." That's when they brought in that wooden portable shed out behind the bathrooms, and we moved everything from the loft to that shed.

After that, I don't know what happened. That's when Father Deane took over everything. He probably took what he wanted—the booths and the chairs and tables—to St. Cecilia's, and what he didn't want he probably either discarded or let the Park Service have it. I don't know.

Was your experience in those first few years of the park as positive as the congregation had expected? Were you able to work with the Park Service?

We had some problems in the beginning with staff, mainly with the superintendent and his assistant. We were a little disappointed at the red tape involved in everything and at not being able to get the things done that we thought they were going to do fairly quickly. Everything took a lot longer than we expected. We had a problem with our money box at one point.

In the church? But the Park Service supposedly has nothing to do in the church.

It was a question of charging visitors. The Park Service did not want us to have a donation box because none of the other units of the park were charging visitors. We argued that the donation boxes had been in place even before the Park Service came in and that this did not represent a fee but a goodwill, voluntary donation, which for us as a congregation was a very necessary thing. So then they wanted an accounting of how much money was coming in over a period of several months, etc. This haggling went on back and forth until finally they relented and let us have our donation box. I think a sign was set up at the ranger station stating that it was a donation or a voluntary contribution and not an admission fee.

But other than that, we really and truly had no problems. They didn't have enough staff to man the ranger stations on Sunday when they would have their Park Service staff meetings, so we volunteered to man the station for them on Sunday mornings while the ranger went to the meeting. I set up a committee and drew up a list of volunteers, and we would rotate the duty. It worked out fine.

What was the condition of those rooms in the convento, the ones that you were using for storage?

They were pretty bad; they needed a lot of restoration. You could see very little of what remained [of the frescoes] painted on the walls.

Could you close them against the weather? Were there water leaks or something like that?

No. And they were always closed. If we went in there after hours we had the keys, and we left them locked afterwards. We understood the problems of such old buildings, and even our kids were pretty good about being careful while we were there. But they needed a lot of work.

So what happened to your congregation then?

Everything was fine for a time. All the priests that came in after Father Peter and Father Bob Markunis, they all worked very well with the park rangers; they would attend the OSM meetings with us and had no problem with the Park Service at all. They basically left the running of the mission congregation to us. There was one priest always assigned as kind of "our" priest, and he was in charge of overseeing the mission, and I guess he would report back to the pastor. So long as that was done, there was no problem.

Can you clarify something? You were part of St. Cecilia's parish, but you had another priest that was in charge of the mission?

No, St. Cecilia had multiple pastors: a head pastor, an assistant pastor, and so on, and one of the priests on the pastoral staff would be in charge of the mission. He was the one who would be consistently coming to give us our Mass, although they were all our priests, and periodically we would see the other pastors also.

When did this situation change, and why?

It all changed when the current pastor, Father Deane,[1] came in. The SCJs [Sagrado Corazón de Jesús], which are the priests of the Sacred Heart, were the ones that were at St. Cecilia's at the time. Concepción was the only one in that situation. The other missions are manned by Franciscans. Concepción was not manned by them because it was so close to the boundaries of St. Cecilia's that supposedly the Franciscans didn't want to step on anybody's toes, so they let the archdiocese have it. But at one point the SCJs came into San Antonio, and they decided they wanted to be at St Cecilia's. I don't know what the details of that arrangement were, but the archdiocese agreed to let them have that responsibility, including the mission.

And they were very good about it. They worked well with us, and they worked well with the rangers. They were, I would say, progressive for the time; they believed in letting the people be more involved in the church, in allowing them to take more of a part in the running of the congregation. They saw the need for that, because there was a shortage of priests.

So they welcomed it when the people asked, "Can we do this, or can we do that?" It relieved them from having to oversee everything, because they didn't have to come to our Posadas, they didn't have to come to our Pastorelas, they didn't have to come to our Stations of the Cross. We had been doing it for so long that we'd just do them ourselves. We knew what to do.

I remember Father Bob regretting that the people at St. Cecilia's had to have someone at each and every one of the church services or functions. He had to tell them, "Look, I can't be with you all the time. There are too many things to do and too many places to be."

And they would say, "Well, then, why do you do that for the mission?"

And he would have to explain to them that he did *not* do that for us, that we took care of it ourselves: "If I can make it, I go, but if I can't, it gets done anyway!" And that didn't sit too well with the people at St. Cecilia's.

But then the SCJ priests had to leave St. Cecilia's; they decided that they were needed elsewhere, other cities that were more needy than San Antonio. So they pulled out and gave the parish back to the diocese. That was in 1986, I believe in the spring. We asked them to tell the diocese about the mission, and they promised they would try to see that we got someone who would understand the situation. But of course that was out of their hands, since this was a diocesan priest coming in.

My husband had bone cancer; he'd had it since our daughter was born in 1975. In 1986, he was really having problems, so we had to leave for Houston, where he was going to go for treatment, in May of that year. And that was about when the change took place. That summer, they brought in a temporary priest. I never met him, but I understand that he had run-ins with a couple of the parishioners right off the bat. So, the whole thing kind of started off on the wrong foot.

I stayed in Houston with my husband while he was in the hospital, and I came back at the end of August or the first week in September, to enroll our daughter in school. That's when Father Deane came in; he'd just arrived the week before or so. That Sunday, he announced he was going to have a meeting after church.

Since I happened to be in town that weekend, I went to church and to the meeting. He explained to us that he was no longer going to have baptisms or weddings or funerals, nothing at Concepción; everything would be at St. Cecilia's. He would continue with the Mass, but as time progressed, he felt that he would probably have to cut down some of these other activities. I could see the handwriting on the wall, and it really scared me when he said, "No funeral Masses, ever again, etc."

So I asked him. I said, "Father Deane, why don't you want to have these services at the mission? In the ten years I've been here, we've only had a total of three funerals. The Park Service opens up the mission in the morning at eight o clock; we have a sacristan who comes in and sets everything up; you don't have to do anything but come in and officiate. You're only a mile or a mile and a half from the mission. What is the reason to curtail these things?"

And he said, "There is no reason. It's my prerogative." And he added, right then and there, "You know, you people think that this is a democracy; this is not a democracy, this is a church. I'm the pastor," and he pointed at us, "and you are going to do as I say. Things are going to change."

So he started demanding keys and taking them away from the people who had held them. He wanted to know where we had gotten all these things. He didn't like the OSM and the idea of our being represented there. He wanted the congregation's money, whatever funds we had left. People were very upset and told me not to give him the money because, after we had worked so hard for it, we would never see it again. But when I refused, he threatened to file charges against me.

I went to the archbishop [Archbishop Patrick Flores] and explained the situation, and he counseled that the best thing would be to turn over the money. So I agreed, but I said, "I just wanted you to understand where we're coming from, and that this is not just my being stubborn but that the people in the congregation didn't want me to turn over the funds." So we gave him the money.

Little by little, he started cutting things out. We didn't have our Virgen de Guadalupe celebration anymore; he started cutting our Christmas Eve midnight Mass, which was our biggest Mass. It went from midnight to ten o'clock, and then to eight o'clock. He sent another priest to inform us after Mass one Sunday, "Oh, by the way, your choir is fired." They were never paid to begin with, but he told us Father Deane had instructed him to tell us that they were fired. And it was simply because they knew already what the routine was, knew what kind of songs the priest liked or would want. And he didn't like that. You *had* to ask him for everything; he didn't want you coming in and taking charge of anything. He didn't see it as you helping him out; he saw it as a threat to his authority, as your "interfering." He didn't see the benefit of all the things that we did, even though we tried to explain it to him. He would have none of it.

I went back to Houston, but I kept hearing these things. And then, in November, my husband took a turn for the worse. The archbishop had come by to see him one time and called to asked about him. He knew Edmon because Edmon had made a painting of the mission several years back and had given it to the archbishop, who then commissioned him to do some other artwork: coats of arms for the other bishops, and so on.

So when the archbishop called, I told him, "I'm very concerned about the problems at the mission. I'm afraid that if my husband dies, I'm not going to be able to have his funeral there, as he would want."

He asked, "Is it the Park Service? Do you think they're not going to want to let you have it there?"

And I told him, "No, the Park Service is not the problem; it's Father Deane." So then I told him what he had said.

The archbishop got real quiet, and then he said, "I don't think you'll have to worry about that."

Sure enough, my husband died, and, when I came back to San Antonio, I called Father Balty, and I asked him, "What am I going to do? I've got to have his Mass there, but Father Deane is not going to let me." He told me, "Here's what you do. You call the archbishop and find out when he's available for the funeral Mass, make arrangements, call the funeral home and tell them the time of the Mass, and after it's all done, you call Deane and let him know." So that's what I did.

I told him I realized how busy he was with his schedule, and I didn't want to take up any of his time, so everything was taken care of, and the archbishop was coming to celebrate the Mass at three o'clock that afternoon. Father Balty was concelebrating, and he wouldn't have to worry about anything. He got real quiet and finally said, "All right." But he was mad! He showed up anyway.

Let me tell you something else. I used to make the bread our congregation used for communion rather than the host. All our priests loved it. I had three ladies that would help me, and we made bread both for St. Cecilia's and for the mission. We'd take it over there, and they'd put it in the freezer so they always had it available. And they'd call me when they were running low, so I could get some more made. No problems. But Father Deane didn't like that. He did away with using it at St. Cecilia's right off the bat; then he did away with it at the mission also. He said that we were committing a sin because this was not consecrated bread and so forth. So we couldn't use the bread, and once more the people were upset because we'd gotten used to it. Many of them had never seen anything else used, and we even had people come to our services from out of town because they thought using the bread was wonderful, that it really was going back to tradition.

For my husband's funeral Mass, which he had nothing to do with and was not supposed to be there for, I made the bread. When it came time for me to bring the bread to the archbishop and four other priests who were concelebrating the Mass, the bread was gone, and there were hosts in its place! I was shocked, and for a moment I didn't know what to do, but then one of the celebrating priests, who was a good friend of ours, gave me a look and motioned me to come anyway.

It turned out that Father Deane came, he saw that they were going to use bread, and he hit the roof. He said, "You are *not* using bread!"

Father Bob Markunis tried to tell him, "Look, this is neither the time nor the place for a scene. You were not even supposed to be here.

This is a private funeral Mass, not only for a parishioner but for a friend of mine, and his family wants to use bread."

"You're *not* going to use bread. This is *my* church. I am the pastor, what I say goes here, and you're *not* using that bread."

In the meantime, here's the archbishop standing there. Apparently, he intervened and recommended that they go ahead and use the host. So he just had to go, just to have the last word. And, as if that wasn't enough, he came to my house a couple of days later to tell me how upset he was and how I had gone behind his back to do this against his wishes. He had never met my husband; he had just heard of him, but he said, "I'm sure that your husband was a wonderful man, and I know that if he were alive today, he wouldn't have agreed with you in having gone against my wishes."

So I told him, "Then you don't know anything at all about my husband! But let me ask you this: if you've heard about my husband and about how much he loved the mission and how much it meant to him, if I had come to you and asked you to allow me to have his funeral Mass there, what would you have told me?"

And he replied, "Well, Margaret, you know the rules: no more funeral Masses at the mission!"

So I said, *"That's* why I didn't come to you!"

And it got worse, progressively worse. Little by little, he whacked at the congregation: he finally took the tabernacle from the mission. And that was originally a discarded tabernacle from St. Cecilia's that we had taken as a hand-me-down. My husband had had it fixed and refinished, and we had had a special ceremony to install it. He said that the mission was not a church, that it was just a mission, and that the tabernacle had no business being there. That it was blasphemy, etc. There was nothing we could do.

When he had done away with everything else, all we had was our ten o'clock Mass. That was it, nothing! We couldn't even meet at the mission anymore, because he didn't want us "hanging around" after Mass without his permission. The rumor started circulating that he was going to do away with our Mass, or move it to 5:30 in the afternoon, which we didn't want. We circulated a petition that everybody signed, but that didn't do any good.

Then one day I called the archbishop. I had talked to Father Balty, and he suggested I talk to him. So I told him things were really bad. This and this had been happening, and now he was taking away the ten o'clock Mass, which was all we had left. He said, "I need proof. *Quiero que le digas a los parroquiales que me hagan unas cartitas . . .* " "I need some letters telling me in the parishioners' own words what is happening, what Father Deane is doing."

I told him, "They're not going to want to do that, because they're afraid of Father Deane. He can be very intimidating."

But he said, "Well, I need proof; that's the only way. And I promise that I will not give him the letters."

So I went back to the congregation and told them, and of course they said, "There's no way we're going to put our complaints on paper! If he finds out, we'll be in worse straits yet." But I told them that the archbishop had said he would not give him the letters, so they finally agreed to write them. I still keep them, letters that the people wrote and that even the children wrote. My daughter wrote one.

We hand-carried them to the archbishop, about ten or fifteen of us. We met in his office. He sort of glanced at them. We pleaded with him. We told him that we realized our congregation did not bring in much money, but that there was more at stake here than just money. Finally he said, "I'll talk to him about this."

And someone asked, "What if he says no? What if you talk to him and he says no?"

And he leaned forward and said, "I am the ultimate pastor here." So we thought that was good enough for us. Well, he read the letters, he called Father Deane in, and *he gave him the letters!* I am sure his reasoning was that Father Deane needed to know what was being said about him, but he *did not* tell him, "Don't do this." So what Father Deane started doing was calling each of the parishioners who had written, one by one, to meet with him, and those whose kids were ready for confirmation or Holy Communion or baptism were called first and told that unless they retracted their lies, he could not in good conscience baptize or confirm their children.

I called the archbishop and told him I'd warned him he would do something like that. "He's holding it like blackmail over the parishioners heads', because you gave him the letters."

Then he told me, "Well, you need a tape recording. You need to record a conversation where he's actually saying these things."

I said, "How am I going to record him? He's not going to go for that."

"Well," I was told, "you'll have to find a way."

It was all to no avail. Finally, Father Deane called us, and I said, "I know what this is about, Father Deane, and I have nothing to retract. What I stated in my letter was the truth." I had already talked with my daughter, because she was already in CCD at St. Cecilia's and getting ready for her confirmation and First Communion. And I told her, "You know that if you don't retract your letter, he may kick you out. You think about it, and let me know what you decide. You have to make your own decision."

She thought about it and after a couple of hours came back and told me, "Mom, I'm not taking it back. If we have to go see him, we'll go see him, 'cause I didn't lie."

How old was your daughter?

She had just turned twelve. So he kicked her out of the CCD program. I had sent my money for her registration, and he sent it back, saying that he could not accept her. I called him and tried to change his mind: "You're not going to teach the class! You're not even going to be in the classroom with her. You won't have to look at her. It has nothing to do with her CCD education."

He said, "It's my church. She will be here in my church, and I will not have it! So long as she feels about me as she does, she cannot come to CCD here." So she lost a whole year when she could have made her confirmation, and I had to enroll her somewhere else.

He also wrote me a letter telling me he did not want me in his church—in effect, kicking me out of the parish. He used the excuse that we lived right on the boundary line of another church, and it would be better if we went somewhere else. He also did that to several others who were well within the boundaries of St. Cecilia's, even just a few blocks from the church. He wouldn't allow them to come back.

So my husband's funeral Mass was the last that was held at Mission Concepción. We had Mr. [Alejandro] Avilés, who was well over one hundred years old, die afterwards, and Doña Luz, who had been there a *long* time and also loved the mission, but, although the families asked, they couldn't have their funeral Masses at the mission.

Also no *quinceañera* celebrations, so the girls who had been going to Concepción and reached fifteen and wanted their celebration there, he would not allow that, either.[2] And the only thing that made my daughter an exception was that she had included just that in her letter: she had said she was afraid Father Deane was not going to let her have her *quinceañera* celebration at the mission. So when the time came and I wrote to ask him whether he would allow her to have her celebration there, he said yes! In effect, he had to. But she was the exception.

I don't know what kind of a hold he has on the archbishop, but we had to do what he said. When we asked him, "We thought you said you were the ultimate pastor!" he said, "Well, he's the pastor there, and you have to learn to work with him. You have to learn that you have to do as the pastor says." He also told another parishioner, "There's plenty of other small churches you can go to; there are other missions." People were very, very disillusioned with him after that.

We even went to an [archdiocesan] advisory board that advises the archbishop, that does the hiring and the firing, so to speak. One of our parishioners is an amateur historian and knows a lot about the history of the missions and about canon law, and he told us about this board. We took our information and everything else there. There were several priests, and one of them said, "He's a fellow priest, and I hate to judge a fellow priest, but I have never, ever seen such abuse in my career as a priest." Another one told us that we had documented everything very well, and a lot better than they had seen in most other such situations. We were told that they would be getting back to us, and for a while we thought that there was a chance, but they also sent us a letter telling us that we had to do as the pastor said.

When was this archdiocesan advisory board? Was it after your meeting with the archbishop?

Yes, not long after it; within a month, I suppose.

And that is your prerogative within the church's structure, to appeal to this board?

Yes. We went to the bishop, we went right up the chain, but nothing happened. In effect, he shut down the mission congregation. Nobody would show up for a 5:30 Mass on Sunday afternoon, which was just a ploy, so he finally shut it down "because not enough people were attending to warrant the Mass." Father Deane had told us in so many words; he once told us, "I didn't bargain for this. When I was assigned to St. Cecilia's, nobody told me of having to take care of the mission as well!"

We tried everything. We even asked, "If you can't come"—because we didn't dare say "if you don't want to come"—"can we find another priest who'd be willing to come and just give us our Mass?" Well, he wouldn't go for that, either. There were a couple of priests who were willing to do that and who even went to him and offered, but he wouldn't hear of it. Father Deane's an Irish priest from the old school, and he had to have total authority and power. You had to ask permission for everything.

What role did the OSM play in all this? Or did it play one at all?

They didn't. That's who we went to first, to Father Balty, to ask if he could be of any help. The OSM was strictly an advisory board for the archbishop on the running of the missions. They could recommend, but that was probably all. In any case, Balty had already talked to the archbishop.

What kind of hold or what kind of influence does Father Deane have that he can get away with something like this, do you suppose?

People say that he's very good at fund-raising; that's one thing he is good at and brings in a lot of money wherever he goes. I guess money talks. And, of course, Deane threatened to leave at one point. He actually told the archbishop that if he didn't get his support he would leave the diocese. You can find priests, but you can't always find a pastor to replace another pastor; they don't always want to take on a congregation. So the archbishop would've been left with the problem of finding a pastor for St. Cecilia's. I suppose that was part of the leverage that he had.

And all this happened in 1987, the year after your husband's death? How long before the congregation at the mission dwindled down to nothing?

By the end of '87, maybe the beginning of '88.

So it didn't take very long.

No.

Where do you and your family go to church now?

For a time we were going to San José, and we still do most of the time. Sometimes we go to St. Joseph's downtown, other times to Sagrado Corazón [Sacred Heart]. I like San José, but I'm not totally at home there yet; I'm still floundering. We're going to church, but I feel that we're just biding our time. We want our mission back!

Do you think there's any chance of that?

Probably not, because Father Deane has asked for an extension, and he's serving the church alone. Sometimes I feel that he's staying there because he knows that as long as he does, nothing will go on at the mission.

What happened to all these people who worked with you on the appeal to the archbishop? Are they still at St. Cecilia's?

Some are at St. Cecilia's. Others are at San Juan or Espada missions. Still others are at San Fernando Cathedral.

So they travel the distance to Espada or San Juan rather than worship at St. Cecilia's?

Yes, even though they used to be within walking distance of Mission Concepción; now they have to get rides or drive there.

It's sad, because we had something beautiful there. The archbishop had been to our midnight Mass and had told us how impressed he was and how we should not lose this spirit that we had there. The kids grew up working with the parents on grounds clean-up projects and other congregation activities. At Christmas we had our own decorations and had our Posadas. People came to visit our congregation because they liked the atmosphere they encountered there. It was familial and close; everybody knew everybody. And what we had there, we could truly say that we worked together to achieve for the mission.

NOTES

1. Appendix A records attempts to communicate with Fr. Deane and to include an interview with him in this collection.

2. *Quinceañera* is the Mexican-American celebration marking a girl's fifteenth birthday.

Jesse and Zoila Sánchez

Jesse (JS) and Zoila (ZS) Sánchez, sixty-five and sixty-three, respectively,
were also active members of the Mission Concepción congregation. They are also
neighbors of the mission, living directly across the street from it. Mr. Sánchez was
born in Crystal City, Texas, but his family moved to San Antonio in the 1940s.
Mrs. Sánchez was born and raised in San Antonio. Their interview corroborates
the story told by Margaret Benavides about the fate of the congregation at Concepción. The Sánchez family had been long-time sponsors of the mission's celebration
honoring Our Lady of Guadalupe, an event that held very special significance for
them and for the community. Jesse and Zoila Sánchez were interviewed on July
26, 1995. The interview was conducted in Spanish.

For many years, Jesse and Zoila Sánchez, who live across the street from Mission Concepción, sponsored the celebration of Las Mañanitas, a midnight Mass in honor of Our Lady of Guadalupe, in memory of a teenage son who was murdered. In this photo from the celebration on December 12, 1985, parishioners, led by Archbishop Patrick Flores, left, and other officiating priests, assemble for the congregation's procession to the mission. Courtesy of Margaret Benavides.

Archbishop Flores and his two concelebrants stand before the congregation. The painting of Our Lady of Guadalupe on the altar was done by Margaret Benavides's first husband, Edmon, and donated by the couple to the mission. Courtesy of Margaret Benavides.

Jesse and Zoila Sánchez spread a cloth on the altar in preparation for the celebration of the Eucharist. Courtesy of Margaret Benavides.

Mr. Sánchez, what is your full name?

JS: My given name is Jesús Z. Sánchez, but I'm usually called Jesse.

And when did you come to this Mission Concepción neighborhood?

JS: In 1946.

And you, Mrs. Sánchez?

ZS: I was born here in San Antonio, on San Pedro Street, close to South Flores.

And what brought you to this neighborhood?

JS: When my family came to San Antonio, in 1943-44, my parents bought a house on this street.

And how long had you been married then?

ZS: No, we married in 1948, and we've been here in this neighborhood for forty-seven years.

And you've been members of the Concepción congregation all that time?

Both: Yes.

What kind of changes in the physical aspect of the mission have you observed in that time?

JS: I think the principal changes have been in front of the mission, and I think they have been all to the good. In the old days, Mission Road ran almost directly in front of the church.

ZS: They moved the street about half a block. In the old days, our house was the fifth house from the corner on Theo Street, but, as you can see, we are now right on the corner of Theo and Mission. The other houses were torn down.

JS: Actually, there were four houses: Mr. Guerra, Mr. Reyes, and Miss Mass, who was right on the corner of Mission Road, then there was Mrs. Ledesma's house and a cantina that was owned by a fellow named Corrado. The road was straight, but when they moved it, they made it go in the big looping curve it has now, in order to give the mission more space in front. Now it looks much nicer than it did before.

What happened to the people who lived in those houses?

JS: Well, they moved to other places in San Antonio.

Who instigated this change?

JS: I think it was the national park, but the work was carried out by the city. They worked together on the project. Now there's a sidewalk along the edge of the property. They've also improved the parking situation, and in 1992 or '93, they built the little visitors' center.

And the properties were bought up by whom?

JS: By the city. I think in Mrs. Guerra's case, they just traded her one house for another. Miss Mass sold out. The cantina and one of the houses actually faced Mission Road; the others had frontage on Theo Street.

ZS: The cantina and Miss Mass's house were torn down; the others were moved away and, I guess, sold.

What effect did this have on the neighborhood?

JS: None that I am aware of. It was advantageous for me, because I ended up on the corner, and I don't have immediate neighbors on two sides.

So it did not cause any changes in the way of life of the neighborhood or in the relations among the neighbors?

JS: No. It's the same as before. But things look prettier now. Before, you could hardly see the mission because it was surrounded by a fence of cedar posts.

Do you mean a solid fence of posts?

JS: Yes, just like the fingers of your hand. But that was a later change, because when we moved here originally, the mission was surrounded by a cyclone fence. It was when Father Balty was here that the cedar fence was built. Now everything is wide open and looks much better.

What was the condition of the mission grounds when you first moved here?

JS: The congregation was very small then. I don't remember exactly what the arrangements were, but I think that my mother and a few other people would sweep out the church, and somebody else did the grounds. But there weren't too many people available to do the work. There was a Mass said on Sundays, but that was about all. I think maybe Consuelo Garza could tell you more about that.

Then, in the 1970s, Edmon Benavides and his wife Margaret joined the church, and they took the initiative to get people together—David Garza, Mario Villaseñor, Lalo Rendón, and others—to mow the grass and keep the grounds clean. By then, the congregation numbered perhaps eighty or ninety people. But the leaders were certainly Margaret and Edmon Benavides.

Unfortunately, later on they had a problem with the pastor. Previously, the pastors, Father Balty and others, cooperated with the people. The mission congregation operated pretty independently: they raised money, they had their own bank account, they gave money to the priest when necessary, and took care of their own expenses. But the new pastor changed things according to his views: he took over the bank account and changed things. Eventually the congregation disappeared, and he stopped saying Mass altogether .

There had been Masses said at the mission since 1950 or before. A delegation of people from the neighborhood went to talk to the parish priest at St. Cecilia's —I think his name was Father McDonald—and to ask him if he would have a Mass at the mission, because the neighborhood was growing. I think the Masses started around 1948 or so, because I remember before we were married seeing people coming back from Mass at the mission.

ZS: And the last one was in 1989, on June 16, 1989. We now have them occasionally—perhaps on December 8, which is el Día de la Concepción [Conception Day], we have Mass, or at least we've had it on that date the last few years, but that's all.

So it went from weekly Masses to Masses just once a year at most?

JS: Yes, and that is only on the mission's patron saint's day, which is something that has been done ever since we moved to the neighborhood, and probably for a hundred years before that. That's like a person celebrating his birthday!

You say that initially the congregation was very small, but when Margaret and Edmon Benavides joined, things started growing.

JS: Well, the congregation had grown already before they came, because we started the memorial Masses for our son Chuíto, who died in 1964, and the church used to be completely full for those Masses. But Margaret and Edmon organized everyone well, so that a lot got done; they really did a lot, and they had everything looking very nice. They were very forward looking and very active.

So how do you see from your own point of view this conflict that led to the ending of the Masses at Concepción?

ZS: It's a very sad thing. Many people cried over it.

JS: The pastor began by canceling our memorial Mass because he said he had no time to come here for it. It had been an evening Mass dedicated to Our Lady of Guadalupe, but he said that Mass was not necessary. People started taking sides, as is usual among human beings. But the pastor could not get along with Margaret and Edmon or with the rest of the congregation.

In the past, the congregation would pass the offering plates twice; the first time went to the pastor, and the second offering stayed in the congregation. The other priests accepted and approved that; we had a treasurer, and everything was very well taken care of. But the new pastor didn't like that, and he forced the congregation to transfer the funds to St. Cecilia's account, where he was in control.

So in the end, the whole thing fell apart. Some people went to St. Cecilia's; others are going to Mission San Juan Capistrano; others have gone to other parishes. There's even some who have stopped being Catholics and have become Protestants, which is something I don't understand. If you can't get along with the priest, then go to another parish, but there's no need to stop being a Catholic because of it.

Let me tell you a story: When I was just a kid, about sixteen years old, my mother, who was very religious, worked as a cook for the convent that is over there on McCullough Avenue. And one time, when I went to pick her up, Father Edmundo, who was the pastor there, started chatting with me. Finally he asked me, "Tell me, son, do you go to Mass?"

So I told him, "Let me tell you, Father. Sometimes I go, and sometimes I don't, and it's because our parish priest offended me. On Ash Wednesday some friends and I went to church, and he refused to give us ashes, because the person who had been giving religious instruction in our neighborhood had reported us for not attending. He threw us out of the church and wouldn't give us ashes."

And he said to me, "You have to remember that, with the exception of the Redeemer, all of us are sinners. You should not hold it against the church because that priest ran you off. Remember that the church does not belong to him. It belongs to God. Don't leave your church because of one priest."

ZS: Here at the mission, when Ash Wednesday came around, the line of people coming to get their ashes extended far out of the church, because people came from all the surrounding neighborhoods to get ashes.

JS: Anyway, our memorial Mass to Our Lady of Guadalupe, as I said, was among the first to go. A lot of people came to those Masses. The Mass started at three a.m., and people started arriving at midnight. Then, after the Mass, we had Las Mañanitas with mariachis.[1] Later on, because we had a lot of older people who wanted to participate, we changed it to start at midnight. We used to make lots of food, we paid for the mariachis and organized everything. But we had dozens of people helping us out, among them Margaret and Edmon Benavides; they were among the first to help. The bishop came here to the house once—something that Edmon arranged—and we had a procession to the mission.

We have to be very grateful to them, because they really gave of themselves. My wife and my mother and I started the Masses when my son died, and we had them for twenty-five years until the pastor suspended them. The best thing that Edmon left me with when he died was his example of being totally lacking in jealousy or pride. He introduced me to the bishop and made sure he knew that I was the sponsor of the Masses. But actually I was only financing the activity; he and Margaret did all the organizing so that the event would really be successful.

ZS: Before, when there were three priests at St. Cecilia, I invited them, and all three of them came. Father Balty also came. At the last Mass we had, there were 250 people in the congregation. The church was completely full, and people were standing outside.

JS: We had all the help we could use for those memorial Masses. Some people came because of the good will they felt towards Margaret and Edmon, others because they knew us and knew that we were the sponsors. The Mass started out as a memorial for our son, but it grew so much that it became a memorial to all those who had died in the past year and before, and a real parish activity.

ZS: And the collection from that Mass was huge. The baskets were overflowing one-dollar and five-dollar bills. A lot of people have great devotion to Our Lady of Guadalupe, and they ask her for favors, so the congregation was especially generous with the collection at that Mass. And, of course, that money went to St. Cecilia's.

It seems to me that the root of the problem with the pastor was the autonomy of the congregation?

JS: In what way "autonomy?"

Well, it seems to me that if the congregation needed something, its leadership figured out a way to collect funds to meet that need, and they did not have to be going back to the pastor and asking for every little thing.

Both: Yes, that's right.

JS: That's what the new pastor did not like.

How old was your son when he died?

Both: Fourteen years old. He was our firstborn.

And what happened to him?

ZS: They stabbed him in school. It was some hoodlum from Burbank High School; he had been expelled from there and had only been two weeks at Page Junior School, where our son attended, when it happened.

JS: His friend told me that they were coming back from lunch at the school cafeteria when three other boys with knives came at them. One tried to stab the friend, and Chuíto grabbed the knife. But the boy stabbed up and hit him in the heart. Then a second one cut him in the neck. Later on I got a letter from the pastor of St. James, where the boys belonged, and they claimed that they had had no fight with my son and that the stabbing was an accident.

ZS: But two of those boys had previous records.

JS: Yes, the principal later told me that the boy who killed him had been expelled from five schools previously. He came here to the house and told me that the director of the school board had instructed him to admit the boy. The fifth expulsion was supposed to be the last, but they decided to give him another chance.

Friends of mine counseled me that I should have sued the school board big time, but I told them I couldn't do that, because I think the head of the school board meant well; he meant to do good, not harm, and you can't attack a person who tries to do good, no matter what the results. He was just trying to help those boys. But if I had been greedy or rebellious, I would have gotten a lawyer and sued, and I'm sure I would have won.

ZS: Someone from an insurance agency asked us, "Did someone pay for the funeral expenses? Because the school should have at least done that!"

Well, you folks are certainly an exception to the rule, because today people can't seem to think of anything but suing for one reason or another. And you certainly had cause.

JS: Perhaps, but the other thing was that I felt that if I went to them asking them to pay for my son's life, it was the same thing as though I were selling him, exchanging his life for money, and I could never do that.

So this was the background of the Masses to Our Lady of Guadalupe; there were none before you undertook to sponsor them?

JS: That was it. And the Masses led to a revival of celebrating Posadas in the neighborhood. One time after the Mass, I talked to Mr. Vázquez and suggested that we do the Posadas, and he agreed. The community had become very united, and many families were willing to help out.

Describe your Posadas here at Concepción.

ZS: The Posadas would start at the mission church, which was the first stop. There, you asked for admittance and a place to stay. Then, in the following eight days, you went to eight different homes and repeated the whole thing, and at each you prayed the rosary. Afterwards, there were *golosinas y chocolate* [Christmas goodies and hot cocoa] for all those who had participated. *Y la gente acababa su comidita y se iba* [And people ate their goodies, and then they would go home]. On Christmas Eve, at midnight, you ended once again at the mission church.

Oh, for the Misa de Gallo ["Cock's Crow" Mass]?

ZS: Yes. All this took place the week before Christmas. A different house each evening.

And how were the homes that were to host each evening selected?

ZS: Well, in church they would announce that we were going to have Posadas, and people would volunteer for a specific day. The names would be listed on the church bulletin, so the parish knew exactly where each night was to be held. But it started at the church and ended there as well. *Y todo el tiempo había mucha gente* [And there were always a lot of people participating]. For many years, we had the Posada on the 23rd always here, and from here we would go in procession to the church.

When you said the rosary on a Posada evening, did the priest lead it, or did the people do it?

ZS: For many years the pastor would come and lead it, but with the present pastor all that came to an end.

It seems to me a shame that something that seems to have been so well organized and that ran so well should dissolve like salt in water in such a short time.

ZS: Precisely.

JS: Let me tell you a story about our neighborhood. I used to rent the cantina that was on the corner before they changed Mission Road around. The oldest person in the neighborhood was Don Alejandro Avilés, who at that time was about ninety-five or so. He was the father of one of my *compadres*, the godfather of three of my children, including the oldest one, who died. Don Alejandro was retired and didn't have too much to do, so he used to come to the cantina to chat with me and help me by sweeping out the place and so on. I used to give him a couple of dollars, and we got along just great.

One day I asked him, "How old are you, Señor Avilés?" He took out an ID card or a driver's license, and it turned out that he was four or

Redeeming a promise to his neighbor Don Alejandro Avilés, the oldest member of the Mission Concepción congregation, Jesse Sánchez threw a big birthday party on Don Alejandro's one hundredth birthday in May 1982. In this photo, Don Alejandro sits in front of the mission surrounded by his grandson (in the wheelchair) and his children; Jesse and Zoila Sánchez stand at left. Courtesy of Jesse and Zoila Sánchez.

five years from reaching one hundred. So I told him, *"¡Mire usted, Señor Avilés, cuando usted complete los 100 años, si yo estoy vivo, le voy a hacer una fiestota!"* [Look, Mr. Avilés, when you reach one hundred, if I am alive, I am going to throw you a great big party!]

"Oh," he said, "between now and then you'll forget all about it." But I promised him I wouldn't. So the three or four years went by, because that's the way life speeds by, and one day he came in and said, "Jesse, do you still remember what you promised me?"

And I said I certainly did, "But why do you ask?"

"Well, because my birthday is coming up soon, and I'm going to be one hundred! It's just a few months more."

So I went to my *compadre* Avilés, who is his oldest son, and I told him the whole story. I said, "I'm not telling you this to ask you to help me

Don Alejandro takes a crack at his birthday piñata. Courtesy of Jesse and Zoila Sánchez.

pay for it, but just so that you'll know what is being planned for your dad." Anyway, we had a great party with lots of food, and mariachis, and a piñata for Mr. Avilés, and a special Mass at the mission, and everything.

The word got around that it was his hundredth birthday, and even Henry Cisneros, who was mayor at the time, came to the party, and people from the congregation and the neighborhood showed up. He even got a birthday greeting from the president of the United States! And the whole thing was held on the grounds of the mission through the assistance of Edmon and Margaret Benavides.

A couple of years after that—because he lived to be 104—I came into the cantina wearing a new hat. Mr. Avilés was there, still sweeping the floor, and he didn't recognize me. When I greeted him, he said, "And who are you?" So I took off my hat, and he said, "Ah, Jesse, it's you! Well, who was going to recognize you with that hat!" Then he said, "You know, you never threw that party for me that you promised me for my hundredth birthday!"

I was sort of taken aback. Then I realized that he was getting forgetful in his old age, and I reminded him of the party at the mission, and the piñata and the mariachis and Henry Cisneros: "Don't you remember that you danced with Miss Mass?"

And he said, "Well, you're right! I *had* forgotten. It wasn't until you reminded me of dancing with Miss Mass that I finally remembered!"

But the fact that he didn't remember stayed in my mind, because I remembered my mother telling me that if one promises something, doesn't keep the promise, and the person dies, it's likely that their spirit will come back and haunt you afterwards. So I went to talk to his daughter Jesusita, with whom he lived. I told her my problem, and I asked her to please remind her Dad periodically that we had had his party. And after that, every time I saw him I always reminded him of dancing with Miss Mass! [Laughs.][2]

So you didn't want Mr. Avilés coming from the other world to claim his birthday party?

JS: Absolutely not. [Laughs.] And later on, one of his granddaughters came and told me that when I got to my hundredth birthday, she was going to throw a big party for me . . . *with the same mariachis!* Although I think she meant with mariachis also, like her grandfather's! [Laughs.] So it is really a shame that that kind of community spirit and the good relations that existed between the priests and the congregation had to be destroyed, because it ran wonderfully for years.

NOTES

1. Mañanitas is the Mexican tradition of presenting an early-dawn serenade on a person's birthday, as well as the name of the tune usually sung on this occasion.

2. From a parish bulletin item on the death of Alejandro Avilés provided by Margaret Benavides: "Alejandro Avilés was born on May 20, 1882 in Ibarra, Guanajuato, Mexico. He came to the US in 1920 as an agricultural worker. In the 1940s he bought a home closer to the city, and settled by Mission Concepción when there were only three or four homes in the area. At that time, carpenters were just building houses along Theo Street."

Monsignor Balthasar Janacek

Monsignor **Balthasar Janacek**, *Father Balty to most people, is probably one of the best-known priests in the Archdiocese of San Antonio, a man beloved and appreciated both within and beyond the Catholic church. Although of Czech background, Father Balty is very much in tune with the Hispanic community. For years, he has been the Church's guardian of the Old Spanish Missions and has represented the diocesan interests in the missions vis-à-vis the city of San Antonio, the state of Texas, and the National Park Service. Father Balty was interviewed at his parish office on July 12, 1995, with a followup on July 21, 1995.*

How old are you now, Father Balty?

I'm almost sixty-nine now. My term here at San Francisco di Paola Church is a six-year term, so I will be seventy-five by the time it ends. I can choose to continue to work then, but I won't necessarily be assigned to a church full-time. Or I can move out to Casa de Padres, our retirement home. Do you know where that is?

Well, somehow I can't see you being put out to pasture.

[Laughs.] It's going to be neat to be able to do full-time research then. That's what I'm hoping to do.

It's just too bad that it takes so long before you can get to do what you should've been doing to begin with! I'd like to hear a little about your background. Where were you born? Where did you grow up?

I was born in a little village called Deweesville, Texas, which is in Karnes County, south of San Antonio, approximately forty-five miles towards Corpus Christi. I was born on a rancho out there. My dad and mom had a little store at what I like to think of as the place where the West begins, because from there on it's mostly ranches. They had a little grocery store, which was used by the ranch hands, many of whom were former Mexican nationals who had come over and had ultimately become citizens.

Out among those people, who were twenty-five miles from the nearest parish church, they did the *Pastorela*. My sister, who later became a nun—she went to the convent when I was about a year and a half old—wrote me once a little history of the *Pastorela* the way she remembered it. The families would come into our store and buy all the supplies they needed for the *pachanga* [feast], and they would invite my mom and dad and the family out there. So I probably went to their *Pastorela* when I was a squirt. That must have been in 1927-28 or along in there.

So this was a spontaneous celebration of the local people there?

Yes, absolutely. It wasn't done by the church, because there was none nearby. There was also a troupe around Lacoste and another around Pearsall, and, of course, there is the one here in San Antonio, but those were areas way out there that probably had nothing to do with one another. I doubt very much if there was any connection between San Antonio and that Falls City area.

And your ethnic background is?

My grandparents came from Czechoslovakia.

Were they Czechs or Slovaks?

Czechs, actually from Moravia, which is in the middle and today ended up being in the Czech Republic. I grew up speaking both Czech and English. My parents spoke and wrote both languages, and my mom used to write for the newspapers, sometimes in Czech, others in English.

Was there a large Czech community in that area?

Not a large one, not where I was born. When I was six years old we moved to a place called Hobson, which was not far from Deweesville. There the "Polish Corridor" was on the east side of the San Antonio River, with Panna Maria, Cestohowa, Kosciusko, and Falls City, and on the west side of the river were the non-Polish families: Germans, Czechs, and a few French families.

I would say that out of the eighty families that made up our parish, probably half were Czech and half were German. So it was a matter of language in those days. The mixture of cultures was not exactly easy. It took intermarriage finally to break through. We also had a few Mexican families in Hobson. No black families whatsoever in that vicinity.

What caused the move from Deweesville?

When I was born, I was the straw that broke the camel's back, because I was the eighth child. My dad needed more acreage so that the boys could have more farmland to work. We had only a small acreage around the store. So in 1929 or something like that they bought bigger acreage further west, in the area of Coy City. But the next year, the price of cotton dropped to eight cents a pound—that was all in those Depression years—so they ended up losing the whole farm. That was when we moved into the town of Hobson. Of course, there we had a parochial school, so I got to go there, and two of my brothers did also. I entered the seminary from there, so it was one of those providential kind of things.

What did your dad do in Hobson?

Farm. For that we rented a farm. We were "third-and-fourth renters," that's what they called it. That meant that every fourth bale of cotton and every third head of corn belonged to the owner of the land. Actually, they ended up selling the corn, and the owner would get a third of the sale price.

Were you the last child?

One was born after me, but she died in infancy. She was the tenth child, actually; the first had also died in infancy, so eight of us survived. And now there's only two of us left. My mother and father both died in the '50s.

Where did you go to seminary?

Right here in San Antonio at St. John's Seminary, right next to Mission Concepción. I went there for eleven years, so I really grew up in the shadow of Mission Concepción. I went to the seminary when I was twelve—it was a high school seminary—and then on to college and postgraduate. It was all on the same campus, so I didn't leave until I was twenty-three, and I only had summers to go home. Living in the area of the missions became a part of my life.

What was your first assignment out of the seminary?

It was in Schulenburg, Texas, about one hundred miles from here. I was there for two years. From there, I went to Edna, Texas, which was still a part of this diocese at that time. Both of those are part of the Victoria diocese now. And I was in Edna for ten years, from '52 to '62. In Schulenburg, during my first two years I almost lost my Spanish, which I had studied in the seminary, but we had a Hispanic family that lived in the neighboring parish, and I used to give instruction to their kids. That way I was at least able to keep my Spanish. In Edna, of course, half of the parish was Mexican-American; it was a real rural area, with farming and ranching both.

Then, in 1962, I came to San Antonio to St. Cecilia's parish, and of course Mission Concepción is a part of that parish. By that time they had begun to offer Sunday Masses on a regular basis. Monsignor Roy Rihn had inaugurated the Masses there. Before that, there was only occasional use of the mission as a church.

When you came to San Antonio as a student, what was the condition of Concepción and the remains of the mission there?

It was always very dilapidated-looking, because at that time the work had not been done on the doors and other things. It looked very much like some of the old pictures you see, showing the abandonment of the missions. There was brush around it, and no kind of restoration work had been done on it at all.

There used to be a caretaker who would come and open the church for visitors during the summer months on weekends. And of course, once in a while, like when we had the Christ the King procession once a year in October, we would leave from there with the Blessed Sacrament and go across the street to the orphanage.

Monsignor Morkovsky was in charge of the missions in those days, when I was in the seminary. He was one of our professors . . . I remember him talking about the missions to us . . . and I have a document from him about the placing of that wrought iron grid in the front at San José, explaining why he put it there. He said he saw holes in the wall and came to the conclusion that there was probably some kind of grid there at one time.

Did the caretaker live on the grounds?

No, no, actually the caretakers ended up being an aunt and uncle of Monsignor Larry Stubben, but they did not live on the grounds. And then later a Mrs. Rogers took over for many, many years, until we amalgamated the missions effort into what we called the Old Spanish Missions [OSM] Committee.

Were any of the rooms that are left standing in the convento there used at that time for anything?

They were used by the caretaker as kind of an office space.

During your student days, did you ever have the opportunity to get over to San José?

Yes. We used to go over there with real awe, because the priest who was over there was an old Franciscan who'd come over and function as sort of our confessor at the seminary. We hiked to San José—we were allowed to hike south from the seminary, but not north into the "wicked city." [Laughs.]

What was the name of this Franciscan?

Father Bonaventure. Ilg, I think, was his last name.

What do you remember of the physical remains out at San José?

I don't remember any clear differences between when I was first there—that would be 1939 and '40—and later on in the war years during the '40s. And I can't remember any clear differences in 1941-42, when the state took it over as a state park. The WPA work had all been finished in the '30s, so the walls and everything else was there, just as it is today.

Then, from '50 to '62, I was completely isolated from the missions because I was out on rural assignments. I don't know that the state park system did much in the way of repairs other than what was done before. The repairs of the roof at San José came in the '60s, I think, when Pete DeVries was there; and I came on board in '67 with the OSM and started going to the meetings of the San José board.

So your assignment as the person responsible for the missions on the church's side began in '67.

In '67, yes.

And what did that assignment entail?

First of all, my direct connection came in '62 already, because I was assigned to St. Cecilia's parish, so I began saying Mass at Mission Concepción on Sundays. In those days, Bishop Steven Leven was director of the missions. Once in a while he would call me to represent him at some function which he was supposed to attend because of his connection with the missions.

Then he turned that job over to Father Herzig, who later became Bishop Herzig in Tyler, Texas. When Herzig was going to be assigned to working with the archdiocese, traveling all around the diocese kind of doing a survey, he resigned his position as director of OSM and recommended to Archbishop Lucey that I be assigned to the job, since I was already connected to the missions through Concepción. So he was the one who really got me into it.

My first assignment was to supervise the work at San Juan, the restoration work that had already been commissioned by Archbishop Lucey. At that time he had what he called the San Juan Mission Committee that was made up of Gilbert Denman, General William Harris, O'Neil Ford, Stewart King, who was a landscape architect, and Henry Guerra. They were asked to raise funds for the restoration of San Juan, and they developed an elaborate plan to do so.

Their first project was to get archaeology done at the site, so Mardith Schuetz, who was already a recognized archaeologist, helped by Anne Fox, was contracted under the University of Texas or possibly the Texas Historical Commission to do the work. So my first assignment was to be a part of what was happening out there, to supervise the work as Archbishop Lucey's representative.

The archbishop supervised everything in a general way. He not only wanted to know what was happening but he would go out there on his own time, and not a leaf would be turned without his knowing about it. He would have his chauffeur drive him out there on a Sunday afternoon so he could see what had happened and what was happening.

I remember going out there once and chatting with Mardith and Anne, who were seated on the threshold of the door into what is today the museum . . . of course, in those days it was nothing but a gutted shell, no doors or anything in it . . . having a cool beer at the end of their workday.

That sounds just like the archaeologists I've worked with!

Yes. [Laughs.] But they were doing the preparatory work for the restoration at San Juan mission. This was in '67.

What was the extent of this restoration?

They restored what is now the rectory, what was for many years the CCD office or the caretaker's residence. Not what's now the museum; that was done later under a separate grant, a gift from Ewing Halsell. The church was restored later because the San Juan Committee wanted to have a real-live Franciscan on a permanent basis out there.

The committee had the idea that they wanted to restore the walls. For that purpose, the archbishop had the rocks from the old chancery building, that was located on Dwyer Avenue, dumped in the compound of the mission. The idea was to make it "a beautiful place for Mexican-American couples to have their weddings." I remember the committee describing this idea to me and telling me what a blessing it would be for such couples to have a beautiful setting for their weddings. I thought the whole idea was pretty insensitive and that they'd be lucky if anyone took them up on the offer, but I never said it. So that was the concept.

As part of it, they wanted their real-live Franciscan, who would walk around in his robe and, I guess, imitate St. Francis. Well, it turned out that they got their real-live Franciscan, Father Jasper Mauss, who is today the chaplain at the Cordi-Marian Villa on Culebra Road. I think it would be interesting to talk to him and get his impressions of the first years of that restoration project.

Anyway, Jasper walked around in his robes, all right. He even planted flowers and everything in his robes, but he also did things that they didn't like, that exasperated the members of the committee. I remember telling them, "You all wanted a real-live Franciscan here, and you got one. If you wanted somebody to just wear the robe and not do anything, you should have put up a statue of a Franciscan or hired an actor to wear the robe. But a real-live one is going to be himself, and that is part of the place being a 'live mission.'" Especially when the church got restored later on, he would do things that they didn't particularly like. It's just like I don't like some of the things that happen at the missions today, but if we have live congregations and live pastors, it comes with the territory that they are going to want certain things their way, and not yours!

Then, my second assignment ended up being removing the stones that the archbishop had had trucked there. [Laughs.]

You mean the stones from the chancery?

Absolutely, and these were stones; they were not pebbles. They were big chunks of limestone that the old chancery was built of. There were fifty-four truckloads all told! All of them sitting inside the compound.

Remember that this was '67. San Antonio was preparing for Hemisfair in '68, and we were being told that we were going to have tons of visitors—and we ended up having tons of visitors—at the missions. So my duty was to get that mission, along with the others, ready for Hemisfair '68. We finally got the fifty-four loads of limestone out of the compound, and they are still back there. Some of it we could use for restoration work, even at the Alamo. Some of them were put into windrows; others went into holes in the bank of the river to help prevent erosion. We know where they are, anyway.

Fortunately, the restoration of the walls never took place. That would have been a real disaster, to try to restore those walls. Meanwhile the museum was falling down, and the roof on the church was in bad shape. The work on the church was done with matching funds from the Texas State Historical Commission. We air-conditioned the church and the museum and repaired the roof. The ductwork was run underground for that project, but the National Park Service recently dug it out again.

What was your assignment insofar as the other missions were concerned? I assume that this was a package deal for all the missions, not just San Juan.

That's right. At that time we didn't use the name Old Spanish Missions yet. I was the connection between all the missions as far as the church was concerned. My assignment was to be the liaison between the archbishop and the mission parishes, because he had to have somebody to represent him sometimes, or to take the blame sometimes, when he would have something done at the missions.

I remember the furor over a statue of the Blessed Virgin Mary at Mission Concepción. It was a wooden statue from Mexico that someone had donated, and Bishop Charles Grahmann, who was the archbishop's administrative secretary (under Archbishop Lucey, and later on under Furey as well), simply put that statue in the mission without notifying the local priest or consulting the congregation. I had to step in and attempt to calm things down and salve hurt feelings. By the way, there's a sort of interesting ending to the story of that statue. A few years ago, someone went into the mission, took the statue down, and beheaded it!

Beheaded it? What on earth?

Yes, sawed its head right off. And the head was never found. The story circulated that "a tourist" had done it, but no one had actually witnessed it. We have some idea of what happened, but the culprit was never caught.

Anyway, as far as my job at the time was concerned, since Hemisfair was upon us, my primary job, as far as priorities were concerned, was to get the missions ready . . .

Make them presentable?

Yes, presentable for the expected visitors. And it was no small task. First of all, Concepción was not open all year long. It was open only during the summer and during special holidays. The other two smaller missions, San Juan and Espada, were never "open" officially, more than any church would be open. In other words, there was no caretaker of any kind, so there was nobody that took care of them other than the parish priest.

San José at that time was already a state park. For San José, I would go to the meetings of the San José Advisory Board, and by that time, Pete DeVries was already the superintendent, and Mrs. Ethel Harris still lived in the house now occupied by Los Compadres, but she was really the "owner"! [Laughs.] She had so much power that she could have the pastor removed at San José if she wished; she had the archbishop's private number.

What was the basis of her power?

She had been the one who helped the archbishop get San José into the state park system. She was a member and a former president of the Conservation Society and had been very much involved in saving San José and in the Conservation Society's efforts there. Somehow or other, she had become very close to the archbishop. As Father Herzig used to say, they deserved each other! [Laughs.] God rest their souls! She could reach him, and if she didn't like what the pastor was doing, she succeeded in getting people "moved along" rather quickly.

Pete became her protégé at San José, and then she got him into being the superintendent. But there was this love/hate relationship: Pete could be her fair-haired boy one minute, but the next she could be just tearing into him. She could run him ragged at the meetings, because she couldn't stand the state park system, even though she had helped arrange making the mission part of it. They could do nothing like she needed it to be done.

So the National Park Service (NPS) became her dream. I don't know whether she ever dreamed that the missions should become part of the national park system, but she arranged it so that the NPS had membership on this board, and she would always use them as her "fall-back" against the state, in the sense that they had more expertise and so on than the state system.

One question: how did she end up living on the grounds?

It was her house.

But how could she own a house on a state park?

No, the state didn't own all of the land. That was part of the problem with San José: it had such a divided ownership situation. Until recently, you had parts that were owned by this or that private individual, and she owned a piece of land there, where she built her house. Eventually she ended up giving it to the state, or some other such arrangement, but reserved the right to continue living there.

And, of course, you know that eventually they had to settle by declaring the inner portion of the compound as "indivisible property" owned both by the State of Texas and the Archdiocese of San Antonio, which it still is. If one or the other gets sued, for example, the other is part of the case. It was a friendly settlement because the ownership situation was so complicated.

But she was the one who, almost even out of her deathbed, ran, or at least thought she ran, San José because she would still call shots through the ladies of the Conservation Society, as much as she could. I got along with her okay. She always let me know that she had the ear of the archbishop, and as long as I respected that we got along. But she came to the conclusion that Pete and I always did things hand in hand, so if Pete was on her good side, then I was on her good side, too.

As far as the other missions were concerned, the problem that we had was that the archbishop didn't think that anybody used to go out to San Juan or to Espada. From the beginning of my tenure as director of the OSM Pete was my consultant because he had experience with the state parks, and he saw that the missions needed to be treated as one unit.

He helped me work out a kind of brochure: a mimeographed sheet for Espada and for San Juan. We reproduced them, and we got Father Larry Brummer at Espada to allow us to put them in the church: he would leave the church open, keep up the supply of brochures, and he would count how many he would put out and how many were taken.

Then, at San Juan we had some summer workers assigned to us under the SANYO [San Antonio Neighborhood Youth Organization] program to do clean-up out there, and a young airman from Lackland used to volunteer to be the supervisor for the SANYO workers, because you always had to have somebody. His name was Ralph Herr, God rest his soul; he has since died. He had met the Franciscans in California and was baptized out there at one of the California missions; here he was a friend of Father Larry Brummer's. He and the SANYO workers used to also hand out our little brochure to visitors. Everything had to be done with volunteers because we had no money.

By the time Hemisfair came along, we got the archbishop to let us build little kiosks, like for a parking attendant, at San Juan and Espada. We had volunteers at each to keep the gate open, and that way we could tell how many people were coming. Initially, the archbishop didn't want us to hire anybody; he argued that people were just picking up our brochures and throwing them away. So we got him to authorize our use of volunteers to do it.

At Concepción we already had a person who was hired for part-time work, but the archbishop allowed us to extend her hours. Pete helped a lot. He had a way with words and could formulate very effective letters. He would keep you busy, dictating them to you.

By the time Hemisfair was over, we had a pretty good account of how many people were visiting. Where before we would have four thousand visitors to Concepción over a period of a year—that we could account for—and nothing at the other missions, during Hemisfair we had between four thousand and seven thousand per month at Concepción, and then, of course, they also went to the others.

And Hemisfair lasted for how long?

One year, 1968. At the end of that we decided to develop a "mission tour ticket," because we felt that if we sold visitors one ticket with four stubs on it, they would stay over another day and use up the rest of the ticket seeing the other missions. Actually, they say that's the way things work in tourism; people will do the strangest things when they are visiting away from home.

In order to do that, though, we had to reach an agreement with the state comptroller's office, because they would be collecting tickets and would have to pay us for the tickets in the long run. We, in turn, would pay them for part of it. The state was already charging something like fifty cents for Mission San José. If we sold the ticket for the four missions for a dollar, then money had to go back and forth between them and us, depending on what part of the ticket was used. I think also that they agreed to give us part of the fifty cents they were charging. I forget now how all the details worked out.

But anyway, we did work it out, and we would get a check from the state every month. That caused some consternation in various quarters, and the church-and-state question was raised, but the agreement stood. This was a real boon for us, because people would really go out to San Juan and Espada.

We advertised, and we sent teachers packets to all the school districts in the state; San José would have them printed, and we would send them out. And the increased visitation helped San José as well. You know those brick pathways at San José? The ones that the Park Service gripes so much about? We put those in with the funds collected.

Before, all we had at any of the missions were gravel paths, and we didn't want to put in regular brick, so Pete and I went to Mexico, and right across the border we found these bricks that were handmade for a nickel apiece. He wasn't allowed to buy material across the border for the state, so we bought them out of the diocesan budget, and the state park people did the work. So it was one hand washing the other.

Then, in essence, Hemisfair provided the impetus for the four missions to be regarded and treated as a unit?

Yes, that's right. It brought recognition to the missions that they had never had, even as far as the diocese was concerned. Previously the archbishop had thought that they were not visited by people, but now we knew that they were, despite the fact that the roads were awful. That's when the archbishop used to complain publicly that you could get lost out there trying to find the missions.

If before Hemisfair there was no signage and no road markers put up, how did people get out there?

By hook or by crook. The signs were really bad, and it wasn't until 1970, when we were going to have the first Día de las Misiones [Day of the Missions] on the 6th of August, that we got some signs up, but they were not official ones. They were signs we got the Boy Scouts to make: on the day before, we got a bunch of them together and we made signs that said "Mission Trail" and had an arrow pointing. The evening before, almost at sundown, we started from downtown and started nailing signs to the telephone and electric line poles along the road so that people could find their way out.

Well, we had fifteen thousand people visit the missions that day. It was the first anniversary of Archbishop Furey's coming to San Antonio. It was also the date of Father Antonio Margil de Jesús death. We were hoping for it to become an annual event, and it was for several years.

It was a free day at the missions, including San José. By then, the mission tour ticket was popular—fifty cents at each individual mission, or a dollar ticket for all four. At all the missions we had something happening every hour, and we had a free bus that started at Roosevelt Park on the hour and stopped at all the missions. We paid for that out of our budget.

But we still did not have permanent signs. After that first event, we contacted the city and started the round of lobbying and meetings, until finally one day someone from the city called me up and said, "Would you make the rounds with me? Let's talk about where you think we should have signs for the missions." We did that, and we got the Mission Trail signs. Then, when the Park Service came in, they got better signage, even though it is still pretty hard to find them.

It certainly is sometimes. It depends which way you're coming from. At some corners, you can see the signs from one direction, but there is nothing from the other. Did your assignment from the diocesan side change significantly after Hemisfair?

No, it just grew. In 1969, shortly after Archbishop Furey came here, Pete and I decided that it was highly important to consolidate the missions while we had them working together. We wrote up a proposal to the archbishop to establish the Old Spanish Missions Committee, that would serve in an advisory capacity to him and also would direct the policies for the old missions.

We included in that initially San Fernando Cathedral, but we really never could get Father Nuevo involved. But, we felt it was necessary to get the diocesan authorities thinking in terms of historic preservation because up until that time, the cathedral had done things on its own.

We also felt that we had to get some control over that San Juan Mission Committee, lest it go out on its own and do restoration out there that would do more damage than good. We proposed some twenty-six members in the committee and set up subcommittees within it: architecture, landscaping, and so on, and we made each one of the members of that group head of one of the committees, but as part of the whole committee. Gilbert Denman was the art man, King was in landscaping, and so on.

We got all this approved by the archbishop and had letters drafted, so the people involved could hardly say no. Then we would all meet on a regular basis, and eventually it turned out to be a very good thing. It helped us to get a superintendent of the OSM sites, and Pete DeVries quit the state park and took over the job. I always used to kid him that he had worked for the two perfect societies, the church and the state, according to St. Thomas Aquinas, and ended up getting screwed by both! [Laughs.]

So that's how the OSM Committee got going, and we were able to keep it strong enough so that, in the end, it was a big help in working out the agreement with the NPS. The preparation of that agreement was done by representatives of the OSM Committee, including the lay people from the various parishes, and we spent hours and hours working on it with the NPS people.

After the national park came into being, we had hoped to continue with the committee, but some of its members began to lose interest because they became members of the advisory board of the park—which was something we had pushed for through the OSM's influence. At one point, we had Margarita Madrid, Janie Garza, Felix Almaraz, and others as members of that board.

Going back to the establishment of the national park, were there any major hurdles that had to be overcome before that could be accomplished?

The first major hurdle came after the bill was signed. There was a problem with a local Baptist minister, Jimmy Allan, who protested monies being spent on the churches. We argued that the money would not be spent on the churches but on other things at the sites, according to the agreement. But Jimmy Carter refused to let the money be released for the actual establishment of the park.

The word, however, got out that *we* were stalling the process! Grahmann, who was auxiliary bishop by that time, had to go into action to get the word to influential people that we were not the cause of the delay and that we were open to making the distinction more clear as to what was to be done and how. So finally the appropriations were allowed.

NPS personnel moved to San Antonio. They set up an office in the Federal Building downtown and began their research work. That was in '81, if I remember correctly. The agreement was finally worked out under Reagan. Since they could not spend money on anything that was owned by the Church, it was decided at the diocesan level that we were willing to give the NPS the missions if we could be granted the concession right to hold religious services there. We were that serious about wanting the national park.

The agreement was drawn up along those lines. Then Reagan came in, and he sent down a bunch of new young Republican lawyers, and they decided that the U.S. government did not have the money to take care of the missions. So we had to start from scratch on a different form of the agreement. We then worked out the agreement on the basis of keeping church ownership of the mission but letting the NPS have the right to maintenance and interpretation. We held on to the right of maintenance, interpretation, and restoration of the church buildings themselves. And that was the compromise that was reached.

What was your working relation with the state, as far as San José was concerned, before the national park became a reality?

The same as it is with the national park. I had to work out the details with them of anything that included San José; I attended the advisory board meetings of the state park and worked out things as they came up.

As far as maintenance and historic preservation are concerned, is it still the same thing?

Yes, because they maintained everything that was not "church." The agreement with the state was really a model for the one we eventually made with the NPS. Archbishop Lucey did a really good job of working that out. It was a tremendous help to San José mission and to the parish, because the parish could not have kept up the park.

But it's also important to realize that the federal government's help had been there from way back: the WPA was a federal agency, and they had done reconstruction at San José and helped save the walls at all the missions. They had capped them and stabilized them.

I've encountered the opinion that the establishment of the national park was, in effect, responsible for the death of the San Juan Capistrano mission community and that Espada did not suffer the same fate because they were fortunate enough to sort of bring their forces together and present a more united front to protect their interests. How do you feel about that?

The San Juan community was, I think, enhanced through the coming of the national park. It was already dying, in a sense, even before that. There were plenty of "For Sale" signs down there all along those roads long before the park became a part of it. Father Brennan Schmieg came to San Juan just before the park was created, and he was the one who built the church community during his time there, who got the church community to pull together.

The national park has had nothing to do with the church community not pulling together, as far as I can tell. There may be those that feel that is the case, but I really don't see how; what it really has made possible is that the place has stayed in good shape, which it wasn't before the park.

The first thing that sometimes people resented was when we pulled all the missions together in the OSM concept. The diocese had subsidized the parish for many years, and it was not until recent years that it began to pay its own electrical bills, for example. At the time, everything out there had to be electrical—there was no other way of doing it—and we thought that was a burden on them, so we helped out. But as the parish built up and began to do things on its own, we talked to them about covering that expense themselves. And that has all happened since the park has been there. I don't know what someone would mean by saying that.

The way it was presented to me was that the community suffered its first blow when the River Corridor question came up and caused large-scale displacement because people's land, or the land where they lived, was going to be involved in the project. I guess the issue then was flood control. But then the sort of coup de grace was that, from what was left, now the park was going to claim another portion to carry out the plans for developing the site within the park. The additional exodus, in essence, weakened the fabric of the community so that it has never recovered.

That may be partially true, depending on how you look at it. The number of families affected at the time the park came in was not that great, but of course, if you're talking about a small number of families to begin with, the percentage may look bad. Physically or geographically, it affected only two or three families right around the mission whose land was purchased.

The Centeno place, which was purchased for the labores [agricultural fields], really didn't affect the community, because it was a case of absentee ownership from long before anyway. I don't remember the families that lived on the Centeno place as being active members of the community, but I may be all wrong. They could still be active, for that matter, because the place was bought, but is still being lived on by families.

The bulk of the families that go to San Juan mission never lived right around the church, because you always had the railroad and other things interfering with the community. The Richter family was the one that lived closest to the mission, and they died of old age, not because the park interfered with them. I don't remember the land taken up by the river channel as being farms, either.

I just think that that may be an overstatement.

**Do you perceive any significant difference between the Espada commu-
nity and that at San Juan, either now or at the time when the park
was being established?**

No, not really. I have not kept a count of how many families moved out, but
I don't see that the national park has bought out a lot of families, either.

When we went through the hearings in preparation for the coming
of the park—it was a colloquium sponsored by the U.S. Bicentennial
Committee, and, of course, the NPS also held hearings—there were
people who fussed because they were concerned about what was going
to happen and because they did not want what they saw as an intrusion
into the community's life. But I don't know that the original observa-
tion is accurate.

**What is your function nowadays with the national park an established
entity?**

Where the parishes are concerned, I continue to be the liaison between the
parishes and the archdiocese. For instance, there is a restoration of the
choir loft at San Juan in the works now, and I am the one who has helped
move that, making sure that it is done with an architect, etc. I'm
probably more involved with it than I want to be because the parish
priest has shifted the responsibility my way.

And I am the liaison for the NPS as well. Every so often something
comes up that needs to be taken care of. Remember that the agreement
has a sixty-day clause, which allows a party that is dissatisfied with the
way things are functioning to give sixty days' notice that it wants to exit
the agreement. We could tell the NPS that they have to leave, and,
vice-versa, they can inform us that they want to exit. And that is done
with the idea in mind that both parties will work to keep the agreement
going because both parties have a lot invested in it. We felt that
otherwise, sore points might be left to fester and cause really major
disagreements. What happens now is that if something is going wrong,
then we have to let each other know, but fast, and we have to try to do
something about it.

Surely the NPS could ruin the parishes if they somehow put obstacles in the way of parishioners using the sites. They could do that
without putting up a wall. So we have to have their continued cooperation to ensure that the missions continue as active parishes. And the
park *wants* them to be living parishes. So that's really where I come in.

For instance, right now, the NPS is not happy that we're not having Mass at Mission Concepción, and they've told us we're not living up to our agreement to keep it as a living parish. As a matter of fact, the superintendent recently told us that if we are not going to have a parish there, then perhaps we would be better off turning the site completely over to the NPS. They could then do the roof and other necessary maintenance jobs. Of course, that is a big temptation, but it is not one that we want to respond to in a hasty manner. That would tie up the mission more than we would like, even though according to the agreement we have the right to use the grounds at the missions for our purposes.

So I'm the liaison between the diocese and the mission parishes, the diocese and the NPS, and the mission parishes and the NPS. That does not keep the parish priests from going directly to the superintendent for things that pertain to the immediate mission, but anything that pertains to or affects the whole needs to come through me.

In general, has it been a happy relationship between the archdiocese and the NPS ?

Oh, yes, definitely. Sometimes there has been unhappiness among some of the people at the parish level, but I'm sure that the Park Service doesn't always appreciate things that happen at the parish level. But that's where we were blessed that we had a few years of working together as the OSM Committee, because that has created the perception that not a single one of the missions is off by itself, that they are all part of a whole.

It certainly has been helpful to the missions physically. I happen to think that it has also been helpful psychologically to the people of the mission neighborhoods, who now think of themselves as being much more important than what they thought they were in the past. In many ways, the city did not appreciate the missions. A prime example of that was that sewage plant that was built right out there on Espada Road next to the mission. And, of course, the city did not take care of the roads in that area for many years, and so on.

In '69, Pete and I decided to do a fund-raiser at the San José amphitheater, and we thought we could try to cash in on all of the businesses that use the word *mission* or the name of one of the missions in their name. We used a pitch in the letter: "Your business benefits from the name and the image of our missions, so help us support them."

I think it was a five-dollar catered meal, and there was going to be a show in the amphitheater. Well, we only got a handful of them to answer! After the bill had been passed in '78 and we were preparing to go into the agreement with the NPS, we immediately started working on an organization called Los Amigos de las Misiones [Friends of the Missions], and Pete developed this squirrel character as a mascot for the missions, because that was an animal that was common to all the missions. We called it Amigo the Squirrel. Pete went out to Disneyland and had the same company that does the outfits for the Disney characters do ours for Amigo. And it ended up that the city took Amigo to Mexico as part of one of these friendship exchanges. I remember the squirrel walking across the Zócalo in Mexico City!

Pete had a lot of ideas, and for the most part they really worked. The Mission Trail ticket worked, the idea of working with the park and getting the agreement together, all of those were things that he either originated or worked very hard on.

Anyway, the idea of Los Amigos was to bring together a group of supporters who would raise money for the missions to help us with their upkeep. After the bill was passed, we were able to get a storefront downtown on Alamo Plaza, where Fuddrucker's is now, for less rent because it was in the process of being sold, and we set up a gift shop. I think all of this helped strengthen our position in the negotiations with the NPS, because we were not dealing out of a shoebox.

And eventually Los Amigos developed into Los Compadres de las Misiones [Godfathers of the Missions];[1] Betty Beuché took that idea and developed it. Ours did not get off the ground after that; you cannot have two groups working for the same goal in fund-raising. And so Los Compadres is *the* group of friends of the missions, and fortunately it brings in monies that we never could get because it gets the attention of people who would not normally be involved with the missions. I sit in the meetings of Los Compadres and see the people who are there, and it's fantastic. We'd never be able to reach them through a Catholic approach.

Yes, of course. They have the advantage of working beyond the borders of denominational affiliation.

Exactly. And they also recognize that their work makes it difficult for us to raise money for our mission churches, so they're trying to help us with that: money for the roof at Concepción and at San José, for example.

When there are major upkeep projects or major historic preservation projects, how is the funding handled?

Anything that pertains to a church building or to a building where priests live, for instance, the NPS will not touch.

So that is entirely the church's financial responsibility?

Absolutely, and that is a big difficulty. Needless to say, we had that before, plus whatever the NPS has assumed responsibility for, so at least we have that much help now.

Restoration projects are not cheap. Supposing you come into a situation where work is urgently needed and the church simply cannot afford it. What happens then?

We're at that point right now. The roof on Concepción and the roof on San José urgently need repair. We are trying to get money through grants. If something were to fall down, then we would have to borrow money and take care of it. We have a small fund that we've been able to hold on to. A few years ago, I guess about ten years ago, we included the old missions in the archbishop's annual appeal for funds, and we managed to hold onto a small portion of that, probably about twenty thousand dollars, to be used for immediate emergencies. I use that in urgent cases.

A blessing that we have also had is this Bexar County Historical Foundation. It was set up by Henry Guerra, Gilbert Denman, and General Harris, who has since died. I think O'Neil Ford may have been a part of that also. They organized it at the time the national park came into being, because they foresaw the time when we would be needing help with continued restoration and repairs of structures that were the church's responsibility. [See interview with Henry Guerra.]

That foundation has been able to collect and disburse approximately three-quarters of a million dollars over the years to use for that purpose. They got money through the Moody Foundation; from Ewing Halsell, who I think came through with a twenty-five-thousand-dollar nest egg to start the foundation; and then we were able to get some matching grants from the [Texas State] Historical Foundation. That's where some of the work done at Mission San Juan and some of the other missions was paid from several years ago.

There's supposed to be some money coming to the missions from an estate, but that is now tied up in the form of property. We applied to the Kennedy Foundation in Corpus Christi for $225,000 to do the

A cedar post fence built during Father Balty's pastorate surrounded Mission Concepción. Courtesy of the Old Spanish Missions Research Collection, Special Collections and Archives, Our Lady of the Lake University.

During "Día de las Misiones" activities, April 29-30, 1971, a priest addresses children from the San Antonio public schools in front of Mission San José. Courtesy of The Institute of Texan Cultures, San Antonio, Texas.

Amigo the Squirrel, here standing in front of Mission San José, made countless public appearances on behalf of the missions and their preservation. Courtesy of the Old Spanish Missions Research Collection, Special Collections and Archives, Our Lady of the Lake University.

roof work, but they gave us $10,000, and that's it so far. I just had a meeting with our development committee last week, and we hope to be meeting with Father Stubben and the archbishop to see if we can develop some kind of real fund-raising effort.

We don't want the parishes to be directly involved in things that pertain to the historical structures, so that they just don't get done this way and that way. They have to be done properly, with the supervision of an architect. So what we do is that the parish priests let me know if something needs to be done, and we get the architect to look at it. Ford, Powell & Carson have served as our architects in the restoration work at the missions.

Well, that partially answers my next question, which was going to be: if you need work done on the roof at Concepción, let us say, what is there to prevent you, i.e., the church authorities, from going up on the roof with tar buckets and taking the easy road out?

Exactly. I was up on the roofs at San José and Concepción two weeks ago with our architect and two architects from the State Historical Commission out of Austin to look at the problem and hear their ideas on what the possibilities are. Right now, we really don't know what to do with the domes in order to do them well so that we don't ruin what's there but solve the problems that exist.

Does the Park Service have any veto over what the church undertakes in any of these projects?

We have to submit the matter to them, and then they give us advice. I guess they could really cause all sort of problems—and so could the State Historical Commission because, since we've gotten money from them in the past, we're obligated to do a lot of checking with them. And all of that is, of course, to protect the missions from any one of us!

But we're really grateful to the Bexar County Historical Foundation, because they've continued to help us on a day-to-day basis with the upkeep of the missions. We pay the bills and submit them to the foundation, and Henry Guerra sends us a check to cover. That has been a tremendous help, because those little things can really eat you up over a period of time.

I guess it's like owning an older home!

Absolutely! If it's not one thing, it's another. Sometimes it's termites: the stairway to the bell tower at San José was found to be completely infested with termites. You would think that stone missions would be impervious to them, but the situation is perfect for termites. The stone in the missions' walls is a veneer, and the centers are filled with dirt, so termites get in through the cracks between stones and make their tunnels through the dirt; then they get at the wood beams, sills, and everything else that's vulnerable.

What changes do you see coming? What do you foresee in the future of the missions?

The big thing I see right now is the question of whether they're going to get cut out because of the "new wave" in Washington. We've heard that there are a lot of parks that are going to be suffering drastic cuts in their budget, and, although our budget is presently not large enough to fall among them, it very well could if the threshold is lowered. That could mean that the Park Service could be forced to drop San Juan, Espada and Concepción and hold on only to San José.

Then the Church would have the complete care of the others again. That could be very expensive. We could conceivably start collecting admission from visitors, but that income is never enough. And we would have to go back to volunteers to man caretaker positions, because we couldn't afford to pay full-time staff. Of course, then, any work on the grounds would have to be bare minimum, like it was before.

What are the prospects for the revival of the Concepción parish?

Well, it never was a parish; it was just a chapel of ease. I have seriously thought about starting it up myself, but I don't know if I want to go through the hassle it would entail with Father Deane. Perhaps just doing it once a month or something like that would be feasible to see how that goes. I think the community would still be willing. A lot of the folks around there go out to San Juan, so I think I could pull them back together. But I think I would have to talk seriously to the archbishop about it.

So there are no Masses being said at Concepción at all now?

I think perhaps once a year. And, although we never spelled out anywhere what a "living parish" is because we didn't want anyone telling us what to do in that area, we would have to work things out with the NPS if they are unhappy with us about that.

In talking to former members of the Mission Concepción, I hear what seems to me is a very tragic story. The way it is presented to me, here was a viable, vibrant, active, small congregation that took the initiative to keep a parish alive at the mission, and with a change in pastor all of this went down the tubes, with no recourse or redress available for the parishioners when they appealed to the church's hierarchy. How does that look from your side?

Unfortunately, that is a pretty accurate picture. There were instances of stubborn actions on the part of both sides, but it surely did happen. The whole thing got entirely out of hand, even affecting kids who were supposed to be attending catechism classes. With the change in hours of the Mass, which supposedly happened because the pastor could not have Mass in two places at once, the community disappeared. Eventually the pastor hurt his leg, and that became the ostensible reason for the final canceling of the Mass at the mission. Thus far, it has not been reinstated.

Looking at it from the parishioners' side, I am told that when they presented their case to the church authorities not only did they receive no support but, in essence, they were betrayed, because their confidences were turned over to the pastor, something which they had been assured would not happen. I'm puzzled about what looks like a total lack of power of the hierarchy over a single pastor in a diocesan situation.

To begin with, the policy of the chancery is that when letters of complaint are written, copies are forwarded to the ones about whom the complaints are being made, which seems to be a fair way of dealing with a situation. It is common practice that the accuser should know his accusers. One way for the person against whom a complaint is raised to deal with that complaint is to see the entire letter and thus the complaint in context, perceiving from whom it comes as part of the context.

To a certain extent, the bishop's hands are tied, because each parish is its own entity. He has some say, but he also has to be prudent how he goes about making requirements within a given parish. The pastor needs to be able to have some autonomy, and this particular pastor insisted that this situation came under his autonomy.

Can you remove a priest if he does not do what the bishop wants? The question is: Do you remove him over a question of a Mass at a given place that he has his reason for not having? Of course, the controversy was not only about the Mass.

It seems to me that the Mass was just the last straw, the last step.

Yes, it was what finalized the breakup of the little community. People started going over to San Juan, and that was it. It was a tragic question of personalities. I guess that's part of the missions' being "living parishes."

Someone I've talked to speculated that sooner or later Father Antonio Margil de Jesús is going to be canonized, and that when that happens, Mission San José is going to become a pilgrimage site, and that this is going to change the visitation pattern at the San Antonio missions significantly. Do you feel that that possibility has any significance at all?

Yes, I really do. If he gets canonized, then whatever regulations the NPS has about statues outside the church won't be able to stand, I believe, for one thing. There will probably be devotions to Margil de Jesús on a larger scale than there is now.

Have there been any moves to canonize him?

Oh, sure, there have been moves. When Father Ben Leutenegger was here, he was the vice-postulator for the cause of his canonization. Since he died, now Father Barnabas Diekemper, who is a Franciscan who was once stationed here, has taken over.

I just got a letter the other day announcing a day of reflection on Margil in Houston, on August 6, 1995, sponsored by Mrs. Mary Davis, a lady from Houston who has been sponsoring prayers for his canonization, and a tour of San José mission here. That is his death date, August 6.

We've tried! I've gotten a book into the pope's hands—Margil's book called *La Misma Nada* (Nothingness Itself)—supposedly through a Polish priest in Rome who is close to the pope. But right after that was when the pope was shot, so the effort got lost in the incident.

I had hoped that he might be canonized when the pope was here, but had not built up my hopes too much, knowing how those things go. And when I heard how things went in California over the fuss made about the beatification of Junípero Serra, then I was kind of glad it didn't happen. First, the church in California spent a lot of money lobbying for the beatification of Fr. Serra, and then, when the word got around that it was about to happen, Native American groups in California raised a stink, because, as they saw it, Junípero was part of a system that had oppressed the Indians.

But I really think it is true that if he were canonized, that would make this a pilgrimage site and certainly could affect the number of people who come to San José. I'm sure you know that he has already been declared "venerable" and that that took place as early as 1826. But at the time that happened, it wasn't to be expected that a Mexican Franciscan would have backing for much more than that. He was Mexican in that he had worked in Mexico and had become very much a part of this area of the world. The Italians over there had enough of their own to postulate, and there wasn't anybody else interested enough to push further than that.

We always thought that the fact that you can't buy sainthood was a factor, and the case of Junípero Serra was a perfect example of that, because I always felt that, if you could have bought it, California would have bought the sainthood for him a long time ago! Junípero hadn't even been declared "venerable," and we had Margil, who already had that distinction. But the pope went on and disproved me, because he went on and beatified Serra without his ever having been made a "venerable!"

In effect, he jumped a notch! [Laughs.] He's already listed in the missal, and I must admit that when I said Mass on the day that was designated "the feast of Junípero Serra," I wasn't exactly as happy as I could have been! [Laughs.]

All I can tell you is that that's California for you! They exist in a different time/space continuum than the rest of the world!

Exactly! Exactly! [Laughs.] I can get along without Margil's being canonized. I'm sure he's in Heaven and quite content and that he can help us from there even if he never gets canonized.

Any final observations about the San Antonio missions?

Yes, I think it's great that the missions have continued to be a vital part of the area and have actually grown in their vitality in so many ways. The diocese continues to use the missions more than ever in the past for different functions, which results in recognition for them from all over the country.

Every time I can, I try to reiterate that the missions represent not only the Hispanic presence in the area but the Hispanic *and* indigenous presence, because the Native Americans were the ones who really built those missions, whose intelligence was put in visible form at these places. They must have been amazing people to have learned as much as they did and to have learned it so quickly. And their work has continued to be with us as a tribute to them.

As far as the future is concerned, the challenge for us is going to be how to integrate the idea of the participation of the Native American in these Old *Spanish* Missions. In reality, we have worked ourselves into a linguistic trap by the name commonly applied to them. We thought that was a clever way of integrating the missions into the community, but one heritage has tended to obscure the other in that name.

A name that sheds light on one aspect of the thing named but obscures another one just as important.

Exactly. But how do we do that now? That is our problem.

NOTE

1. In the Hispanic world, the terms *compadre* and *comadre* describe the relationship of a child's baptismal sponsors to the child's parents; that is, they are *padrinos* and *madrinas* to the child, but *compadre* or *comadre* to the parents.

Margarita de la Guerra

Margarita de la Guerra, a spry seventy-two-year-old, lives in her retirement home in Pipe Creek, north of San Antonio. Rather by accident, she ended up in the city and living at Mission San José during the Ethel Harris era, and offers some interesting information about the mission as a state park. Mrs. de la Guerra was interviewed on June 21, 1995.

Tell me something about your background. Where did you grow up?

All over the world. My mother and father were both doctors, and they died when I was very young. My grandfather then raised me. He was a geophysics engineer, and his idea of how to raise a wee one was to drag her along with him. He went everywhere around the world, with perhaps the exception of central and South Africa, and I went with him.

And how were you educated?

Mostly through tutors.

And what happened then?

Well, I grew up and married a sailor. I had been told that nice girls didn't marry sailors, but I didn't believe that. And I was also told that sailors have a girl in every port, so I made sure mine had the same one. He served thirty years in the Navy, and out of the first twenty-two of those thirty he had only eleven months on dry land, but I was along with him as much as I could.

Did you do this on your own, or were you able to get the Navy to send you along?

On my own.

Two questions: Any children? Is your husband living?

No to both of them.

Where was your husband from?

He was born in the East. To the best of our knowledge, he was three-quarters Cherokee Indian, but we had no idea how he got the Spanish name.

How did you end up in San Antonio?

When he retired, we had gone to Tehuantepec, Mexico, to retire, but all of a sudden he developed a dermatitis that the doctors down there could do nothing about. So we ended up having to leave there and come to the closest military hospital complex, which was here in San Antonio.

On our way here, at Tamazunchali, where the roads start on the flat and go straight up into the mountains, we were pulling a twenty-two-foot travel trailer behind our car, and when my husband tried to brake on a wet road, we went into a skid and skidded right into an oncoming truck. We had to take the car to Mexico City to have it repaired; then we had to ease the travel trailer up here for repairs. So we got stuck here in San Antonio.

The doctors at Wilford Hall told him he couldn't travel anywhere, because his dermatitis was something they didn't have any record of. It was something he had apparently caught in the Aleutian Islands. So he ended up under their care for ten or twelve years. They finally got it under control to where he could at least live with it.

And you've lived here in San Antonio since?

Well, more or less. This has been home base.

Now, what is your connection to the San Antonio missions?

When we first came here, friends of ours—Nita and Roy Jones, who owned the Oaxaca Courts in Oaxaca—were also friends of Ethel Harris, who was superintendent of the San José Mission State Park at the time, so they told us to stop and see Ethel when we got here. Of course, we were living in a motel, because our trailer was being repaired, so she said, "There's no sense you living there when we've got the cottage here, so you may just as well move in." We moved into the cottage right there on the mission grounds. It's right behind the back wall, near Ethel's house. It was a four-room cottage built out of limestone blocks. That's where the peacocks that Ethel had around the mission would roost on the roof at night, and the slightest little mouse that went across the grounds would set them off screaming bloody murder. When we first moved in, we levitated about ten inches off the floor every time it happened!

What year are we talking about?

It must have been 1954.

And you lived there for how long?

I guess about a year or so, and while I was there I went to work for the state parks in the front office, doing office work, and being ticket-taker and question-answerer.

There were two or three maintenance men working there at the time, and one, Cástulo Ochoa, who lived on the grounds. The others lived on the Pyron Drive side. One of them, in fact, died in the late '50s or early '60s. He had a house that was built against the east mission wall. I was told it had been a Spanish land grant. Most of the men who worked there spoke no English and understood very little, even though most of them, like Cástulo, were third or fourth generation. His great-great-great-grandfather, as I understand it, once owned the property that the city hall in San Antonio is built on. Anyway, this poor little man apparently didn't know that he could get supplemental help from the city, and he starved to death! He was maybe in his late seventies or eighties, and Ethel kept him on the payroll. The maintenance men raked the lawn and picked up trash and so on, but apparently he got to where he couldn't work anymore, and he starved to death.

You've told me that Cástulo and his wife María also lived at the mission. Where did they live?

In the walls [the Indian Quarters]. As you come in the main gate, you go past the beehive ovens. Well, the first one was at her front door, and they occupied three or four other rooms along that wall. They had cut through the connecting walls so that they had a kitchen, living, bedroom, etc.

Did they have any children?

Not there. As I understood it, they lived at the mission some twelve or fifteen years altogether and raised their children there. The children had already grown up and left them. Her daughter from another marriage lived just outside the walls, just out of the west gate, where there was a small house. She raised her children there, so of course the children were in and out of the mission constantly.

There was also a small school operating just outside the east gate. It must have been a church school.

What kind of administrative staff did the park have then?

Ethel was the superintendent. Then she had a woman friend of hers who lived with her also on the staff. It was also about that time that Ethel started with the idea of the amphitheater, of putting an amphitheater in.

Was that constructed while you were there?

They started on it. It was funded by the State Parks Department.

What did Ethel do as superintendent?

The whole nine yards! She oversaw everything, from the kilns and the pottery making to the sale of the pottery at the gift shop, all the way through all the paperwork and bookwork that was required. She had the tendency to ask you a question and walk off onto something else before you finished telling her, so sometimes you had to grab her and hold her down until you finished your answer.

How old was Ethel at the time?

I guess she must have been in her sixties.

Was there a priest assigned to the mission?

Oh, yes, the priest's house was outside the east wall, where the Franciscan monastery was located.

Anything special going on at the time?

Not unless you want to include the man that got hung!

He "got hung," or he hanged himself?

No, he couldn't have hung himself. You know the garden in front of the cloister? There is a well there, and one morning, when people got up and started moving around, they discovered that there was somebody hanging in the well. That was the second time that had happened, as I hear it.

Was he identified?

Oh, I think so.

Did you see the body?

I saw at least the feet, when they brought him out!

What kind of visitation traffic did you get at that time?

It was mostly out-of-town visitors and an awful lot of military people. They were people who were stationed at Brooks or at Lackland, especially people who were attending special schools there. Brooks was very, very active then, and people from both bases were brought in to see the missions.

Do you have a feel whether your out-of-town visitors were Anglos, Mexicans, foreigners, or what?

I think it was a polyglot mixture of everything. Given a period of a month's time, you could see people from most anyplace in the world.

Was visitation heavier on weekends?

No, it was pretty steady throughout the week. It was heavier during the summertime than the winter.

Did you keep in contact with Ethel Harris after you moved away?

Oh, we'd see her every so often. Her home was right outside the mission grounds. I don't know whether she had gotten archdiocesan permission

WPA reconstruction of the Indian quarters in the West wall of the Mission San José compound, ca. 1932-33. A small frame house can still be seen just beyond the tree in what will become the mission's outer wall. Courtesy of the Institute of Texas Cultures, San Antonio, *The San Antonio Light* Collection.

or permission from the State Parks Department to build her home abutting the amphitheater. She had lived for years in the walls themselves, close to the granary.

It doesn't sound as though it would be a very comfortable place to live.

Actually, she had it set up very nicely. The only thing was that she didn't have any windows. But with Ethel, most of her work was outside anyway, overseeing all the work around the place, so all she did in her apartment was eat and sleep and powder her nose. And, if you've lived in Spanish colonial-design houses, the setup is pretty much the same, and you never think anything of it.

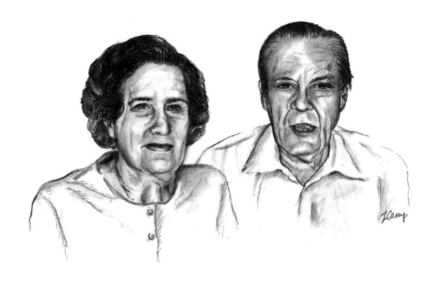

Donald W. and Trudy Harris

Ethel Wilson Harris was one of those figures who attain mythical proportions during their own lifetime because of their energy, their strength, and the single-minded dedication with which they pursued causes or goals they were convinced were right. Her youngest son, **Donald Harris** *(DH), sixty-eight, and his wife* **Trudy** *(TH), sixty-seven, give us an intimate viewpoint of Ethel Harris's background and work and also provide an interesting picture of conditions at Mission San José in the years immediately following the completion of the WPA's reconstruction of the mission compound. Mr. and Mrs. Harris live in the Castle Hills area of north central San Antonio. They were interviewed on July 24, 1995.*

Mr. Harris, which are you among Ethel Harris's children?

DH: I'm her fourth child, her youngest. The other children are Arthur L., Mrs. Henry C. Witte, and Robert Harris.

And where are they?

DH: Arthur died about ten years ago in the Dominican Republic; he had an accident on a grader or something like that. Mrs. Witte is Helen Harris; she lives in Memphis, Tennessee. And Robert Harris lives in Washington state.

What was Arthur doing in the Dominican Republic?

DH: He worked for American Airlines as a troubleshooter and ended up in Puerto Rico. He found he loved it in the Caribbean, and he bought a big ranch in the Dominican Republic. He was going to raise cattle, and he also started a refrigeration company to serve the little islands down there. While working on the ranch one day he was operating a bulldozer, and the machine turned over and killed him.

Helen's husband died about eight years ago, and she continues to live in Memphis. Robert is an architect. He used to be here in San Antonio and practiced with O'Neil Ford and his group.

Arthur was how much older than you?

DH: Seven years older; Helen is five years older, and Robert is two years older.

You were born in San Antonio?

DH: Yes, at the Baylor Hospital on the San Antonio River, on June 30, 1927. We've lived here all our lives, aside from my years as a student in Austin at the University of Texas and a few years in Corpus Christi. My father, Arthur Lewis Harris, died when I was twelve years old. He was a major in World War I and later taught in the San Antonio public schools. When they opened Jefferson High School about 1931, he taught there, but he had taught elsewhere prior to that.

What can you tell me about your mother?

DH: Ethel Wilson Harris was born in 1893 in Sabinal, Texas. Her family moved to San Antonio when she was still a girl, so she attended public schools here and then went for a couple of years to San Antonio Female College, which is now Trinity University. By age twenty she played the violin with the San Antonio Symphony. And at age twenty-five, in 1918, just after World War I, she married my father.

What sort of family did she come from?

DH: Her father started out as a telegrapher for the Southern Pacific Railroad, and he ran the station there in Sabinal for many years. Then he came to San Antonio and opened the West End Lumber Company, and aside from selling materials, he soon also became a home builder. Wilson Boulevard, over by Jefferson High School, is where his first house was.

  Then he financed his son into the movie theater business, and he built the Harlandale, the Uptown, the Highlands, and other suburban theaters. Suburban theaters were a big thing then to begin with, but the Depression sank them all, and the lumber company also almost went down. Grandfather died about then.

Where did your family live in San Antonio?

DH: Well, we lived on East Craig Place, about half a block from the river. Our playground was the eleventh hole of the Brackenridge Park golf course; that was our front yard. Then the Depression caught up with the Harrises, and we moved to the Hettie S. Brown Country Day School, which doesn't mean a whole lot unless you've lived here all your life. It was located right on the river and was a very free-thinking school where they did things like teach kids to write, not in longhand but in "manuscript" or printing. My father had been diagnosed with cancer, and the day school had closed because of the Depression, but the people who ran it allowed my mother to move in while my father was in the last six months of his illness.

What year was this?

Both: It was 1938.

DH: Then we moved into my grandmother's house, which was over on Cincinnati Avenue right near Woodlawn Lake. This would have been mid-1939. Then, when she became custodian of the mission in 1940, we moved out there.

What was your mother's background? Was she a housewife? Did she teach?

DH: [Laughs.] My mother was an entrepreneur. She always seemed to be on the edge of things. She told a story about becoming the first woman to drive a car in San Antonio when she was only fourteen, the first woman to get a driver's license in Bexar County. The car was a bright yellow Apperson Jackrabbit, a car you could hardly ignore, and every time she had to wait for her father in town she was embarrassed, because people would cluster around and stare.

TH: First of all, she supervised the WPA [Works Projects Administration].

Are you talking about the reconstruction at San José?

DH: No, no. When the WPA came on strong here in San Antonio, they wanted someone to develop the cultural part of it. Some of the WPA's work was building bridges and the like, but another was culture, to keep cultural matters alive. Anyway, in 1931 she had opened a business, the San Antonio Mexican Arts and Crafts at 1002 North St. Mary's Street. The business was housed in an old stable, the old Lewis Barn, which had been restored under the sponsorship of the Conservation Society.

The WPA came along and hired my mother to run the business as the Arts and Crafts Division of the local WPA project, so she became an employee of the WPA. She made tiles and pottery, and her production was well-known across the state. In 1933 she went to the Chicago World's Fair and later to the New York World's Fair, where she exhibited the things her studio was producing. Her tiles have gone all over Texas: they're at the King Ranch, they're at the O'Connor Ranch in Victoria, in the XYZ Ranch in West Texas near the New Mexico border. They're in several places in San Antonio: at Alamo Stadium, on the Riverwalk, etc.

TH: Both Alamo Stadium and the Riverwalk were WPA projects, done when she was managing the WPA. The pieces produced then are marked "WPA" instead of showing the century plant that became her trademark when the WPA closed and she started her own business again.

Are you talking about glazed tiles?

DH: Yes, all glazed tiles. She used Mexican craftsmen to make these things. A lot of her pottery was made on the wheel, although later on, to make the larger pieces, she had them use molds. After World War II, when the WPA closed down, she had been president of the Conservation Society and had been very active in it, so when the society suggested that she move to San José, where she would have space for her business,

Ethel Harris stands by a panel of decorative tiles made in her workshops. Courtesy of the San Antonio *Express-News* Library.

have a place to live, and get paid as custodian to boot, she moved out there, and a lot of her employees moved with her.

Where did she find these craftspeople? They were not local people, or were they?

DH: Yes, they were local people. But she spent her life making many, many trips into Mexico, taking pictures and traveling all over the country. We have never determined how she learned all she knew about crafts, who developed the glazes that she used, and so on. We have some of her record books, and the formulas for the glazes are in my father's writing. He was a graduate of, I think, the name is Bates College, in Cambridge,

Massachusetts, and we think that he somehow was responsible for the glazes. He had done some design work himself, but primarily he taught school.

And what was his subject?

DH: English.

So it wasn't chemistry or something else that might explain it.

DH: No, it wasn't that. But he died when I was so young that I don't really know that much about him. All I know is that he taught at Washington Irving High, and when they opened Jefferson High School he became head of the English department. But we really never have found out how Mother became interested in arts and crafts and in making pottery and tiles.

TH: No, but I think your father had some influence on her in that respect.

DH: All I know is that it had to be in the early '30s, because it was just something that was always around me as I grew up.

She wasn't a potter herself, so in essence what she did was to bring these craftspeople together and market their product.

DH: Yes, but where she became the most important person in the production was in the fact that she fired the kilns herself. And growing up at the mission was an experience in just that respect alone, because on the night that the kilns were fired—particularly for the glazed pieces, not so much the ones that just had the bisque—we were up all night.

They would fire them on, let's say, starting on a Monday morning, and by Tuesday night they would've gotten to about one thousand degrees, and then you started being careful and watching them. About every hour you'd go out and check the temperature cones, and when they fell over you knew that you had reached a certain temperature.

She would check them every hour. Of course, we didn't have TV or anything like that, but she would read to pass the time away between the inspections. We'd usually go with her and help her with what she needed. Sometimes, for example, we'd take the firebricks away to create more draft to get the kilns hotter. It was a ritual we went through.

It certainly would be interesting to find out how she learned that, because it is a very technical aspect of pottery making. Glazes and firing are not something that just any idiot can do. They require experience, and they require trial and error and a certain degree of sophistication in knowing how to handle heat, and what certain materials require, etc.

DH: As far as we know, when she went to the San Antonio Female College she took some business courses and then went to work as a secretary at Camp Stanley, which was where she met my father.

So there was no chemistry or arts background?

DH: No arts background; she was not a painter or an artist. I don't even know where she learned about pottery-making, or about glazes and temperatures. I'm sure she read a lot, but to the best of my knowledge she never had a tutor or someone to really tell her what to do. But she did all the final work.

I remember going out with her to Elmendorf many times in her old station wagon to get the clay that she used. There was a quarry down there, and she would look at the different colors of clay. She had a little water with her, and she would test here and there to make sure that the clay had the right grain, that it didn't have a lot of heavy aggregate in it.

Then she would have someone with a pickup truck, and they'd go out there and shovel the truck full from that particular section of the quarry. She'd take it home, dry it, and then put it through a pug mill so that it came out as a powder. From that she would mix and prepare the clay they needed.

I think if there's something about her business that will carry on as unusual, that would have to be her colors. She had some very dramatic shades of red and other colors. You could hold a Geiger counter to some of her red pieces and it would go like crazy, because the material was radioactive. It contained uranium oxide, which was what gave it its distinctive red color. During World War II, the government came around and confiscated all of it they could find. Her colors are so distinctive that I can tell the difference between her own production and imitations of it.

So she provided the basic materials for these people who were making the crafts?

DH: Yes.

How many people were involved?

DH: Oh, I'd say she had ten or twelve who worked there at one time. My mother was also very much involved in helping to keep many of the Mexican traditions alive here. As a youngster, I remember that many Christmas seasons we'd go out to the west side. Today, you might be frightened to do that, but in those days there was nothing to fear. We'd go and stay all night to watch the performances of Los Pastores. In those days it was really something. It was all in Spanish, but after so many years of watching it, we knew what was going on. Now they produce it every year for Christmas at the mission.

And she was big with the Chili Queens also.[1] She thought that was a very important part of San Antonio, and some of her tiles showed scenes with the Chili Queens on the square in town. And she was also big on other cultural things.

There were two very well-known Mexican dancers here at that time, Fernando and Carla, and he was one of her workers. He did most of the Mexican designs, and I think I also can tell his original designs from imitations because of the way he showed the features on his human figures.

Were these craftspeople schooled people or naive craftsmen who had learned from someone else?

DH: No, they were not trained or schooled. One of them, Angel Rendón, worked for her for years. He was an all-around guy who could do many things, but one of his best crafts was weaving with palm leaves. All of the furniture pieces that my mother made that used palm leaves were done by him. She'd go out on Woodlawn Avenue when the city was trimming the palm trees and collect the fronds, take them home, keep them wet a little bit until they got just right, and then Angel would take them, twist them, and weave with them.

My mother used to take us to the San Antonio Symphony frequently. She would get nicely dressed, and we would also be dressed up. Then, after the concert, we would go up and down the alleys behind the stores downtown, scavenging to collect the cardboard that the merchants would throw out after unpacking their goods. We would load all we could find in our car—she had one of the first station wagons in San Antonio—and later my mother would use that material to ship her tiles all over the country.

So she was into recycling long before the idea became popular! One thing I wanted to ask you was this: Some of the pieces of your mother's production that you've shown me, the bowl and the tiles, show a great deal of sophistication in their design. They're not designs that could have been produced by what one might call primitive craftsmen.

DH: I don't know if I would call them sophisticated, but certainly they were typical of Mexican designs of the period, or at least Mexican-inspired designs.

Now, tell me more about your family's move into Mission San José.

DH: We moved into the walls at San José in 1940, into a section that was called the prefecture, adjacent to the granary. Around 1935, the Conservation Society had put Mother in charge of the granary, which had been restored by the society using government-paid labor from the relief rolls of the day. Almost at the same time the reconstruction and restoration of the church was done, and also the reconstruction of the compound walls and the Indian quarters.

The biggest thing I remember about it was that it was a very different and unique place to live, because of the unique ceilings and the four-foot-thick walls. We had fun listening to the tourists speculate about who lived there, and why they couldn't go into that section of the Indian quarters, and so on. Of course, when we first moved there, Pyron Road went right through the compound and through the east and west gates of it.

So in 1940, even after the WPA reconstruction, there was a road going through San José?

DH: Yes, it was a dusty county road, and cars went back and forth over it through the mission. I thought the neighborhood was pretty wild at the time because there were people constantly going back and forth through there. The mission grounds themselves were open. On the south side, the Catholic church had built a fence right down through Pyron Road and then turning at the granary and catching the north end of the church.

When Archbishop Lucey came in, he and my mother conceived the idea of a state park at the mission. The county was going to close the road, and the granary, which had been managed by the Conservation Society, was to be added to the complex. The three different institutions—the Church, the Conservation Society, and the city and state agencies—were going to form a sort of triumvirate to administer the place. To begin with, the gate was opened between the two parts, so you could come through and go into the church, and finally the whole fence came down.

So the part that belonged to the church had been fenced off from the rest?

DH: Yes, it had always been fenced off. Then they opened a gate so that you could go in through the granary, then down to the mill, and then through the open gate into the church. I guess the problem was separation of church and state, because a lot of people didn't want the church and state to be mixed together. But they finally got it all together and agreed that the mission could operate as a church and be closed to the public when they had Mass or when they had funerals and things like that. They took the fence down, and everything was open. The gate to the compound used to be on Pyron Road but was subsequently moved to the southwest corner, where it is today.

I have heard that before reconstruction of the walls there had been private homes in the compound and elsewhere around the mission. Were any of those left when you moved out there?

DH: I don't know about before reconstruction, but, no, there were no private homes left when we came.

What major differences in the mission compound would strike an observer of today, if he could see the mission at the time you moved there?

DH: The main thing would be the road through the compound. Of course, there were a lot more trees there then, but nothing other of significance.

And you say that your quarters were in the corner of the compound, after you pass the granary going in the direction of the church?

DH: That's right.

Describe your quarters.

DH: The walls were very thick, three-and-a-half- or four-foot walls, plastered and painted white on the inside. The ceilings were all cedar branches, stretched over the rooms from the sides. Over that was a layer of tar paper, and above the tar paper they had put dirt for insulation, then a roof on top of that. There were no closets built in at the time, so we had free-standing wardrobes.

How many rooms did your family have?

DH: We had three bedrooms, one of which I shared with my brother before he went in the Navy: a living room, dining room, and a kitchen, and that included the little patio outside, just before you go out to the mill. Our kitchen was set up there. There was a "keep out" sign, indicating that these were private quarters. I remember it always being cool there, because the walls were so thick, and Mother had a ventilation fan that would suck air through.

TH: That was really a terrific fan. That was before air conditioning, but it certainly kept the place cool.

Did your mother move in there with four children?

DH: No. The oldest son had gone into the Air Force earlier. My other brother joined the Navy shortly after we moved there, and my sister attended TWCU [Texas Women's Christian University] and got married right from there, if I remember correctly. I was the last one to leave the nest. So let's say that she moved into the mission with two children.

Where did you go to school out there?

DH: Well, I started out for a short time at Huff Avenue School, and then I went to junior high at Harlandale. My father had known all the principals in San Antonio, and he also knew the superintendent of schools; I believe it was Mr. Thomas Portwood. Someone came to my mother and said that they wanted me to attend Thomas Jefferson, where my father had taught.

So I commuted. I would walk from the mission down to the bus stop, which was where the golf club starts. That was the turnaround for the bus route. I would take that bus, then transfer and catch the Woodlawn line to Jefferson and then back home every day. And I graduated from Jefferson; we only went three years then: ninth, tenth, and eleventh grades.

What was it like living at San José Mission as a teenager?

DH: Oh, it didn't lend itself to having a heck of a lot of friends from school, because they were the equivalent of a thousand miles away. But I had the mission grounds to run around in. It would close around six o clock, and then I had the place all to myself. I enjoyed it, but it did not produce any longtime childhood friends, because I didn't go to school with the kids who lived closer by, and the ones I did go to school with lived so far away. I don't guess I missed anything, but it was different.

I had gone to elementary school at McKinley over on Magnolia, and in high school most of the kids I knew lived along Woodlawn Avenue. At that time, though, there were only three students with cars in the high school. Fortunately, I knew one of them.

What were your mother's duties at the mission?

DH: Of course, she kept the pottery and tile making business going. During the early period, when she was in charge of the granary, she opened it every day and made sure it was open seven days a week, or she had someone open it. Then, when the mission was made a state park in 1941, she became manager of the park, so she supervised the state employees who worked there. They had a gatekeeper, maintenance people who cleaned the place or did work on the structures. When more extensive work was needed, she would send the state a requisition.

Then she had a little shop there where she sold the things they produced. Sometimes I would run the gift shop for her, and one of the extra bonuses was that then I had access to the soda water they sold and the food. [Laughs.]

Where was the pottery making actually located?

DH: It was in all those walls, as you are walking towards the old mill. That's where the pottery was, where the clay was mixed and the pug mill was located, where the large kiln was. As you go through the arch, the store was on the right. Then, over in the walls, just south of the west gate on the Pyron Road side, she had about three rooms in the wall where they also made pottery and did other work. A lot of the decorating was done there.

There's a woman, Lucille Carmona, who worked with my mother from day one, and she may be able to tell you more about where the different work areas were. She must be in her late eighties now, but she still lives in a little house on Pyron Road.

How much traffic was there at the mission in terms of visitors?

DH: I'd say, during the week, maybe 75; during the weekends, 100 or 200 people, sometimes going as high as 350. The admission was something like twenty-five cents. She actually got the Conservation Society, which owned the granary, and the Catholic church, which owned the church, together first. Then the county, which owned the walls area, joined in, and finally the state came in also. I think it was a quarter to get into the granary and a quarter to go through the little gate I told you about earlier into the church area.

So, in other words, the whole compound at San José, before it was taken over by the state, was put together sort of like a jigsaw puzzle?

DH: Exactly. And, of course, among her duties was to see that the money was counted, that the ticket stubs were counted, the bookkeeping and so on. My mother had a friend, Helen Cox Christian—they had grown up together as girlfriends—and they were both widows, so she came to stay with my mother after I left. She took over the second bedroom, which had been my sister's for a short time, and she did the bookkeeping. I guess I left in '44.

TH: She also did decorating on the tiles.

DH: Yes, in the cold, cold weather in those little rooms with no heat, so they wore newspapers under their clothes to keep themselves warm.

Your visitors to the mission came individually, or in groups?

DH: They came in small tour buses, and in families and other small groups.

Was there someone there to take them around, or did they just get to tour the grounds by themselves?

DH: No, there was a guide there, and for your quarter he took you around. And we had a canned speech [begins repeating from memory]: "This mission was established in 1720 by the Franciscan order of Spanish missionaries . . ." Then we'd tell them about tufa stone; then we'd show them the Rose Window and tell them the story about Rosita [see Appendix B] and how it was named; then we'd take you to the cloister, show you around, and then let you go on from there.

During the weekends, my mother always had Mateo, one of the potters, with his wheel there making pottery, and he would make it look like magic: he could make things big or small; he could make the little Mexican hats they sold for ashtrays, whirl them off, and then cut them off the wheel with a string. She also had Angel doing his palm weaving, but until all of the different organizations got together, visiting the mission was sort of catch-as-catch-can.

Before, I don't know if the church had someone to guide visitors through the mission, but they did have someone there collecting admission. But afterwards there was a formal guide to squire visitors around.

Of course, the well is famous out there, because during the time it was open they found a dead body down there. It's the so-called wishing well.

Were you there during that time when the body was discovered?

DH: Yes.

Okay, tell me more about this dead body in the well.

DH: I think it was someone you might call in today's parlance a punk, a low-level hood. The well in the cloisters area had a grate over it, but it was easy to pick that grate off it and for somebody to just dump this person in.

Did he drown, or what?

DH: No, there was no water in the "well"; they found a blow to his head. But I don't recall any more details. You can probably find out more about it in the newspaper archives.

Well, I can tell you that you're not the first person who has mentioned this dead-body-in-the-well to me.

DH: We had a sheriff here by the name of Kilday, whose brother was a congressman, and the thing I best remember is that he was the sheriff then. I thought he was like Roosevelt: Roosevelt was the only president we'd ever had, and Kilday was the only sheriff we'd ever had. But they did discover somebody in there; I believe he was some low-level punk, but I can't tell you why. I was not actually there to see it, though.

Most of the time when I was in high school I had a job after school downtown in a radio store, and I'd catch the bus home, stop there, and work until whatever time we closed. I was a radio nut, had ham radio equipment, and this way I got to work and got money for it.

I can't think of anything more about living at the mission, except that it was a wonderful place to grow up in. As far as I can remember, it was open all year round, and at Christmas time the church had a special Mass, and they had processions. It was nice to see the weddings that were held there.

And, of course, Mother had peacocks all over the place, and you could hear their peculiar screams all the time. She also tried to have sheep, tried turning them loose in the compound to help keep the grass and weeds down. And they had to be put away at night. And she also had Chulita; she was a donkey. She became famous later because she always was at the Night in Old San Antonio [NIOSA] festivities, which were also a result of my mother's efforts.

What about the amphitheater at the mission? What's the story behind that?

DH: My mother designed and built that theater. She was able to get money from the state to finance it. It finally became the Texas Historical Theater or something like that, and they had some fairly good plays on stage. The first thing they did was a play about the Alamo, and this fellow, Clu Gulager, whom you can see on TV still, was the star. Paul Baker, who became a well-known director, also worked with her. He was at Baylor University then. Then they did *The San José Story*.

Were these productions backed financially by the state?

DH: No, they had local commercial sponsors. And during intermission they served Mexican foods and pink lemonade.

She also got involved in producing Los Pastores on an annual basis at Christmastime, and she always insisted that it be done in Spanish. And at intermission they served hot chocolate and sweet things.

Was this done at the theater also?

DH: No, this was at the mission, and everyone just stood around, because there were no chairs. Later on they brought in bleachers for the performance, but at first everyone just stood, like in the old days. I guess the Conservation Society was the sponsor, but she certainly was active in it.

You told me when we first talked on the phone that when you first got married, you took your bride to live at Mission San José. Why did you do that?

DH: Well, because when I got married, I was going to school on the GI Bill. There is an old house there behind the walls on the north side. It's a little bitty box, and half of it has been destroyed, so it's all boarded up now, but at the time it was sitting there, and it was available. When I first got out, I got a job with the Cliquot Club Bottling Company on South Roosevelt Road.

Children from the San Antonio public schools make the acquaintance of Chulita, the Mission San José donkey, during Día de las Misiones activities, April 29-30, 1971. Courtesy of The Institute of Texan Cultures, San Antonio.

Then my older brother, who was married and also lived here in San Antonio, started a business called San Antonio Vending Machine Company. We had vending machines at Kelly, Lackland, and Randolph, at the Alameda Theater and all sorts of different places in town, so I joined him to be more or less the manager of that company. He did the PR work with the generals and the other people in charge so we could stay at the base. Anyway, my job was on South Roosevelt, I had a wife, and the house was available, so what better place was there to take her? [Both laugh.]

[To Trudy Harris.] And you agreed to this?

TH: I can't imagine why, but I guess I did. [Laughs.] You know, before I met Miss Harry—which was what we all called her—I was very nervous. Donald was such a fussy dresser when we met that I imagined his mother as having crocheted little doilies all over her furniture. I just dreaded meeting her, and I spent a lot of time choosing what I would wear, so I would look "decent."

When we got to San Antonio, here comes this car to pick us up—a huge old station wagon—and when Miss Harry got out she did not have stockings on, because she never wore them, even though in 1946 it was "the proper thing" to wear them. She also didn't wear gloves, and she had on this sort of shapeless denim dress. I just couldn't believe this was the mother of the guy I had been dating! She was too much like I was! So we always got along fine. We never had any trouble.

And you got married in what year?

DH: 1948.

And you lived there with your new wife for how long?

TH: One year.

What kind of a house was it?

TH: It was a stone house.

And do you have any idea how old the place was?

TH: No, I don't.

How big was this little house?

TH: It had one bedroom and a living room with a fireplace in it. There was also a kitchen, and we ate either in the kitchen or the living room; there was no separate dining room. There was also a bathroom. And that was it. When Pete DeVries took over, he moved his family into that house, and he enlarged it. Then later on they tore part of it down; the rock part is still standing. But I don't know who built the house or why.

DH: I think it was during the time of the restoration project.

How long did your mother continue to live at the mission?

DH: What happened was this: I came back from the Navy probably in 1946, and some time later she started to build her own house.

TH: It was in 1953, while we were living in Corpus Christi. Her son Robert designed the house for her. It's the house where the Los Compadres organization is housed today. There is some of her tile work in the kitchen there.

And how long did she live out there?

TH: It must have been until 1976 or '77, when she left. She had gotten too old to live alone.

DH: She needed to have somebody supervise her. She lived out there by herself, which was not a good thing.

How old was she at the time?

TH: She was eighty-four.

DH: She got to where she couldn't drive, or shouldn't be driving. She was healthy, but she needed to have someone to help her out and look after things. So we just thought it better to have her move into an apartment.

When she moved, I went to Pete and asked him to get me a dump truck, because we had to cope with decades of collecting stuff. I started out at one corner one day and would pick up each thing and ask, "Is this of any value? Does it mean anything?" If it did, I would save it; if it didn't, I'd throw it in the dump truck. But the more I went through, the more stuff I set aside. I didn't save any of her paperwork, but I saved a lot of things.

I don't know how many weeks or months I spent moving everything, because she was incapacitated and couldn't help. I think Pete took four loads to the dump for me. What we set aside, I went to one of these self-store places, and we must have filled two or three of those compartments. In her will, she had instructed that I should put together anything she had that was of any value and then have everybody in the family come and divide it as they wanted. So my sister Helen and my brother Bob were here, and, of course, they had some of their kids along.

My attitude was to let everyone take what they wanted, and what was left, we didn't want to keep paying for storage, so we brought it to this house and have it stored here. That's why we have these remnants of tiles and such that we have shown you. Unfortunately, a lot of the stuff is incomplete, and you cannot reconstruct much of any pattern with what there is.

And what happened to the pottery wheels and the other equipment of the crafts production?

DH: That is a mystery. I didn't know anything about this until recently, when the park people called me. I went out there, and they told me that there was a lot of her stuff still locked in some of those rooms along the wall. I found potter's wheels, her molds, and a lot of other equipment. No one had ever paid attention to this stuff, but there has been talk of having a permanent display of her production, and for that they would have liked to have this material. Los Compadres wanted to get it, but my sister said that these things had been given to her, so she has moved everything away except for the big potter's wheel. If no one else claims it, I may dismantle it and store it away.

And where was all of this kept?

DH: It was by the west entrance, about the third door down from the gate. But I knew nothing about it until about a month ago. It's too bad, because as long as the material was together, it would have made a wonderful display.

Your mother sounds like a pretty formidable individual.

DH: Oh, she was something, all right. She stood up against H. B. Zachary when they were going to turn Travis Park into a great big concrete parking garage. She went right up to him and told him that they were not going to let him do it. She was pretty formidable when she set her mind on something.

If someone were to ask me about her personality, I would have to say that she was very proud. She moved in rather high circles of society, but it was on the strength of her work and her achievements, because she had no personal funds or fortune to give her that position. And she was well-respected and liked by many. She could move with the richest of the rich or the poorest of the poor, but she only respected sincerity; she cared nothing about frauds.

She started the "Night in Old San Antonio" celebration, which was connected with her work at San José. Chulita the donkey and her cart were stored at the mission, but she was one of the "stars" of NIOSA. Mateo did craft demonstrations there. María, who was the person behind "María's Tortillas," was our maid at the mission for years. She helped my mother with her housework.

How old was she when she died?

DH: She was ninety-two. And her funeral was a fine time that she would have loved. At the end, she had tubes in her, and she could hardly speak. I saw her the day before she died, I guess.

She had always wanted to be cremated. I called Mary Ann Guerra and asked about Henry, but he was in Washington and not scheduled to come home till the next day. So I met him at the airport and told him I needed him to do something for me the following afternoon. My mother's ashes were going to be brought to the granary at San José, and we were going to have a party in her memory; I wanted Henry to be sort of master of ceremonies over the affair.

The place was full of people, and Henry talked about the things she had done. It was certainly not a religious ceremony, but it was a beautiful memorial. The ladies from the Conservation Society came out, and they did a sort of miniature "Night in Old San Antonio" there between the wall and the mill. The place was all decorated with Mexican paper flowers and cutouts. I had ordered margaritas, and our sons and her other grandsons helped with other things. Someone had arranged for mariachis, and I think there was even a "stand-in" for Chulita, who had died in the meantime. It was a real party, and everyone had a wonderful time. And it was really what she would have wanted! She probably regretted having missed it!

TH: Later on, the Conservation Society planted a tree in her memory. It still is there by the granary with a plaque explaining why it's there.

NOTE

1. "Chili Queens" were women who operated open-air chili stands in old San Antonio.

Henry Guerra

*More than likely, everyone in San Antonio knows **Henry Guerra,** seventy-six, not only as a radio and TV personality but also for his participation in all kinds of civic causes and activities. In this interview, Henry discusses his involvement in bringing the National Park Service to the San Antonio missions. We also learn something about the Mexican-Italian heritage of his family. Henry and his wife Mary Ann Noonan Guerra live in the Monte Vista Historic District of San Antonio. This interview took place in their home on June 26, 1995.*

Would you give me your full name and your age?

My legal name is Henry A. Guerra, Jr.; that's the way I sign my name on
　　my checks, but when I give an autograph for those few fans that are left

I write "Henry Guerra." I am seventy-six years old and will be seventy-seven come October 27 this year.

I was born in San Antonio, on Uvalde Street on the south side, where my father and mother had just gotten a house after their marriage. They were married in 1917, and I arrived in 1918. A year later we moved to Johnson Street, still on the south side, near the river, and my sister, who's eleven months younger, was born there.

We had to move out of there after the flood of 1921. I don't remember any of the details, but the river came up a good two or three blocks to hit that house, and I remember being carried out by the firemen. All I can remember is seeing the tops of the trees above the water. I think the flood was in September.

Then my mother found a house on the north side, 715 Howard Street, and we lived there until my sister left to get married during the war. After the war I came back to that same house and lived with my parents until I got married at age thirty-seven in 1955. We tried living with my parents, but that didn't work because my mother and my wife didn't always get along.

We looked for apartments on King William Street, when my grandmother, Benigna Saldaña Pizzini, spoke up and suggested that we live upstairs at her house, where my sister had already lived when she was first married and had her first batch of kids. So we lived upstairs at 1915 San Pedro. We even had our own address: 1915½ San Pedro Street, and we lived there from 1955 until 1960, when the twins came along.

By the way, we knew we were going to have twins, but it was too late to buy a Lloyd's of London policy against having twins, which had been suggested to me months before by my brother-in-law, Martin Noonan. Once we knew we were going to have twins—by then I could drive a car—I took my wife over all the bounciest streets in San Antonio, trying to get the twins to arrive so I could claim them for all of '59 on my taxes [laughs], but they didn't come until January of '60.

After they came, we were crowded. We lived at 1915½ San Pedro long enough for them to become walkers, but they started climbing down from the second floor. One time we heard the doorbell ring about three a.m., and I went to see who it was. It was the twin boys, who had managed to get out of the house even though we had a gate on the staircase. [Laughs.]

How did you know you were going to have twins?

The doctors told us, but they told us too late to get the insurance. The same year we got the twins, 1960, we found this house, and we've lived here ever since. As you see, the place is cluttered with books. We have here my book collection and my wife's book collection and all of the papers of her father and grandfather, both of whom were judges. Plus I have some papers from my mother, who was a member of the San Antonio public school board from 1917 until she finally had to give it up in 1925 to take care of her two children.

I grew up doing a lot of reading, and I remember the Tom Swift books, some of which I still have, and Tom Slade and other children's classics. But I got interested in reading very early, because when I first went to school at the Luken Military Academy in Alamo Heights—that was in about 1926 or so—I didn't know how to speak English. That had been deliberately done by my father and mother, both of whom were bilingual, so that I would never lose the Spanish, because they knew I would have to go to school in English.

I made my living for more than fifty years as a news announcer on WOAI and other stations, both radio and television, in English, of course, but I speak, read, and write Spanish. Not very well, because what I speak, read, and write is Tex-Mex, as my cousins and friends who live in Mexico never cease telling me! [Laughs.] But I can make myself very well understood in Spanish. I've toured in Spain, and people there understood me quite well.

What was it like, going to school and not knowing any English?

One of the reasons why my parents sent me to military school in Alamo Heights instead of to a Catholic school was that they had a lady there who spent my whole first year teaching me English. By the end of the year, I could speak English.

Was that a pretty common occurrence?

No, but the school had chocolate-brown Mexicanos going to the school, as well as other white Mexicanos. For example, among the students who went there were grandsons or nephews of Mexican President Carranza. Of course, he had been killed already, but his relatives were at the school. Those boys became aviators later, and they both crashed. Anyway, these kids arrived knowing no English, and this lady had specialized in quickly bringing them up to speed in the language.

And the military academy went from what grade to what grade?

It graduated high school, but it closed in 1931. I spent the last year the academy was open in bed with the flu. No sooner would I get up than I would get sick again, so I was delayed one year. Otherwise, I would've graduated from university in 1939 instead of 1940.

My parents, looking for a place to send me, found a grade school at the St. Mary's University campus on Woodlawn. They had a grade school and high school, so I was enrolled there for the sixth grade. When I was ready for the seventh grade they closed the school, and eventually I wound up at Central Catholic, which was opening a brand new Brothers of Mary school. I graduated from Central Catholic in 1936.

I was going to go to the University of Texas, so I went up to Austin and took one course, algebra or something I was weak in, and I sat in such a big class that we never did see the professor because he sent a graduate student to teach the course. At the end of the semester I decided that I would rather go back to the Brothers of Mary and their small classes, so I came back to San Antonio and attended St. Mary's University. I graduated from there in 1940.

In the meantime, as an undergraduate I did a program for my mother. She called me one day frantic—I was the editor of the *St. Mary's University Rattler*, the student newspaper, and had been doing a lot of amateur theatrics and emceeing—and she said, "You have to help us out. The man that WOAI was going to send to read our script took one look at the script and threw up his arms and refused to do it." The program was a gift of the consul of Mexico and was the first exhibition of all the Indian costumes of Mexico, all the states and provinces. The costumes were being modeled by local Hispanic girls. The announcer took a look at the script, with all those Indian and Spanish names, and gave up . . . and he was an NBC guy! They had to send a taxi to get me, and I took one look at the script and said, "I can do this!"

So they hid me behind a curtain, because I had just been delivering the forms for the student newspaper and I was all smudged with ink, and among the people who had been dragged to this luncheon program was Mrs. Hough's husband, Hugh. And at the end of the program, he talked to Paul McSween, the manager of the St. Anthony [Hotel], where this was taking place, and told him, "You know, that man who was doing the announcing, I never saw him because they had him hidden behind the curtain, but he has a very good voice. Send him to see me. I may have a job for him."

I was nineteen at the time, but I went to see him, and at first we couldn't agree on which courses I would drop. Then he called me again, and we decided that I would drop one course. In reality he saved my life, because that course was ROTC, and if I had graduated the next year, I would have been a second lieutenant in the field artillery, and I would have gone to Java. Three of our boys [classmates] got killed there.

He was shocked to find out that I was an undergraduate and had no experience, so they trained me in the back rooms of WOAI. I had a rough time at first reading from news copy I had never seen before, but finally in November of 1939 they threw me on the air the day that Russia invaded Finland. I decided that there were few Russians and no Finns in San Antonio, so I read all those names as I thought they should be pronounced, and I never had a complaint. After that, I managed to stay on the payroll. When I told my grandfather about my job, he couldn't fathom that they were paying me for just talking!

After the war I went back to the station for a time, then was director of development for St. Mary's University, later went back to radio and television. When the TV station I worked for was sold, my former boss, the general manager of the station, had gone to the Hemisfair and offered me a job. Even though it meant a cut in pay I accepted and went to the Hemisfair, because it was such an interesting job. Initially, I was doing public relations for the event, but I ended up working with the architects in developing the foreign exhibits for the fair. I stayed there from 1966 to '68. Then Channel 12 made me an offer, and I did special shows for them for two or three years. By that time my mother needed me at the funeral home, so I got out of broadcasting for a time. When around 1972 or '73 WOAI was bought again by local interests, I found I could make room again for radio, so I did on a part-time basis, and I did that until I had my heart attack in '91.

I was not active civically until after the war, when my mother got me involved in the tuberculosis movement. After that I became very active.

What can you tell me about your grandparents?

I have both Italian and Spanish/Mexican ancestry on both sides. My father was born here, and so was my mother, but on my father's side, his father, Ramón Guerra, came as a bachelor to San Antonio from the ancestral lands on the Rio Grande, at Roma and Mier . . . Roma on the Texas side, and Mier across the river in Mexico. At that time the border was not patrolled, and people ran cattle on both sides. My grandfather came in the 1880s and later on brought over at least two brothers and probably more of the family. They left the dusty acres of south Texas and came to San Antonio.

The cousins who stayed down there, however, stayed until Gulf Oil came along and punched holes in the ground in the '20s! [Laughs.] I remember as a boy being taken to meet the cousins at the St. Anthony Hotel in San Antonio. They had just finished a round-the-world cruise, and we had to go there and be very respectful to the cousins! They lived in the [Rio Grande] Valley and still do. We have many relatives down there, but we don't have much to do with them.

Grandfather wound up as a fire captain and retired from that job and, with his savings and the aid of Mr. Reby, who was in the funeral business, he opened the West Side Funeral Home in 1910. In the city directory of 1910 he is listed as the employee of some clothing store, but in the 1911 one there is a big ad for his new business: Agencia de Inhumaciones Guerra [Guerra Funerary Agency], which was on Dolorosa or one of those downtown streets on the west side, a couple of blocks from Shelly Funeral Home. One of Shelly's daughters later married Porter Loring, who had been a railroad clerk along with my father, and that's how the Porter Loring [funeral] business got started.

By the time of the flood of 1921 my grandfather had died, I think in 1913, and my father, Henry A. Guerra, took over as head of the funeral home and became a licensed funeral director and licensed embalmer. I never got a license because I came into the funeral business late. I already had a career on radio and television and didn't go down to help at the funeral home until my father had his first heart attack in 1952.

He stayed alive with nitroglycerine pills, but he kept active, not only with his business but with a host of other things. He was in the Knights of Columbus, where he was a Grand Knight; the Alhambra; he was head of the Fiesta Association; president of the downtown Lion's Club and founder of the West Side Lion's Club, and stayed very, very active until he died in 1962.

By 1952, I had gone into the funeral business for a while, working at the funeral home to help my father. Then, after his death, my mother decided to keep the place open, so I went to work for her, and eventually she made me president of the Angelus Funeral Home.

My mother, Elvira Pizzini de Guerra, and my father had married in 1917, after she was elected to the school board. She was elected as a young, single woman, and, although her name was Italian, she was really Hispanic. She spoke perfect Spanish, read and wrote it also, and perfect English. She was a graduate of the high school at Incarnate Word College and then also of the college, which at that time was a two-year college. Her father was Frank Pizzini, who had a very prominent store on Produce Row.

Selling what: comestibles, food, and so forth?

Yes. He would import from various places in railroad cars: chiles from Mexico, etc. After my grandfather's death, my mother ran the store for my grandmother, and I remember, after the war, going with my mother to get the Italian spaghetti that they sold at the store. They sold Mexican spices, chiles, and herbs, and they sold Italian and American foods: canned goods and whatnot. I still remember the sacks of Pioneer flour. We went to the store quite often because my grandparents lived behind the store, and also my mother's sisters and her brother.

You said there was an Italian connection with the Guerras, too.

Yes, after my Grandfather Guerra came to San Antonio and became a fireman, he married Giuditta Degasperi, who was born in Italy but came here with her family as immigrants, not through Ellis Island but with the same group of Italians that had included the Pizzinis.

They were imported by the Mexican government, through an agreement between the Italian and the Mexican governments, to settle Italia Irredenta ["Unredeemed Italy," i.e., any territory settled by Italians but not contiguous to Italy itself]. They all came from northern Italy, from the Italian Tyrol, which was under Austrian rule at the time.

The reason most of these families came, the Pizzinis included, was that the older boys were about to be inducted into the Austrian army. Nonetheless, my grandfather always kept a likeness of Austrian Emperor Franz Joseph in his home, and he sympathized with the Austrians in World War I and II, until Italy got in the war on the Allied side. Like most immigrants, he ultimately became a citizen before World War I.

So my Grandfather Pizzini came to San Antonio from Mexico. His father and mother had come to Mexico in 1881 with their five sons and two daughters. The Italian colony from which he came was an agricultural colony that was going to teach the Mexicans the modern methods of agriculture that the Italians had developed . . .

Where in Mexico did they settle?

Around Veracruz, which was a mistake, because a lot of the Italian settlers died from yellow fever and other tropical diseases. Eventually they moved to the plateau, to the coffee plantations around Córdoba, and there to this day there are Pizzinis still living. One died a couple of years ago, Tino Pizzini, a cousin whom I knew, a son of one of the guys who left Italy.

My grandfather was of that generation. He grew up in Mexico, and he spoke more Spanish than Italian. He played bocce and Italian card games, and he could converse with the Italians here, but he never went back to Italy.

When he was about seventeen or eighteen years old, he and a friend devised a scheme to travel around Mexico selling merchandise, and he got his father's permission to leave home to do this. He came to San Antonio around 1888-89 and with a friend, Joe Bolner, settled around Mission San José, and both got jobs working on the railroad laying tracks.

They saved their money and bought a ranch near Mission Espada. Shortly thereafter he met Paul, or Pablo, Broggi and, probably as two Italians meeting far away from home, became friends. Eventually Broggi gave him a job in his grocery store, which was right on Military Plaza in the center of San Antonio, and in the city directory of 1891 he is listed as a clerk in Broggi's store.

The house where Broggi had his business was an old colonial house that was later moved to the grounds of the Witte Museum for preservation. That house was where the first public schools were held in San Antonio, first under the Spaniards and later under the Mexicans. The Ruizes lived in that house; then they sold it, and by the time Pablo Broggi came along, he could buy that house or rent it as his store. I remember as a boy sitting with one of the grandsons, Jake Rubiola, Jr., on the sacks of beans and whatnot that were on the front porch of that store. The store was right across from city hall, and this must have been around the 1920s.

Although working for Broggi, Grandfather kept his ranch near Espada, and apparently Broggi would lend him a horse and wagon to go out there on weekends and keep an eye on the place. When he returned to the city, he would bring corn and other produce to sell at the store.

Anyway, Grandfather Frank Pizzini saved his money, and by 1892 he opened his own store on Durango or Dolorosa. Then later he moved his business to Produce Row, probably by 1895. He leased the store from the French family that had built Produce Row, the Arnauds. They were an old San Antonio family that has died through the years. We buried the last of them, Eli Arnaud, who was a professor at Our Lady of the Lake, two or three months ago from our funeral home.

Grandfather Frank Pizzini married a Mexican born in Durango, and they had their first child, my mother, in 1895. I grew up in the houses of both grandparents, but most of my time was spent with the Pizzini ones. As usual, my mother and Grandmother Giuditta didn't get along too well. Women do that, and I can see why: if you're a son, and especially an only son, then the mother resents the woman who married her son, I don't care who it is. I could have married someone else and my mother still wouldn't have gotten along with my wife, and my mother ran into that, too.

Are you still working today?

I still go to the funeral home, and I attend the rosaries and the funerals. I go everywhere except for the cemetery anymore, on the very good theory that I might not come back. You see, I've had a quadruple bypass operation, and I've had an operation for cancer of the colon, so I don't go to the cemetery any more than necessary.

And I only go to the cemetery for people I know through my family, or for people who call the Angelus Funeral Home. Very rarely would the friends of my wife or of my sister call us. We had the disappointment while my father was still alive that good friends of hers that she had gone to school with had a death in the family, but they were Anglos, and they called another funeral home. So we wouldn't go to the funeral.

To this day, I get calls from the Alhambra or the Knights of Columbus to tell me of a rosary for one of the members, and if it's being held at [one of the Anglo funeral homes], I just say, "Well, thank you for letting me know." I only go to funerals at the Angelus Funeral Home. Now we get Anglos, and we get Belgians, and Italians . . . everything except blacks. The black funeral homes would resent our taking black business, so we don't go after it. It isn't that we wouldn't bury a black! After all, money is green, but we don't go after the business because we don't want to take it away from the black funeral homes.

You mean to tell me that there is that kind of division among funeral homes: Anglo funeral homes and Hispanic funeral homes and black funeral homes?

Yes, there is. For example, old man Porter Loring wouldn't bury my old man. He was anti-Mexican, as were other Anglo funeral directors, but if you had the money they would bury you. We've buried lots of Anglos who were personal friends, but the average Anglo would not think of calling a west side funeral home. Even after we changed the name from Guerra Funeral Home to Angelus we were considered "west side" even by the banks. Even after we moved to our North St. Mary's Street location, most of our business is still Mexican. Things are changing, but the old divisions still persist.

I'm interested in this division between Hispanics and other groups in San Antonio.

This is something that is gradually dying out as the Hispanics get more money and become more numerous. There have traditionally been very few Hispanics that made good money or could hang on to money, and, for those few, nothing was closed to them. In other words, the St. Anthony would take you if you had the money, especially if you were one of those "white" Hispanics. If you looked like a peon, then they didn't want you at the Plaza, at the St. Anthony, at the Gunter. But, if you looked like you could pay for the bill, well, hell, they'd welcome you with open arms. That was not always true of blacks, but now it's true of blacks also.

So the difference was still based on appearance and on financial power?

Yes, until recently. Nowadays, however, I don't envy a hotel clerk, because millionaires can look like bums!

One hears about Hispanics being discriminated against in Texas. Have you experienced that yourself ever?

One time! It was because we had some cousins who came up from Mexico, and they were kind of brownish. We went to the Terrell Wells swimming pool, which was owned by a friend of my father's. We used to go there all the time. But this time my father wasn't along; I think my aunts took us there. We were kids, and we were speaking Spanish, and they threw us out of there. So we never went back, and I think my father's friend wondered why we didn't come back. But it was because his employees threw us out for speaking Spanish.

However, I grew up taking dance lessons at the St. Anthony. I grew up eating in the finest restaurants in town. The Pizzinis or Guerras were people who were never rich, but we had enough money. In fact, my grandfather made so much money in his grocery business that he could afford to send one of his daughters, my Aunt Esther, to school at LaSalle College in the East, where her date was a young man with the last name Ludens, from the family that made the cough drops. We used to ask her why she didn't marry him, because we could've had free cough drops all around! [Laughs.]

If you were rich or from the ruling classes in Mexico, you seldom ran into difficulties in Texas. In fact, the reason we had a Good Neighbor Commission was because a Mexican consul from San Antonio—he was well dressed, but he was dark—tried to eat breakfast in a small Texas town, and they wouldn't serve him. Boy, did Washington hear about that from Mexico City! And the Secretary of State, Cordell Hull, called the governor of Texas, Coke Stevenson—this was during the war and said, "What the hell are you people trying to do down there?"

And they called on that mayor and told him, "You *will* apologize, and right now, because otherwise we may not have anyone in our fields to pick up crops!" All our guys were gone and in the Army, and we had a *bracero* [agricultural worker] contract with the Mexican government, so they were threatening to pull all the *braceros* back. They really had a pistol to our head.

So the governor of Texas got a call from the Secretary of State, who said, "You straighten that out, and straighten it out tonight!" And that's how we got the Texas Good Neighbor Commission, on which a number of Hispanics have served. I have been a chairman of the commission; Dolph Briscoe named me, not because I was Hispanic but because he had to have someone who was on his side. The chairman and the guy who was executive secretary were actively working for someone else.

What is your first memory of a connection with the San Antonio missions?

My Grandfather Pizzini kept his ranch near Espada mission. It was right on the Espada ditch and ran down to the river. His former partner leased the land from him and farmed it, but we went out there on weekends to the mission and to this ranch, and we swam in the river, where there were snakes. There was an old house with an arbor there. I also learned to play pool and drink beer at a bar that was in the walls of the mission. This was in the 1920s.

What did the rest of the complex look like then?

Well, the chapel was there, as restored by Father Bouchu. There was a house for the priest, and there were even some modern places where they had a school, a parish Catholic school, but the bar, built where walls were still standing, was rented out to the fellow who ran it.

What happened to your grandfather's land near Mission Espada?

He had to sell it during the Depression, and he sold it to the same fellow who had leased it from him.

How else were you connected to the missions?

I got interested in reading about the missions as a kid, and by the time I was in high school my mother gave me an etching of the Rose Window at San José, which she inscribed, "To my son, who loves his San Antonio missions." When I was in college I got active with the Conservation Society.

Later, I was already a member of the board of directors of the San Antonio Chamber of Commerce when at some cocktail party Archbishop Lucey was complaining in general that he had invited several of his colleagues, fellow bishops from California, and was going to show them his missions, and he got lost trying to find them and almost broke the axle of his car because the mission roads were in such poor condition. He was wondering who the heck was going to fix them. I took this story to the executive secretary of the Chamber of Commerce, and he decided that we were going to do something about it. So a committee was formed, called the Mission Road Committee, and I was named chairman.

The Conservation Society had been restoring the granary at San José; the church had been doing what it could to do some work. The church is often not given credit, but it actually led the way in trying to restore the missions. Anyway, the Mission Road Committee of the Chamber of Commerce turned out to be a permanent assignment, and I was chairman of it for many, many years.

We never got a road built, but our efforts led to several repavings of portions of the roads, to new portions of the road being built, and to the linear park that is there now leading from the Espada dam to San Juan

Capistrano. We did a survey of all the owners. In the process, we brought together people and entities that used to be at odds before. The River Authority, for example, is part of the effort now to build a Mission Road.

But in 1966, we were informed by the Department of the Interior that we could not apply for funding for the Mission Road because the neighborhood of the missions was so deteriorated. That was when we switched, at the suggestion of the late General Harris, to the idea of attempting to get the National Park Service involved.

I remember one time when we were at the Institute of Texan Cultures and took off our shoes to walk all over a map of the area, trying to decide where a Mission Road should go and where a national park could go. I was there, and so were our two congressmen, Henry B. Gonzalez and Chick Kazen, and a couple of other people from the city.

Many, many people were involved in getting the national park here, including Senator Yarborough from out West, Washington or Oregon, who included the funds for the park in a bill funding something for a project in Washington, D.C., that President Carter had to pass.

When you began your work with the Mission Road Committee, how difficult was it to convince people to cooperate in that cause?

Well, at first we had a lot of trouble with the city managers. One of them took the money that had been passed for it in a bond issue and used it to repair streets. But that was not enough to build a road anyway. Then the Chamber got behind the effort and got a $250,000 appropriation passed, which was used to build those portions of the road that are there, to repair, and to extend others. Gradually, we got other people convinced, and now the city is all for it. We will get a Mission Road one of these days, but in the meantime we've got something that's very valuable: we've got a national park that includes the missions.

Right now they're putting up a new tourist information center. Sometimes it's hard to see what the Park Service has done, but they've brought in new people, new resources, they've brought studies of the missions, they've uncovered and restored some of the paintings on the walls that were covered over, etc. They've done a tremendous job.

Tell me more about how the Department of the Interior and the National Park Service got involved.

They got involved because the Chamber of Commerce, the Conservation Society, the Catholic Church, and all sorts of other people were brought together, largely by the Chamber, and they agreed to pursue the matter. It was studied by all sorts of attorneys: for the Department of the Interior, for the archdiocese, and so forth, and a deal was worked out whereby the state of Texas—which still owns part of the park, by the way; they legally own San José—turned over this Texas state park they didn't have the funds for.

The compromise that had been reached to restore San José mission, whereby the Church, the County of Bexar, the City of San Antonio, the state of Texas, the Conservation Society had signed what amounted to a treaty, served as a model. By virtue of that agreement, the Church was allowed to have the mission church, although it had been repaired by WPA labor, a governmentally funded agency. Today's constitutional question did not even arise.

That question, of course, is how to repair church buildings that are included within a national park and that are going to be in constant need of attention. Because we saw that question coming, General Harris, Gilbert Denman, and myself formed a funding committee[1] through which could be channeled Catholic and non-Catholic money, since some people just will not give money directly to the archdiocese, to repair the church. This committee has raised more than five hundred thousand dollars.

The Department of the Interior will not allow one penny to be used for that purpose. The checks nowadays are signed by Mr. Denman and myself, and when they have something fall out, or they need a new roof or something, we approve the expense. But we don't do that automatically just because the archdiocese wants it. At one of the missions, the resident priest wanted to build a shelter for his car; he didn't get a penny out of us for that. If he can raise the money from his congregation, then he can do it . . . if the Department of the Interior okays it, and they've turned him down. And they have the right to do so, in the part they control, which is everything but the actual mission church, if it is not in keeping with their restoration standards.

We've also turned down the archbishop several times, but the truth is that he was glad to be freed from restoration expenses at a time when the church was concerned about working with the poor. As a churchman, if you weigh the needs of the poor in your congregation against the need to preserve a historic monument, the historic monument is going to lose out. So that is one of the things we accomplished.

On the other hand, the archbishop cannot touch the mission churches for other than historic purposes unless the work is approved by the National Park Service, and without that approval we won't sign a check. He could use his own money, but he probably won't. So that is something we achieved.

Was it an easy matter to get a national park established here?

No, it took a lot of work, both on the part of the Church, which wanted the mission churches to be living monuments, i.e., working parishes, and of everyone else involved. That was a requirement established by Archbishop Lucey and continued by Archbishop Flores. That had to be worked out with the Department of the Interior, which at first balked at taking even the rest of the mission complexes. But an agreement was finally reached laying out the specific conditions under which these missions are part of the National Park Service.

Curious things can happen. For example, in 1936 and again later, the Knights of Columbus and the Church had a celebration at the Alamo, not inside the Alamo but right in front of it. Well, in 1976, there were celebrations at all the missions, including church services. They knew better than to ask for the Alamo itself, but they wanted a Mass said in front of the Alamo. They were turned down, and do you know why? Because the DRT [Daughters of the Republic of Texas] at the time said, "Don't you know this is sacred ground?" [Laughs.] So they had their Mass out on the street.

Whatever arrangements were reached, Congress still had to get involved, isn't that right?

Oh, they had to be approved by the whole government, and they were. That's why the bill signed by the president was actually a rider attached to the Washington, D.C. bill. [See interview with Betty Bueché.] Senator Douglas was the guy that got that through. But the legislative father of the bill was Congressman Kazen, with the aid of Henry B. Gonzalez and other congressmen. Carter, under the influence of the preacher from First Baptist Church here, might have vetoed it, but he couldn't veto the Washington bill. But the basic idea here has gone through three different archbishops.

You were raised here in San Antonio. Do you remember the Conservation Society restoration work at San José?

Oh, yes. My mother was very active in the Conservation Society at the time, and we would drive out there and look at the restoration. I've lived through a very interesting time. When I was a child, some people kept a cow in their backyards, and we had a shuck house [a place to keep the corn shucks used to wrap tamales] out in back for the tamales. I've seen cars from their beginnings, and lived through the age of flight, and the age of space. Lots of changes.

NOTE

1. The Bexar County Historical Foundation.

Mary Ann Noonan Guerra

Mary Ann Noonan Guerra, *seventy-three, is the wife of Henry Guerra. Daughter and granddaughter of district judges in this part of the state, she was led early on to join in the efforts of the San Antonio Conservation Society, an exemplary organization to which the city owes the survival of many of its historic structures. Aside from being a wife and mother, Mary Ann has become a one-woman local history publishing machine, keeping both locals and visitors supplied with well-researched, reasonably-priced publications on almost every aspect of the city's history. Mary Ann was interviewed at the Guerras' Monte Vista home on August 29, 1995.*

Tell me something about your parents and grandparents, Mary Ann.

Well, my father was born here, and so was his mother. She was born in an old house on the San Antonio River. Her father had bought land in Texas in the 1820s. He had been in South America for a while but came back to San Antonio and bought what was later known as the Bowen's Island in 1840.

Where is that?

It's where the city water board is located and what is now called the Tower Life Building; we used to call it the Smith-Young Tower earlier. That used to be a five-acre peninsula, and that's where my grandparents lived. We have photographs of the place. My grandmother was born there, and that's where my father used to spend time as a boy.

My grandmother, who was a Bowen, was sent to Philadelphia and then to Europe for her education. She came back and met a judge here in San Antonio by the name of Noonan—he was originally from New Jersey—and they were married. They had two sons, and one was my father.

My father went to law school and ended up as a county judge west of here. The family had property west of San Antonio, and he was asked to run for office. He got elected and stayed in office for fifty years, so I was born out there. But I came to San Antonio for boarding school and then was sent other places. Actually, I grew up like on a seesaw: we'd go back and forth. My grandparents had a house here, and they had a house in Castroville and another on the ranch, so we went back and forth from one place to the other.

Where "west of San Antonio"?

In the town of Hondo; it's only some forty-odd miles from here. My grandfather was about twenty-eight or thirty years older than my grandmother when they married; she was only about twenty or twenty-one. As a judge, he served a district that went all the way to El Paso and Laredo—we're talking about the 1850s and '60s. They didn't marry until the 1870s. Grandmother would run the ranch while he was gone, but they kept a house in San Antonio, and she would go back and forth from one to the other. As a young person she went away when she was only nine or ten years old and didn't come back until she was twenty.

My father grew up here and in the family's place in Washington, D.C., because my Grandfather Noonan was a judge for thirty-some-odd years and then became a congressman. Father went to school out east. Then they came back here. The whole thing sounds luxurious, but it was actually a very simple life.

He also became a judge and had part of the same district that my grandfather had had. You have to remember that in those days you didn't go to school to become a lawyer. I don't think my grandfather ever went to a university. He "read the law" with a firm, and that's in his papers. My father, however, went to the University of Texas.

Grandfather rode a horse to hold court out in Uvalde and wherever it was being held. We have his diaries, and they are delightful. They are full of names from the period, but one must bear in mind that in that period there weren't very many people from here to El Paso except for the Indians. He talks about the Indians, and he actually was instrumental in working out an agreement between the Mormons, who had come to settle at Bandera, and the Indians of the area, who opposed them. Grandfather got the two groups to make peace, and in thanks, the Mormons made and gave to him a table and a beautiful tool chest, and the Indians gave him a ceremonial bow and arrow. We still have these things and are now in the process of trying to figure out whom to give them to!

In those days, you could be an attorney if you read the law, or a doctor if you carried some quinine around, but my great-grandfather was a university man, University of Pennsylvania. He came through San Antonio as a young man in the 1820s and went on to Venezuela, where he lived for seven years and learned the hide-tanning business. But he got involved in the Venezuelan movement for independence from Spain and was thrown out of the country. I guess he was lucky to get out with his life. He came back to Texas, where he had already bought some land around Llano, and that's when he came back to San Antonio. That was in the 1830s, after the Revolution, and things were beginning to settle down. He's identified in the charters at the beginning of the early 1840s as handling the mail and functioning as city treasurer, and that's when he bought the five acres of land of Bowen's Island in what is today downtown San Antonio for three hundred dollars, and that's where he built his home, where my grandmother was born.

I had the advantage of growing up in the small town of Hondo, where everybody still had a cow and a horse and a pig. It was a very pleasant, quiet life. But I could come up to my grandmother's, where President McKinley came to call on them. My grandfather was pretty close friends of both Cleveland and McKinley; we still have little mementos given by them to my grandparents.

We also have books from Grandfather's library from the time when he was in Congress. Among them was a marvelous set on the Civil War published by the U.S. government after the war that we gave to the St. Mary's University library. It contained a listing of all of the Union and Confederate armies—each company, where they came from, where they served—and there was a companion book of maps that was just magnificent. These were enormous volumes. My grandfather's set was rare because, although it's relatively easy to find sets of the rosters, it's not so easy to find the maps with them.

Have you ever done anything about transcribing and publishing your grandfather's diary?

I've transcribed it, because, of course, it was all handwritten, and Dr. Joe Franz, who was at the University of Texas and later at Corpus, looked at them and was very interested. I also have Grandfather's letters. Dr. Franz said that we needed to do a lot of "cleaning up," because, as he put it, "all diaries in Texas start out, 'It didn't rain today'!" And Grandfather's diary *does* have a day-by-day report of the weather in San Antonio. But there's marvelous material in it, and some very humorous entries. He had a wry sense of humor that often comes through in his writing. Also, as Dr. Franz pointed out, they are almost a catalog of names from that period.

When he traveled around like that, did he just camp out, or did he stay with people?

He mentions the towns where he would stay. He would always travel with a black servant named Tim, who lived with them. Grandfather was both a very strong abolitionist and a Union man from the word go. He ultimately was defeated in an election because of his stand for the Union.

I remember many stories my father told about Tim and his relationship with my grandparents. At one point, after the Civil War, the judge told Tim that he could not stay anymore, and Tim's reply was, "I have no intention of leaving; I'm staying right here!" And stay he did.

Many people in this region apparently owned slaves, but my people didn't believe in slavery. It's even reported in the family obituaries that they were abolitionists and Unionists. My great-grandfather was threatened at one point by the infamous Knights of the Golden Circle; they were the people who came in the night and burned you out. It was reported that the only reason they didn't burn him out was that he practiced both law and medicine, so he was too valuable a man to lose. Apparently, the family was very advanced in their attitudes for their day.

So this Tim had never been a slave of the family?

I really believe that he must have been at one time, but we have no record of it. For instance, when my great-grandfather came from New Jersey, we have lots of information about him but no indication that he brought a slave with him. Perhaps it was someone who attached himself to him when he came down here.

The reason for his coming here was that in his twenties he was diagnosed as having consumption and was told he had only a year to live. So he decided he would go around the world and find a place where he could live. He traveled quite extensively, came through South America, Central America, Mexico, and Texas, and went on to New Mexico. He stayed in New Mexico about a year, and he said the best place he found was the area between Castroville and San Antonio, so he came back here and lived to be ninety! [Laughs.] So, so much for being given the death sentence!

There's all sorts of stories about his holding court. He was the judge, for example, at the trial of Ben Thompson, the notorious gunslinger. You can imagine that if you were the district judge in those days, a lot of your cases would have to deal with horse stealing and cattle rustling, or with hanging some poor man without a due trial.

And this is all in the records; I'm not embroidering here. According to the family, my great-grandfather ran one of the stops in the Underground Railroad that was used to get black slaves out of the South. That's one of the reasons why the Ku Klux Klan, or the Knights of the Golden Circle, threatened to burn him out.

My grandfather, who was his son-in-law, wrote for the German newspapers here. He was an Irishman born in New Jersey in 1808 or so, but he spoke German. His parents had come to the United States right after the American Revolution. He was one of those people who apparently had a facility for languages, because, as far as we know, he taught himself. But anyway, he wrote for the German newspaper, and he has an entry in his diary about walking around the plaza eavesdropping on conversations to see what the opinions were on his editorials. He wrote under a pseudonym because as a district judge he shouldn't be taking open political positions. The paper was a Union paper, and, by the way, it was burned out for that reason. There were two such papers here that were burned out.

How many of these relatives were you fortunate enough to have known personally? Did you know your grandfather, for example?

No, he died before I was born; in 1912, I think it was. He was about thirty years older than my grandmother. She died at eighty-something in 1931 or '32. My father was seventeen years older than my mother. So when I speak of my great-grandfather and my grandfather, even though the generations should be closer to each other, they are not, because they go way back. They were much older than their wives, although I think that was not altogether unusual for that period.

My great-grandfather married twice. His [half-]brother died in a plague that we had in the 1840s, so he married his half-brother's wife, adopted the children, then they had children of their own. It sounds complicated, but you have to remember that in those days there were relatively few people in this area, probably only a few thousand people. It was not only a matter of there not being enough marriageable women, but also from an economic standpoint, such a marriage was a way of keeping a property together, or protecting related children, because what was a woman to do if she was left a widow with children? And she was originally from Philadelphia, so she was not even from this area.

And as for my father . . . we were really country people, although it sounds like we moved around a lot.

So you grew up between Hondo, San Antonio, and Castroville?

Yes, I still have property there.

Where did you go to school?

I went to school in Hondo for the most part. We had a Catholic parochial school connected with the church. It was run by Irish nuns, and it was a real old-fashioned school: we had to bring in the wood, we had to build a fire in an old stove, we were all in one room together . . .

Boys and girls together?

Yes, but boys on one side of the room and girls on the other. We had to wash down the blackboards in the evening, and we had to sweep up the floors in the evening, using a kind of greasy sweeping compound made out of sawdust and something that had a very strong and very distinctive smell.

You mean sweeping compound to keep down the dust?

Yes. Every time I get a whiff of that smell somewhere, I can just see my old classroom. If someone came to the door, the entire school would stand up and say, "Good morning, Mr. So-and-so!" And you would stand until you were told you could sit down again. The nuns were what we now call Holy Spirit nuns, although we used to call them Holy Ghost nuns, and they were strong in discipline, deportment, and education.

My father's closest friends, other than the few hundred people in the town, were Irish priests who were parish priests in the area. They always came to the house and were included in our Thanksgiving or Christmas celebrations. So when it comes to education, I guess the Irish were the strongest influence on my childhood; I was brought up almost entirely by them.

Then I went to boarding school at Incarnate Word.

The one-room school in Hondo was through what grade?

I went there through grammar school, and then I went to Hondo High School, which was a very small public school. You knew everyone in town, but we thought we were a big school because in our graduating class we had thirty-six people.

We had a lot of wrongdoing, even in Hondo, in those days, but the Mexican kids came to our school, although that was not the usual thing in Texas in those days. They were in the football team and participated in everything.

By "wrongdoing" you mean discrimination, don't you?

Yes. But I mention that because, at least in this instance, we had a kind of mix. I think it is good to bring these things in, because sometimes in reporting history, certain things are omitted that could give a different perspective on the situation.

We had a separate school for blacks out on the road to the cemetery, and it was one room. Our parochial school was brick; we went to school downstairs, and the nuns lived upstairs. There was a frame schoolhouse for the Mexican children, but later they came to the one high school.

I had a friend whose name was Tomasine Grant, who was a black teacher. Her husband used to cook for us. He ran a barbecue place. Our family had a big camp, and when we went out there, he would come with us and cook for us. He was a good man.

And Tomasine was the teacher who broke the color line in 1952, when so much was going on. She went to court asking to teach in the public schools, not the black school but the general schools. And she won her case. Then either Associated Press or *Life* magazine and others wanted to tell the story, because she had done it in a small town and had done it without there being a lot of burning and confusion. But she refused to cooperate with them because she said she would not be exploited.

Tomasine died about four years ago. She had retired. I was already in my sixties, and she was in her eighties by then, but we had stayed friends over the years. She called me just a few days before she died, and I told her that I wanted to do a story on her. She said, "Well, maybe so," and we made a date for lunch in several days. Unfortunately, she died not long after our conversation, so her story never was done.

I mention these things because you hear things that were bad, but you do not often hear about good things that happened in the midst of the bad things. I also had a friend, Thelma Lynch, a schoolteacher who spoke Spanish and taught in the Mexican school. This was in the 1930s and '40s. She worked with her kids so that they could get into the public school, and this was done without a lot of commotion.

Thelma Lynch was not a Hispanic, was she?

No, no, she was an Anglo, but as a schoolteacher she used to emphasize English with her Mexican students so that they could get into the high school. Thelma would come to the house often, and she would be frustrated, not only because of some of the things that the Anglos were doing but at some of the things that were happening among the Mexicans.

Why did you have the Mexican kids together with the Anglo kids in Hondo's high school? That was certainly not the norm for the time in Texas.

Well, one of the reasons was that for some reason we were going to lose our accreditation if the Mexican kids were not accepted, and my father, who was county judge, appeared before the school board and argued for accepting them. Finally he told them, "Gentlemen, you can do as you please, but if we don't do this, I can always send my daughter to boarding school." In the end, they passed it. I finished high school in

1938 or '39, and I don't remember when the school integration law was passed, but it was certainly long after that.

So you graduated from high school in Hondo, and then?

I went to Incarnate Word. I didn't stay very long. The war broke out in 1941, and we had an airfield in Hondo. I had already worked summers for the rationing board—that was my first job—so I went to work at the airfield, and then I went to Washington, D.C. to school.

In the meantime, however, I had thought I would go to school in Mexico but ended up being a tutor instead. One of my oldest friends from Incarnate Word was from Mexico City, Ruth Hoerig, the daughter of a German manufacturer down there. She tried to talk me out of going to school there because she said I would end up associating with all the Americans who were down there and wouldn't learn anything. She suggested I get a job instead as a tutor in English.

So I went and stayed with a very distinguished family; the father was the former Mexican ambassador to Switzerland. We started reading the want ads and found one for an English tutor to go up to Taxco, where all the silver mines are, in the state of Guerrero, and work at a mining camp with the children of the mine owner. Mr. and Mrs. Hoerig made an appointment with the family and with lawyers, and they interviewed me and we interviewed them, and finally it was agreed that I would go to Taxco.

They came for me in a limousine, and here I was, all of nineteen years old, sitting in this limousine with the owner of the mine, driving on these curvy Mexican roads. It was awful, and I started to get carsick, so I asked, "May I sit in the front seat with the chauffeur?" The owner told the driver to stop the car, and we got out, but he told the chauffeur to get in the back seat so he could drive. He would not let me sit in front with the chauffeur. When the chauffeur got out to exchange places, I noticed that he was fully armed.

We finally arrived, and we had to leave the car a long distance from the mine, but they had sent mules and horses to transport us the rest of the way. When we got to the house, the house was built sort of into a cliff, but between where we arrived and the house itself there was a barranca with a creek running through it, and on the other side, on this marvelous patio overlooking the creek, were all these little children—about eight of them—with bouquets of flowers to welcome me. When I got there, they all said, "Welcome, Missy!"

Sounds like something out of *The Sound of Music!*

Well, I swear that's the truth! [Laughs.] It proved to be a very interesting job. The family was from Spain originally. The laborers were all Mexican, except that their foreman was from Brooklyn, New York! And one time they invited me to come to their barracks for supper. I had a good time with them. And on my birthday they had a big celebration, with roasted pig and all sorts of food.

While I was there, I noticed that there were always strangers coming through, and one time I asked who they were. I was told never to mention it again. It turned out that these were people who were fleeing Spain as a result of the civil war there, and they were being funneled into Mexico through the mine. I was never allowed to go anyplace without a guard. If I even took a walk after supper, which I liked to do in the evenings, I had to have an armed man with me. [Laughs.] It may sound like I'm making it up, but it is all absolutely true!

What did your job consist of with the family?

Well, I tried to teach them English, but with my youth and my limited education, I don't think I was very effective. I think the parents actually wanted me as much to fill out their game of bridge as to teach their children, and when it turned out that I couldn't play bridge, they were furious! But it was a very charming period in my life.

What about your friend Ruth Hoerig and her family?

That was another story. When I was visiting them, I was called upon by both the British and U.S. consulate and was asked not to associate with those people because they were blacklisted as Nazi sympathizers. In fact, when I visited their factory, I was introduced to a German fellow with a patch over his eye who clicked his heels when he greeted me. I was later told that he was a famous former German pilot. And Ruth's brother later flew for the Germans. I told both consuls that we were old-time friends, that our friendship had nothing to do with politics, and that I would not not be with my friend.

What year was this?

This was before the war broke out. One time they took me to a famous club, and the floor of the club had the Nazi insignia lit from underneath, so it really stood out. I don't feel I was being disloyal. I was just visiting an old friend. Later on she sent her son here to San Antonio to school, and he visited us, and we threw a party for his graduation. But I haven't been in touch with the family for about ten years.

And what happened after Mexico?

I went to school in Washington, D.C., and took classes at George Washington and at Catholic Universities. I stayed there for a year.

Did you ever get a degree?

No, I guess I'm lucky if I have three years' worth of credits. But I've gone to many schools! [Laughs.] I was very fortunate in not having parents who believed I *should* do this, or I *should* do that. In fact, when I went back to Hondo to work at the airfield, it was my mother who said to me, "You can't stay here; you have to get up and go!" That's one of the reasons I ended up in Mexico. I guess my family was a little odd that way.

I have three children who don't have higher degrees. One of my sons took the GED when he was a junior. We had sent him to Ireland to go to school, and he came back and took the GED and passed it and enrolled at St. Mary's University with just two years of high school.

My daughter Marina, she also has a GED, because she went to school in Mexico and Italy. And my oldest daughter doesn't have a high school diploma, because she went to school in Italy and Ireland, but she was a candidate for a Rhodes fellowship. She speaks five languages. My youngest daughter speaks four. We sent them to school in various places, and in some of them you are examined both by the government and the school itself.

How many children do you have? I know there's a set of twins in there somewhere.

The oldest is Graciela, she's thirty-nine. She works for Time/ Warner, Incorporated in Rockefeller Center in New York. She has been with them several years. The twins are two boys: one finished high school, the other never did but has all sorts of credits. The other is working on his M.A. now. The youngest daughter lacks only one semester from getting her degree from the University of Turin. She came home and married a young Peruvian fellow. She takes her children backpacking in the Iquitos rain forest in Peru. Her husband works for Southwest Research; he's a computer engineer.

What happened after you came back from Washington?

I went to work for Frost Brothers Department Store. I came home for the Christmas holidays, and I got a call from the store telling me that they needed a live model for furs because their model had gotten sick. They used to sketch from life for their ads. The head of advertisement knew me and my family, and she knew I had done some modeling before. One thing led to another, and they asked me if I would stay on. I agreed. They asked me if I could type, and I could. They asked me if I could write, and I could. And within six months I was writing their advertising copy.

I stayed there several years, and I only left because the Hondo newspaper needed an editor. The owner was also a friend, a man who owned several newspapers in Texas. He asked me if I would consider being the editor. I told him I had never been an editor, but he said, "Oh, it won't take you long to learn!" So I went out and was made editor of this newspaper when I was just in my twenties, and I had all these people working for me who really knew much more about it than I did. But I didn't stay long, and that's when I went to Europe and lived in the Convent of the Holy Child in England and in Italy.

But along the line I also took classes at the old Trinity University in the old Express Building along the river. I remember that during warm days we used to open all the windows in the classroom and look out on the river. I studied journalism there with Charles Ramsdell, who was a marvelous teacher and a great journalist, and I credit him for a great deal of what I have been able to do.

At one time in a previous conversation, you told me that you had lived near Mission San José.

When I went to work for Frost Brothers, and they asked me to stay on, I lived for nine years with my relatives, Mrs. Elizabeth O. Graham, her daughter Wanda Graham Ford, and Wanda's husband O'Neil Ford. O'Neil Ford had come to San Antonio to be the architect for La Villita, had fallen in love with the city, and had decided to stay.

Wanda is only about four or five years older than I am. I was in high school when she was married. Her father and my father were cousins, and her mother and my father were also cousins, and our grandmothers lived together for years after they became widows, so the family relation is very close. We've had some disagreements over the years, but nonetheless I truly admire them, because without people like them and others, nothing would have been done. They contributed time, effort, and money absolutely freely whenever it was needed.

I had two interests at the time, and one was the missions: my parents and my grandparents had always been very interested in them. My grandmother, in particular, who had grown up in England and France, was always taken with them.

Anyway, I lived with my relatives behind Mission San José, and I would go to Mass at the mission. O'Neil Ford always used to tell me he could not understand what kind of Catholic I was because I went to Mass at the mission, and then I went to the Unitarian Church. I would tell him that I thought the Unitarians were teaching something that I thought was very important. In any case, my great-grandfather had been a Unitarian who married a Catholic, and a devout one, so my going to both services didn't bother me in the least.

In any case, I lived near the missions, went to San José on an almost daily basis, and was there when really great things were going on. We had fund-raisers on the mission grounds, and I remember the first performance of Los Pastores there. We didn't even have chairs. We had blocks, and planks across the blocks, for people to sit on. And even before the Conservation Society built its booths, we had sort of a framework with a fire in the center, and we sold the chocolate and whatever we had.

But when the play was being performed, we were there so close that you could almost reach out and touch the Hermit or Beto or one of the other characters. In those days not many people came, but so many of those who came knew the music that the audience would sing along. Later on the Conservation Society printed programs.

And then, around that time, my cousin Wanda was elected president of the Conservation Society, and she asked me to be vice-president in charge of publicity. We put on a play called *A Cloud of Witnesses*, by Yelvington. It was one of the most beautiful evenings of my life. We had the play against the walls on the immediate north side of the church, in a small area. But we had a full moon, and the peacocks got up on the wall and started making their peculiar sounds. *Life* magazine came and covered it, not because I asked them but because the editor was an old friend of O'Neil's. It was one of those memorable things when everything worked: the setting was beautiful, the sounds were beautiful, everything was beautiful.

It was the story of the fall of the Alamo. I have the script, which, frankly, I wouldn't dream of publishing today, because it has a bit of the redneck in it. Our attitudes have changed so much over the years. But Ramsey Yelvington was a good man from Boerne, Texas, a very good man. And as you know, history written in the '30s is quite different from history written in the '60s or the '90s.

More and more we're learning to widen our point of view. So much of earlier history was written strictly from the Anglo victors' viewpoint: you'd have thought there weren't any Mexicans here except for Santa Anna's soldiers. And how people saw Mexicans in those days was almost unbelievable, mostly because in those days you had pockets of people: Mexicans here, Anglos there.

I was just lucky enough to be born into a family where that kind of pigeonholing did not make any sense. I was taught to realize that there are all kinds of Anglos, all kinds of Germans, all kinds of Mexicans, all kinds of Irish. I'm descended from the Irish, but there are some Irish that I wouldn't touch with a ten-foot pole! Unfortunately, people generally did not make that kind of distinction: there was one kind of Mexican, or one kind of German, or one kind of Anglo; that carried on and still does to a certain extent, although I think we're slowly learning.

I guess we were lucky enough to come from very educated people. And I don't mean that strictly as a reference to going to a university. It was more your associations, the way you lived. Your outlook was broader; you'd see people for the way they would talk or behave rather than the way they were dressed or whatever.

Of course, through Elizabeth Graham and Wanda, my interest in the missions grew. When Henry and I were married, we had the reception at Willow Way, their home. Many of the people in my wedding party were from Hondo or Castroville, but we had about two thousand guests! [Laughs.] You have to understand that I couldn't invite just two people from Castroville; I had to invite practically the whole town. The same thing for Uvalde and Hondo. My father had about five counties, and in those days you really got to know people. I'd go to Bandera with him, and to Kerrville and other places to hold court, and in each place you met and made friends with people. So between Henry and me, the list of guests was shocking!

Sounds like a real Cecil B. DeMille production!

Of course, Henry was also very much interested in the missions. But our interest intensified when Archbishop Lucey came in. He was transferred here from California and invited some fellow bishops from California here. He was so proud, and he wanted to show his buddies the San Antonio missions, but in the process he got lost and couldn't find them! He called Henry and said, "Henry, it's a mess out there! There're no road signs, nothing!" So Henry went to the Chamber of Commerce and asked them to set up a committee, which they did, and the chamber had a Mission Road Committee. Before that, there had been another group that had wanted a road to the missions, and I'm talking about way back in the '30s, but it wasn't until Lucey came in that something happened. Henry was made chairman, and he remained chairman for about thirty-five years. They just kept him on it.

But you should understand that the missions are really a gift from the San Antonio Conservation Society.

Why do you say that?

Because I think that without the Conservation Society, we wouldn't have them.

I know of their connection to Mission San José through their purchase of the granary, but what else was there?

That's where it started. The thing about the Conservation Society is that they never dropped the ball. There was a time when the Chamber of Commerce was thinking of dropping certain committees, one of them the Mission Road one. And the phone in this house rang about eleven p.m. one night. It was Vivian Terrett, who, I think, was president at that time of the Conservation Society. She told Henry that she had heard the committee was being dropped. And she said, "You've got to do something!"

So Henry called John Bennett, who was president of NBC. He was a marvelous human being. He told Bennett what was going on and asked him to go to the chamber meeting with him. Of course, with Bennett's support behind it, there was no way the chamber was going to drop the committee. And, of course, it was vitally important that the chamber remain involved.

And there were other organizations and entities that contributed. The county was very cooperative, and so was the government, but it took an engine to drive this effort, and the Conservation Society was that engine. They never let it go. And then from there on, the archbishop put as much money into the missions as the Church could, and fortunately, as time went on, particularly in the last several years, we've had Los Compadres, and I think they are terrific.

We've been very lucky. One thing has led to another in a good way. Los Compadres are doing today what needs to be done, just as the Conservation Society did when it was their turn.

And, of course, I had the good fortune of watching Elizabeth Graham in action, because I was living at her home on Willow Way. She would hold a meeting at the house at the drop of a hat whenever she thought it was necessary for the missions effort. She had the talent never to antagonize or make an enemy unnecessarily. For example, Walter McAllister was a prominent businessman. Elizabeth and Walter grew up together. That was in the early days, and Walter McAllister thought that conservation was bunch of nonsense, as most businessmen did. John Bennett was a notable exception. The point is that here's Elizabeth on the side of conservation and there is Walter, a very strong businessman. But Elizabeth and Walter grew up together on Slocum Street, and he called her "Bib." When she died, the first person who walked into the house was Walter.

But you had people who were totally on the other side of the fence on this particular issue, but they had respect for each other, and they were able to still talk to each other. They would have knock-down, drag-out battles, but they could maintain their connections. And those Conservation Society ladies were geniuses in that respect. They didn't go out of their way to make enemies; they just stood their ground. They would simply say, "Well, this is what we want to do." And you might as well cave in, because they wouldn't give an inch. The other side of it was that there were several women in there whose husbands were also very strong conservationists. They saw it differently. But it was the ladies who led the way.

It was a great time. It was not only the missions and the Conservation Society, but it was also the time of the organization of the River Art Group and other organizations that continue to exist today and to do good work.

Were you yourself involved in the Conservation Society?

I've been a member for over fifty years, from a time before I was old enough to be a member. And because I lived with Elizabeth Graham and Wanda, I was pulled into many of their involvements.

Have you been involved in any of these other committees or organizations that have had to do with the missions? For example, I hear there was a group that was working toward the reconstruction of Mission San Juan.

No, but Henry was. He was made an honorary lifetime member of the Conservation Society years ago. I think it was in 1977. He was also involved in many committees that came at it from different directions: through the Catholic Church, through the Chamber of Commerce, through the Conservation Society, and so on. I helped him when I could.

You have written about the missions, about the San Antonio River, about Market Square, and a host of other local topics. How did that come about?

I've been writing since high school and getting some of my work published. Even when we first were married, I wrote for the Girl Scouts; for Frost Brothers, doing their ads, their radio show, publicity releases, and a lot of other things. I also had started doing some political writing for several people.

In 1972, the archbishop called me and told me that they were getting ready to celebrate the completion of the renovation of San Fernando Cathedral and asked whether I could do a pamphlet for them about the cathedral. I did a preliminary survey of the topic and went back to him. I told him that there was so much history there that I didn't see how we could do just a pamphlet. He asked me what I wanted to do, and I suggested doing a book, or at least a booklet.

He asked me if I would do it, and I accepted under one condition: that he should not hang anyone around my neck that I would have to deal with, except as scholars who could check what I produced. He gave the go ahead and asked how much I wanted for it, and I told him it would be my gift for the occasion. I asked what the deadline was, and he set it at two weeks before we needed to go to press with it.

He gave me Monsignor (later Bishop) Grahmann and Father Neumann from St. Mary's University as the two persons who would go over my work. So I wrote the San Fernando publication with the help of several people, chief among them my brother, who was not only an attorney but also a real historian. He and I spent countless hours at the Bexar County historical archives. Henry also helped greatly, and, of course, Father Neumann, as a historian himself, was just great. And we put together this book, which I designed. In retrospect, it was not a good design, but we had collected the pertinent photographs, and the archbishop let me spend money freely on having copies of them made.

That publication came out and sold out. But in doing the research, when I wanted to look up something about Mission San Antonio de Valero, I found that there was not much available on it as a mission, or as the Alamo. I was particularly bothered by the fact that it was so difficult to find the pertinent photographs in one place. I mentioned that to Henry and told him that I intended to sit down and do something about it.

So I did, and in 1974 or '75 I put together a book. I was scared stiff, because when I went to the printer, he wanted $3,500 to do it. I couldn't believe that sum, particularly when I had children in school and so on. But we decided to do it anyway. When the book was finished and I took it down to the Alamo, they told me, "Well, we'll buy two dozen copies." I sold them the two dozen, and within a few days they called and asked for two dozen more, then three dozen, and after a while, they called and said, "Okay, we'll just buy them by the box!"

Then I thought I would do the same for the missions, complete with photographs, and that's how I got started. You might say that Archbishop Furey got me into the business of writing books on local history, even though I've worked for some of the best magazines in the country. I've done work for *Vogue*, for *Harper's*, for *McCall's* magazine, and many others. This, however, was a different thing. It was historical writing, collecting photographs, then the production—typeface, graphics, etc.— end of it, and finally the matter of sales. And although what I produced was nothing I would enter in a contest, it did win the highest award in the state for its research, because we did dig and did some good research.

So everything you've done has been self-published?

Yes, I've paid for them, I underwrite them. I found that any number of people would underwrite me, but when you have an underwriter you own the copyright, but you don't have control. And it was not that I wanted control from an ego standpoint; I wanted control from the standpoint of telling the story as I found it in the records, from the standpoint of accuracy. I was really concerned with educating people about what we have in our city.

Another thing that pushed me was that in talking to people I found that many people actually thought that the way they were today was the way the missions had always looked. Even parishioners sometimes thought that! They didn't realize that they had fallen down over the years or that they had been used as cowpens and pigpens or as targets for soldiers' target practice. And I felt that that was what I could do to help bring it back, and to point out what happens when you don't take care of it.

And I think I have helped to create interest. There have been a host of other publications since mine, and I won't say mine was the earliest, but it was from a different point of view. I tried to point out that there were heroes in the Mexican army as well, and there were all kinds of people on both sides.

Another thing I got into was reprinting other publications that were of local historical interest, like William Corner's work, Sidney Lanier's story of San Antonio, *Viva Tejas*. The last one was a disappointment. The newspapers have always been good in zooming in on my books and giving them publicity, but a lot of local people didn't pay any attention to it, among them some of the leading Mexican-American teachers and teachers of Spanish. I think my publications opened a window, which was what I intended them to do.

I really should say "we" when I speak, because I've always had a lot of help. My kids have always read my things, even if sometime they complain that they don't know what I'm talking about. Henry has also been a very useful critic and editor. And I've always had readers who are first class: I had Carmen Perry on the river; I always have Claude Stanush, who is a first-class editor; and in every case, if we have statements about law in a book, I always consult with a lawyer to make sure that what I say is correct. We've been pretty careful, and we haven't had many problems. This has all been since 1972, so twenty-some-odd years.

Henry mentioned "Alamo Press" to me in an earlier conversation. What was that?

Oh, when I started out, I told Henry that we ought to do it ourselves, because an underwriter would want to sell a book for so many dollars, while I wanted to move the books and make them available. The first few years I had the Alamo book, I sold it for $2.25 a copy. Then I realized that

I'd better protect myself, so through the Library of Congress I went through the proper paperwork in the 1970s to become the Alamo Press.

Sometimes I get phone calls, and people ask whether they can speak with some department of the Alamo Press, and I have to tell them that I am the only department! My daughter translates when necessary and rereads material; my sons deliver books when necessary; and my son-in-law takes care of all the accounting: invoices, checks, and so on. The only paid "employee" is my CPA, and he is only on duty twice a year! Other than that, the entire staff of Alamo Press is sitting right in front of you!

Well, at least your business is compact; you can take it anywhere you go!

The big advantage, as I see it, is that if I had gone with a big publisher—and I had offers from some—the books wouldn't be available today; they would be either out of print or priced out of the market. Three of the biggest publishing houses—Doubleday, Random House, and Texas A&M—have been interested, but a board member of one of the big presses, who is a friend, said to me, "I'm going to give you some advice: We can publish a book of yours, but we'd have to sell it for $25.95. You would sell quite a number of them, but that would be it. What you re doing is right; keep doing it just that way."

And I've done it that way . . . but I'm getting tired. Those printing bills get bigger and bigger all the time! It seems that I just get finished paying one and the next one is due!

Robert Walker

From the 1960s on, the Rufus Walker Company was involved in preservation work at the Alamo as well as at the four other San Antonio missions. "Old Mr. Walker" died in April 1985, but his younger son, **Robert Walker**, fifty-three, remains at the head of the company. The purpose of this interview was to attempt to gain an understanding of the Walker firm's involvement in repair and conservation projects. Robert Walker kindly allowed access to his father's files on the missions, and attached to the interview is a sampling of documents from these files and a description of the projects mentioned. The documents are not meant as an exhaustive catalog; they should just give the reader an idea of the work involved. Robert Walker was interviewed at his office on July 11, 1995.

Your sign outside says "Construction Specialties." What exactly does that mean? What kind of work does your company do?

RW: Construction Specialties really got its name back in the late '20s, when my dad was in the waterproofing business. He would waterproof and caulk windows and such in commercial buildings. He started that little business, and he was, of course, good friends with general contractors who, at the time, would order materials by mail from companies all over the U.S. The materials would be put on trains and shipped down here, but it could take them forever to get their materials.

As materials were developed for construction, people would ask my dad to order some of the stuff and stock it so they could buy it from him, and that's how this business grew. We handle a number of technical items, such as epoxies for injecting into concrete to strengthen it; construction tubes, cardboard tubes into which concrete is poured; expansion joints; joint-sealing materials; water repellents, which require a knowledge of stone and concrete, and the properties of those materials. That's really how he got into helping with the missions. He used to do that kind of work around the late '30s.

The connection came through his knowledge of waterproofing?

RW: Yes, and of the properties of stone and mortar, and being able to waterproof those materials.

So the firm has been in existence for how long?

RW: Since 1929, since the height of the Depression.

Do you deal primarily in materials, or do you also take on projects?

RW: We deal in the materials, but we still maintain the end of the business that does waterproofing and caulking on a contract basis. Of course, construction has changed so much in the last twenty to thirty years that today a lot of it is really putting together pieces that have been pre-formed somewhere else. Highways, for example, are like big Erector sets.

I remember when people in highway construction would pour all their slabs and shore them up. Now all they do is pour a few columns and put the other parts on top of those. It's tremendous work and requires a lot of technology, but most of your "Ts" are poured off-site, trucked to the site, and loaded and placed with cranes.

But my dad's main knowledge was in mortar and in reintegrating stone masonry, which, of course, the missions around here were made of because there was an adequate supply of stone and of lime from limestone.

What projects exactly did your company do for the missions?

RW: My dad did this work in conjunction with Harvey P. Smith, Sr., a local architect. Harvey would do the architectural work, and my dad would carry it out. He had a number of men who were familiar with the materials and were very good at rock masonry. They could make a new piece of work look very, very old.

In the process of carrying out these projects, he discovered a number of people who could do specialty work, such as Curt Voss from Voss Metalworks, who made some of the steel door latches and hinges and things like that that went on the Alamo. My dad and Harvey Smith did work on every one of the missions in San Antonio, all five of them. It was mainly during a period from 1960 through 1966 or something like that.

A lot of this was done through trial and error. I know from hearing their conversations about some of the obstacles they encountered. For example, one problem was dealing with the three entities that had a say: the City of San Antonio, the Catholic archdiocese, and the Conservation Society. I'm guessing a little here, but the city wanted these things preserved for the sake of tourism; the Catholic archdiocese wanted them as missions, because that was their function; and the Conservation Society wanted them preserved with nothing changed. But in actuality, the three of them working together did a real good job. They made them accessible to people, and they managed to preserve a piece of the history of this area.

You say that your father worked at each of the missions. Do you remember specifically what was done at each one, if we go down the list?

RW: Yes. Actually, I have a file on each one from my dad's records, so I can dig those out and tell you exactly. Normally, it would involve repointing stone mortar, which means chiseling out the old mortar and replicating it to match the existing mortar, doing it through trial and error, as far as coloring was concerned; putting it in place; and going on from there.

He had a crew of real interesting people, and probably the best mason was a guy named Santiago Domínguez. He could do anything. He had a good sense of humor and spoke very broken English.

Is he still alive, by any chance?

RW: No, he passed away a long time ago.

Was he a local person, or did he come from Mexico?

RW: I think he came from Mexico. My father was from Alabama, and he never learned Spanish. He knew just a few words. But I grew up here and was interested in it, so I grew up speaking it, and I could never understand why Dad couldn't pick it up. I guess some people have an easier time with language than other people.

During those years, a lot of people just wouldn't try to pick it up. I would work on ranches in Mexico and pick up a lot of it that way. But with my dad there would be a communications barrier sometimes. Of course, then other people would step in and translate.

The people who worked on those missions had a real good fraternity, and my dad had a lot of respect for the Daughters of the Republic of Texas [DRT], who really saved the Alamo. He told me in the late '40s that he had been asked to go to the missions, mainly San José, where there was a fresco on the wall, and he was asked to duplicate that fresco with the materials that were used to create it. The formula that he came up included ocher for red and indigo for blue, and he would mix his pigments with water and milk. He was out there trying to paint but could never get it to work; he kept failing. And some old Mexican man saw him one day and asked him what he was trying to do, so he explained. And the man told him that his problem was that he was using the wrong kind of milk. He was using regular cow's milk, but he should've been using goat's milk! And that was it. After that his formula worked![1]

Which fresco are we talking about?

RW: I guess I'm using the wrong term. I'm talking about the designs that are on the face of the bell tower at San José.

I suppose that we are talking about a time way before the National Park Service came on the scene.

RW: Yes, certainly. I remember one project we worked on at Espada, where we had to rebuild the ceiling of the chapel. In order to replace the beams, they found a bunch of old railroad ties and ripped those railroad ties to expose the weathered surface and used those as beams. They were perfect!

When did you start becoming involved in the company?

RW: I was involved from 1963 on, so about thirty years.

Did you by any chance work on any of these mission projects?

RW: Yes, I did. I would go down to the worksite and delegate responsibility for the work my dad had instructed me to get done, deliver materials, things like that. And since this was not really the focus of the company, I guess you could call it his hobby more than anything else, but he got quite involved in it.

I suppose with each project, he and his crews acquired a body of knowledge that helped on the next one.

RW: Oh, yes. And I remember that it would be fun to work through the sites with him, because he would be constantly pointing out something that he thought deserved attention.

Of the craftspeople who worked with you on these projects, are there any of them left alive today?

RW: No, except for possibly Manuel Dávila, but I am not sure. These guys were real artists. When it came to cement and limestone, they could do anything—just beautiful work. It seems to me that those things are appreciated now, where they were not appreciated then, or even thirty years ago.

Since your tenure, has your company had much to do with the missions?

RW: No. I would occasionally see bids for other historical preservation projects from, say, Texas Parks and Wildlife, but not for the missions. They would order some of the modern materials that can be used to forestall the capillary action that draws moisture into old structures, which is a common problem at the missions.

We're actually lucky that the missions were built where they are, on the south side of San Antonio, because if they had been built in the Hill Country, for example, there would have had been much more freeze/thaw damage over the course of time, and they would have fallen apart a long time ago. But the distance of about fifty miles to the south has really put them beyond that problem.

The problem we have here and in most large urban areas is the problem of sulfur dioxide in the atmosphere. It mixes with moisture in the air and produces almost a sulfuric acid, which will really eat limestone up.

[Calls in Mr. Jesse Hall, a long-time employee of the company.]

RW [to JH]: He was asking about some of the crews who worked on the missions projects.

JH: They were basically the same crew that worked at the Alamo and then went on to the other projects. I think it all started with doing something at the Alamo, restoring some of that north wall and doing some waterproofing. They had leaks, and the rock was deteriorating. Those waterspouts that divert water from the roof off the walls: some were broken, others were cracked or missing.

Domínguez, who was the main mason, carved replicas out of rock just perfectly; then they would do some work on them to make them look old and match the other ones. These guys were amazing at what they did and at finding ways to do it. You couldn't make them change their procedures, but they got things done.

I was supposed to take care of supplies and equipment, and when I saw them carving those water spouts, I thought for sure the next request would be for scaffolding so they could install them. But the next day I went out there, and the water spouts were finished and installed! I asked them, "How did you get them up there?"

And what they told me was, "You shouldn't worry about that; you didn't have to help us!" [Laughs.]

At Espada, they wanted a more substantial ceiling that wouldn't rot, so what they came up with was splitting railroad ties and using those. At Concepción, when they were using the church as a chapel for those kids at St. John's Seminary across the street, they wanted to modernize and put in a tile floor, and to do that they had filled the floor in with dirt and put the tiles on over that. When they started restoring the church, the Conservation Society got in the act, and they wanted to bring the floor down to the original level, so we came in and had to dig all that dirt back out again and haul it out to where the Park Service office is now, where there used to be a slope.[2]

At most of the missions we did the roofs, because they were all in bad shape, but we also did walls and other things.

What did you find under the dirt at Concepción?

JH: Flagstones, or limestone in flagstone shapes; that was the original floor. That architect who lived out near San José, O'Neil Ford, he consulted a lot for these projects.

Document Excerpts from the Files of the Rufus Walker Company[3]

1960

January 15
From: Harvey P. Smith, Assoc., Architects
To: Msgr. Bernard F. Popp, Chancery Office
Re: *Inspection tour of San José* with Mr. Walker, "since he has done all of the repair work there several years ago."
Work involved:

- fill in and seal cracks in cloister arches, walls of church, and convent
- fill in holes or open joints with stone, mortar, and seal
- revitalize all membrane waterproofing along top of walls, arches, etc.
- put in new drain ditch and connect to existing drain extending from back of wall of convent to acequia, so as to prevent water standing against cloister walls
- rebuild or replace worn stone sills at sacristy doors
- various repair projects in cloister
- indications of leaks from dome
- vegetation is growing out of walls and parapets

September 19
From: HP Smith
Re: *Inspection trip to Espada* with Mr. Walker, Fr. Tom Collins
Work needed:

- roof leaking badly in several places
- bad cracks in rear wall, which is leaning slightly
- vertical crack through facade above door and between arched openings
- two head stones above front door have slipped down an inch
- brick floor in nave cracked and sunken in several places
- sanctuary wood floor rotted and caved in in places
- windows, doors, and frames in dilapidated condition

November 4
From: Rufus Walker
To: HP Smith
Re: *Second inspection of Espada,* Nov. 2
Conclusions and work needed:
- impractical from cost standpoint to tear down and replace badly leaning west wall, except for patchwork to prevent further disintegration
- available funds not enough for rebuilding transept on North elevation, replace incompatible windows, or replace roof
- minimum work on front elevation will fill in cracks in facade, rework
  tower and strengthen anchorage of bells to make them operational
  again, and replace window above entry door
- North and South elevations: regrouting and patching of walls and buttresses, repair of existing windows, repointing, and waterproofing
- repair roof

1961

January 12
From: HP Smith
To: Msgr. Popp
Re: *San José mission*
Work needed:
- cost of new lamppost to duplicate those in front of church to be made
  by Mr. Voss, repairs to existing ones
- someone has broken through gate on circular stairs to choir loft and
  damaged the organ. Suggest Mr. Voss make a wrought iron sliding
  bolt.
- remove rotted boards and timbers on platform in front of vestment
  case in sacristy
- caulk windows around dome; water damage along base of octagonal
  stone walls of the dome

June 15
From: Msgr. Popp
To: Rufus Walker
Re: *San José mission*
Work needed:
- recent rains have shown leaks, particularly in window above main al-
  tar

July 11
From: Msgr. Popp
To: Rufus Walker
Re: *San José mission*
- partial payment for work performed included

- repair to platform in sacristy will be paid by pastor, Fr. Merald McCormick, since it is the responsibility of the parish
- repaired dome still leaks

October (no date)
From: HP Smith
Re: *Espada mission chapel:* outline specifications of repair work
- West wall: remove entire wall from vertical crack in North wall to similar crack in sacristy West wall down to approx. 3 ft. below grade, pour new footing, and rebuild reproduction wall using same old stone
- Southeast and north walls and interior: remove extraneous "modern" items, remove entire ceiling boards of nave and rotted portions of truss ends in walls, remove entire brick flooring of nave and sanctuary, open holes through walls for water spouts
- fill in holes, cracks, joints
- apply waterproofing to exterior masonry surfaces
- roof work
- mill and furnish new windows and doors of native red cedar
- communion rail of same wood

October 14
From: Rufus Walker
To: Msgr Bernard Popp
Re: leaks in dome at *San José mission*
- has come to conclusion that leaks are not from the dome, but from windows of the tower, whose frames had no protective coating when installed and have probably decayed seriously. Windows are extremely hard to reach, and will require special scaffolding

1962

January 10
From: Rufus Walker
To: HP Smith
Re: reintegration work at *Espada mission*
- delays because of inability of fabricators of handmade antiqued items, especially mill work items, to meet scheduled delivery
- Chancery has decided to add same ceiling, vigas, floor, and window to sacristy as to the chapel
- some detail work may be required for conversion of the newly added North transept to use as a confessional

February 19
From: Rufus Walker
To: HP Smith
Re: additional work at *Espada mission*
- zapatas and iron bands added to beams of chapel
- Sacrarium for sacristy

- tile base for chapel
- cabinets and shelving for sacristy
- work for creating confessional out of North transept
- removing paint and oil antiquing treatment from front doors
- limestone font at South side of entrance doors
- new rock wall on portion of rectory yard
- flagstone walks to areas of rectory yard
- new pews for chapel

1963

February 21
From: Rufus Walker
To: HP Smith
Re: possible restoration of stone house at Northwest corner of *Espada mission*
quadrangle.
Work required:
- much of front wall facing chapel has fallen away; what remains is leaning seriously and must be torn down and rebuilt
- metal roof, timber framing, and ceiling are beyond repair
- all windows and doors have long disappeared
- North, West, and East walls are intact, but badly cracked and must be reintegrated
- cement floor is cracked, but usable; possible later placement of tile on it
- research shows original roof was flat with a stone parapet; can be reproduced using old utility poles for vigas, small cedar poles or cypress shakes for ceiling

March 19
From: HP Smith
To: Archbishop Robert E. Lucey
Re: projects requiring immediate action at *Espada, San José, and San Juan Capistrano*
- understands decision not to rebuild small house on Northwest corner of Espada quadrangle, although it is part of the continuous outer wall of mission quadrangle. However, points out that two South corner walls are sagging badly, and is afraid school children or visitors may knock out prop and cause walls and roof to collapse on them. Recommends tearing down roof and these portions of walls immediately.
- continuous dampness on East wall behind altar at San José. Repairs have been done above this spot, but leaks continue. Suggests a drain pipe built into wall from the roof has been punctured by bolts holding the reredos. Recommends remedial work short of opening up the wall to search for such a leak.
- Community Room at San Juan, for which complete restoration as a parish hall was proposed, is going to pieces. Galvanized-sheet roof has blown loose; walls on proposed kitchen are disintegrating. Patch work should be done to at least preserve the structure, to include re-

moval of pitched roof and putting in a flat one with beamed ceiling, plus patching and stabilizing walls

March 29
From: Rev. Charles Herzig, Chancery Secretary
To: HP Smith
Re: recent visit of Archbishop to *San Juan Capistrano*
Questions:
- Archbishop disturbed at dark coloring of walls, wonders if it will wash off, or whether some other dye should be used
- wonders whether Smith is satisfied with job of capping reintegrated walls done by Mr. Walker
- wonders if glass domes in the church are in good condition, or whether they can be replaced with plastic ones if present ones leak
- concerned with gap in west wall towards south end of mission walls; may have been a door or window, but framing stones have disappeared

July 31
From: Rufus Walker
To: HP Smith
Re: Cost survey of proposed work at *Concepción mission*
- historic building medallion monument under construction
- pews contracted out to others; Walker will install
- replace all cement, tile, and common brick floors in church, baptistry, bell tower room, sacristy and stair room to second floor with brown flagstones
- spray stone facade with silicone
- paint interior walls of church
- pointing stone in main altar and stone steps in sacristy
- refinish enameled crucifix on main altar

October 18
From: Rufus Walker
To: HP Smith
Re: Chancery has decided on additions to work on *Concepción mission*
- new windows and doors
- communion rails
- electric wiring
- light fixtures
- heating

1966

April 22
From: Rev. Charles Herzig
To: Rufus Walker
Re: three items at *San José mission*
- go ahead on door for the sacristy

- downspout recently broke off and must be replaced
- cracked area around the pivot of mission entrance door

July 12
From: Rev. Charles Herzig
To: Rufus Walker
Re: *San José mission*
   - call from Pearson DeVries, park ranger at San José Mission State Park reporting more plaster falling in sacristy

NOTES

1. Ernst Schuchard was an engineer with Pioneer Flour Mills in San Antonio, who developed a deep interest in the subject of the decorations that originally adorned the San Antonio missions. In the 1930s, he conducted a chemical analysis of the pigments, and using his findings, produced some demonstration designs on the facade of Mission San José. Mr. Rufus Walker assisted him in this.

An articled entitled "Church Wall Color Restored" appeared in the *San Antonio Light* Monday, November 7, 1949, accompanied by a photo of "volunteer artisans" Schuchard and Rufus Walker at work, and describing their efforts:

After faithfully transferring [the designs], Schuchard and Walker mixed earth colors with milk for the final painting. The milk ingredient binds the color to the mortar—a fact which the mission-building padres knew and used when they erected the building centuries ago. The result is as close to the original as possible.

2. A photograph in the Alamo Messenger of October 18, 1963, shows workers Leopoldo Esquivel and Santiago Domínguez replacing the floor at Mission Concepción with flagstones.

3. Reprinted with permission of Robert Walker.

Ross Hunt

Ross Hunt, forty-five, born and raised in San Antonio, is a most impressive man. He is a member of a family with a four-generations-long tradition in the masonry trade and credits both that tradition and his growing up in close proximity to the San Antonio missions with the final direction his career has taken. Ross is a rarity in our modern world: a man so emotionally involved in his work that he occasionally chokes up when talking about it. After several years in Atlanta, Ross, his wife —who is also a San Antonian—and their family have returned home to the city and its missions. They have just moved into a home in Alamo Heights, where this interview took place on September 1, 1995.

What is your full name, Ross?

It's Cary Ross Hunt, although I usually go by Ross.

In what neighborhood of San Antonio did you grow up?

Are you familiar with the hacienda-style home just two properties down
   from Mission San Juan Capistrano in Bergs Mill? The house is several
   hundred yards off Villamain Road. My brother, Curtis Hunt, owns it
   now, but it was built by my grandfather. That's where I lived from the
   time I was born until I was six years old. Then in 1956 my father bought
   some property out towards Elmendorf, and we moved out there. I lived
   there until I left home to join the service in 1969.

How long did your grandfather own that property?

He owned it until the day he died, but he bought it in 1924. He had built a
   two-story wood-frame structure right on the acequia—between the
   acequia and the San Antonio river—and the house burned down in
   1925, right after it was completed. Then he built the present masonry
   home.

At the time, he was the contractor on the fourth-story addition to
   City Hall. That job was done in structural masonry, bricks, and limestone, and he was able to get a good deal on the volume purchase of
   bricks, so the same bricks that were used to build that fourth story were
   also used to build his home. Of course, those bricks are stuccoed over.

How much land is included in his property?

Fourteen acres, give or take.

Did he farm on the side?

He might have grown a hay crop and run a few cattle, plus goats and maybe
   a couple of sheep, but that's all. It was a neat setup, because it was a
   family compound. There was my grandfather's house; then he had built
   a second home on the property, which he rented to an aunt; and he had
   built three small cottages after World War II began, which he usually
   leased out to airmen from Brooks Air Force Base.

But it seems that one member or another of the family lived there
   on the property at any given time. Then, when grandchildren started
   to come along, he started the custom of giving each grandchild a year's
   free rent when they got married, sort of as a "start-you-out" gift.

Was there any particular reason why he ended up out there in the neighborhood of the missions, or was it just pure chance that he had the opportunity to buy the property?

I don't know. Before moving out there, he lived on what is now Martin Luther King Drive—I think it was Nebraska Street then—and the house is still standing there that *his* father had bought. I'm not clear, but I understand that my great-grandfather owned property toward the west side of town where Hunt Lane is now, but they moved into town, and my grandfather was raised on the east side. Then as far as I know, his next move was out to Bergs Mill.

We have a lot of German blood in us, and I think there was a small German community there in the Bergs Mill area—the Geigenmillers and whatnot—and that may have had something to do with his decision. And, of course, that was real rural living at the time, and again that may have been the factor.

How far back has your family been in this area? Was your great-grandfather the first family member to live here?

I wish I knew more about that. As I understand it, my grandfather's mother came down from Pittsburgh and down the Mississippi on a packet boat, and two of her brothers accompanied her. As far as I know, they went to New Orleans or Galveston and then on to San Antonio. That family's name was Wurzel.

And then we always heard this romantic story that my grandfather's relatives on his father's side came down here from the Tennessee/North Carolina/Kentucky area and that they may have been ne'er-do-wells or maybe were on the lam, but he met his future wife, Miss Wurzel, here in San Antonio, and they were married sometime in the 1880s.

I understand that one of the brothers continued and went out to San Diego, where he opened a brick-making operation. The family trade seems to have been to be masons even then. There are also Hunts in Oklahoma City who have a large masonry contracting company as well.

How many siblings do you have? I know you have a brother.

There's my brother Curtis and three sisters.

And your father was also Curtis?

That's right. He was Curtis Hunt, Jr. So my brother is Curtis Hunt III, and he has a son who is Curtis Hunt IV.

I had gotten the impression from talking to you earlier that masonry was a family tradition for three generations, but apparently it actually goes back four generations.

Right.

You intimated in our phone conversation that your grandfather had had a connection with work at the missions, that your father has had that connection, and that now you have developed the same connection. Can you tell me more about that?

My dad told me stories of being sixteen years old in 1932, when the WPA was doing the reconstruction of the mission compound at San José, the Indian quarters surrounding the mission church. There was also a pretty extensive project to rebuild the granary, which had collapsed over the years. Dad was able to get on those projects as a laborer over at the granary. That was his earliest involvement.

As we were growing up, and we had moved from Bergs Mill out to Elmendorf, it was our habit for my brother and me to spend at least two weekends out of the month with my grandfather back at Bergs Mill, and during the summer we would probably spend two months out of the three months vacation with him. It was just a great place to live and grow up on the river, playing around the railroad tracks and the missions and climbing the walls and whatnot.

Grandpa was pretty much semiretired by then, the early to middle '60s, but he never stopped working. He stayed pretty active right up into his late eighties or nineties, doing masonry work. Oftentimes, he would load up some sand in the back of the truck, and we'd load up some masonry tools and equipment, and we'd go up and do work on the missions. I don't remember his ever asking anyone, or anyone asking him; he just did it because he apparently thought it was necessary. And we would help him.

I remember one summer he spent time doing some work on the Espada aqueduct. And, of course, as a kid I had no idea at that time how significant that structure was. As a matter of fact, sometimes I resented having to spend my free time during the summer doing that hard work: making mortar by hand and everything. I thought I should've been swimming and running around. But Grandpa did that a number of times.

And, of course, as a property owner, he was very concerned about the condition of the acequia. I never got the sense that he was concerned with the historical significance of it, although he very well may have been, but it ran through his property, and he looked upon it as an asset. So he would work extensively on sections of the acequia well off his property and up in the Bergs Mill area, trying to patch the side walls and so on.

Later on, he was president of the acequia association along Villamain Road and joined the association in a class action lawsuit, I believe against the River Authority, over some of the things that they were or were not doing with the acequia, water rights issues and so on.

Was this when the San Juan dam was destroyed? Was that the cause of the lawsuit, or was it something else?

I think that entered into it. I'm not very familiar with that story, but I think that's when the dam was destroyed and the water was cut off to the acequia. I think the River Authority had agreed to make repairs, but it never did and so on. He was up to his neck in involvement with that.

Let me make sure that I understand you correctly: Your grandfather would do these repairs to the missions as a private individual on a volunteer basis; he wasn't contracted by anyone to do that kind of patch-work.

No, he didn't ask anyone if he should do it; he just went and did it. That's the kind of guy he was.

By the way, what was your grandfather's name?

He was Curtis Roff Hunt, Sr., then my dad was Curtis Rulf Hunt, Jr. I don't know if the difference between the middle names was a misspelling at the hospital or what.

What kind of contracting work or what kind of masonry work did your grandfather do on a regular basis?

He did mostly commercial masonry: churches, schools, banks, hospitals, that sort of stuff; a lot of large masonry projects. Dad worked for Grandpa and became partners with him. They did a lot of work along the Highway 90 corridor—Uvalde, Sabinal, Brackettville, Eagle Pass—between here and Del Rio, down through Laredo, and along the border towns.

So your father continued the business. Has your brother taken it over, or is he doing something else?

Curtis started off on his own business. Dad was continuing working and was getting towards the end of his career. There were times when Curtis would run a job for Dad as a foreman or superintendent, and at other times Curtis would take on his own projects. And I operated the same way. It never would have worked for all of us to work together too long. That wouldn't have lasted at all.

Dad did not chase work at all during his last ten years; it would pretty much come to him. He was one of the leaders in the preservation movement early on here in San Antonio, when it first started getting attention in a big way, in the early '60s. I'm not talking about the things that Hugman[1] was doing down in the Riverwalk and whatnot in the '30s. But when preservation became a popular issue across America, San Antonio was already going strong and had a good program going. Dad was involved in that early on.

Late in his career, people would approach him to do work, and he could sort of pick and choose what he wanted to do or turn over some projects to my brother or to me.

When did your father pass away?

That was in February 7, 1983.

So, regarding what you heard from your father about working at San José during the WPA reconstruction, do you have a clear idea of what he did there? Was he just a laborer?

I'm sure he was, because he would've been sixteen years old, so, although he would've been familiar with the trade, I'm not sure he would've had the skills to have been on the wall necessarily. But as he described it, times were tough in 1932, so he was just happy to get any work he could. Apparently, in 1930, when he was fourteen, he had left home, hopped a freight train, and started riding the rails. He came back in '32, worked at San José, and then left again and rode the rails some more before coming home and settling down.

At times when I've worked there, they have had several displays at San José of photographs from that period, and I've searched hard to see if by any chance I can spot him in those pictures. The WPA also has an association of former members, and they have rosters of everyone who worked on the organization's projects, so maybe I should try to track that down and see if there's any record of Dad and his involvement.

You say that your father was involved in preservation. Can you be more specific? What projects was he involved with?

Our family has done almost all of the masonry work on the Alamo since the early '60s. Dad did several contracts in the King William area, at Blessed Sacrament, and on some of the older structures around town.

Did he ever do any work at the missions?

I can't recall any specific projects there, but one of the things he did there was to help a YCC [Youth Conservation Corps] class one summer. I think that was 1978, because I did it the following year. He made arrangements for his lead man, Raymundo Rodriguez—or Mundo the Maestro, as we called him—to lead the group. He was my dad's right arm. Raymundo had to deal with this group of YCC kids for about two months, and I think it proved to be too much for him. It was just him and these twenty-some kids.

And what were they doing?

They were repointing the east interior walls in the Indian quarters of the San José compound. The project quickly got out of hand; Raymundo took care of it day by day, and Dad would come out once a week to check and to see that they had the materials they needed.

The following week, my brother-in-law, my wife's brother Steven, who is a mason also, went to work for the missions and cleaned up some of the things that these kids had done the year before, took on a new group of kids, and continued down the south wall on the interior.

And when you had the YCC group, were you doing the same thing?

Right. The YCC kids were there for about two and a half months in the summertime, and when they left we continued working there, doing some masonry repair on the interior of the mission compound.

And I hope you were doing this under some sort of agreement with the National Park Service, not as a volunteer like your grandfather!

[Laughs.] Well, the state had the mission at that time. This was before the national park was created. Betty Jo Calzoncit, or, I guess, Bueché since her divorce, was the superintendent at that time, and she had talked to Dad about taking on this YCC project again in 1979, but he had had enough, so he declined. Then Steven and I took it on. We were actually state employees for that period, and there was enough funding to continue with the work.

In 1980 or '81, maybe '82, we did have a contract at San José that Dad entered into with Guido Brothers, Cosmo Guido and Company, to do some masonry preservation there on the mission itself. We did some work on the drum of the dome on top and some masonry repairs around the bell tower. I had forgotten all about these when we mentioned projects before.

Then, tell me something about your own career.

Well, I had no interest in getting into masonry. I left home in 1969 and joined the Navy, got out in '73, and lived in Corpus Christi for a while. Susan and I were married, and our youngest daughter was about four years old at the time. I had gotten a job at the Naval Air Station down there as a civil servant and did that for a couple of years. Another brother-in-law of mine, who is a bricklayer, suggested that I quit working for the government, come back up to San Antonio, and work with him doing masonry. Of course, I had spent numerous summers working for Dad and doing jobs all over town.

I was ready for a change, so I came back to San Antonio and started to work with George, my brother-in-law. Then he up and moved to Hawaii! [Laughs.] I guess he wanted a change also! He sort of left me holding the bag, because I was still trying to learn, and we were doing a lot of work on the north side, building fireplaces, putting in Saltillo tile floors, etc.

Then Dad asked if I would help him with some small projects for a few days, and I started running a job or two for him. Dad got to the point where he didn't like to get out of the house and come into town, and he would take contracts but never set foot on the job from beginning to end because he had people he could depend on—my brother, or me, or Mundo—to do the work and do it right. We would talk a lot at the end of each day about what was happening and how to proceed the following day and the week ahead, and discuss different approaches or techniques to solve problems in preservation: mortar mixes, and let's try this and that technique or the other, the handwork or craft work of the job.

He started getting some nice jobs. In '82, he got a contract to restore the facade of the Alamo, the shrine itself, which of course was a huge job as far as its significance and the planning required to make sure that it was done correctly according to strict preservation standards. And, of course, the sort of peripheral requirements of the job were also daunting. I remember that we had to keep our scaffolding to a minimum and had to tear it down every night.

Actually, the DRT [Daughters of the Republic of Texas] was interested in our getting in and getting out as quickly as possible, before the press got wind of what we were doing, because they're always walking on eggshells about that sort of thing. Although we were operating under very strict standards, they felt that the less publicity the better.

Immediately after the Alamo, we had work over at St. Joseph's—or, as people call it, St. Joske's—on Commerce Street by the Rivercenter Mall complex. That was actually one of Dad's last jobs.

What was required there at St. Joseph's?

Again, that was a contract through the Guido Brothers, where we were doing a lot of stone patching. It's a technique used in the preservation of limestone where the core limestone piece has started to wear and deteriorate. It's a restoration technique where you go in and you use a mixture of crushed limestone and lime and maybe small amounts of cement. My father and Raymundo developed these mixtures and formulas and would use them to restore the shapes and profiles of these stones.

Raymundo was an absolute master. Like a sculptor, he would take this plastic, semiliquid material and apply it to what was left, the good, sound remnants of a piece of limestone, and do this tremendous job of restoring the shape and profile of the piece. His work is all over town. On the bell tower, the steeple of St. Joseph's, there is extensive restoration work, and also on the walls and the facade of the church.

Is Raymundo still working?

He's semi-retired now. He's sixty-seven, sixty-eight years old now and lives on the west side of the river off of Roosevelt Avenue. And in addition to being this fantastic artisan, he's a tremendous human being, a great guy. I consider him a great friend, one for whom I've always had the utmost respect. I start to tear up when I talk about Raymundo, because he taught me so much and he is such a wonderful person.

Well, you were telling me about your career.

Yes. Dad died in '83, and we were in the middle of a couple of projects, one of them down in King William on the Groos House for Charles Butt.

We continued on with that; my brother came in and took over a portion of that contract with his own company, and we finished it with no problems. My mom was not interested in continuing on with the business.

Now, this is very interesting, because it led to my involvement with the National Park Service and the missions. The NPS had taken over the missions, and José Cisneros was the first superintendent, with Betty Jo [Beuché] as the assistant superintendent. An architect, a woman from the regional office in Santa Fe, came into town and was doing some preliminary studies, because when the NPS comes in and takes over a site there are certain things that have to be done within the first couple of years to bring it up to standards and so on.

One of the things that needed to be done was the preservation of the masonry walls at Espada, San Juan, and San José. So she was doing some preliminary work, and just as a friend of the mission I would come around and see how things were going, visit with people and so on. I ran into her—I don't remember her name now—and she would ask me technical questions about different approaches to different problems, and I would help her with that. And one of the things the Park Service has always been concerned about is letting out a contract to do preservation on sensitive historic fabric, some of the stuff that is not in too good a shape, because contracts can get out of hand very quickly.

One evening I got a call from an individual at the regional office in Santa Fe who asked if my mother was part of the Section 88 set-aside program here in San Antonio with the Small Business Administration. Do you know what that is? It's the minority set-aside for contracts. I said she was not, and he suggested I go down to the SBA and get her involved. I asked Mom about it; we made a few phone calls and found out she was not eligible. A couple of evenings later, I get another call, eight or nine o'clock at night. The same person asks how it went, and I reported that it didn't work. A couple of weeks later, another phone call: he tells me he wants me to go and meet Oscar Venegas, who was from El Paso, Texas, new in San Antonio, etc., has started his own business and is a pretty sharp guy.

I wasn't quite sure what was going on, but I knew something was going on. I called Oscar and met him, and he and I became very, very good friends. We did a number of contracts together. But to make a long story short, Oscar got the initial contract to do the masonry work at the San Antonio missions and bring the masonry up to standards, and, of course, I was his subcontractor. We did that in six months, and everybody was very happy with our work, so we were asked if we would be interested in bidding on other projects for the Park Service in other parts of the country. These weren't set-asides; they were big contracts. We did that for a while. We made a good team and worked well together.

The work at the missions included the exterior walls and the Indian quarters at San José and the exterior walls at San Juan and all the walls and ruins at Espada, but, of course, no work on the churches themselves. That had to be a separate contract entered into by the Church. Interestingly, that contract went to my brother Curtis, so at the time I was doing work on the walls he was doing work at Espada, San Juan, and San José.

So, in essence, you sort of fell into historic preservation?

And I liked it, I liked it a lot from the very beginning. Working with Raymundo and everything that I learned or picked up from him pointed me in that direction. And then I have a love for history and a sense of our history here in San Antonio.

I have never had any desire to do concrete block work or brick veneer or that kind of modern stuff. You know, when you're doing historic restoration and preservation, you're standing in the footprints of ghosts long gone, men who dedicated a portion of their lives to that piece of our history. You're right there in his footsteps, and you're helping that piece continue on by preserving his efforts.

So I look at these structures in different ways. One: they represent the history of a time, but there is also the significance of a particular structure in its setting, since there may have been significant events in history that occurred here. Two: they're significant to me personally because they represent the height of the efforts of the common man who, with his own hands and ingenuity, produces something. This is particularly true in this area which was once a far frontier. Artisans dug the stone out of the ground—over where Trinity University or the Zoo or the Sunken Gardens are now—and, sometimes under amazingly difficult conditions, used their hands to create something beautiful.

Look at what Huizar did at San José in the 1730s, out in the middle of nowhere, with his sculpture! I got to reconstruct the jack arch on the back side of the Rose Window, and that was a tremendous thrill for me. You know the story behind the Rose Window [See Appendix B] . . . [Ross is so involved in his story that he chokes up, and we have to pause a moment.] The darned thing is a monument, and it should be there a thousand years, long after you and I are gone at least, and here I am, being able to contribute to that!

You've used a technical term that I've never encountered before. What does it mean?

Jack arch? The Rose Window is on the exterior of the structure. It dresses an opening into the interior of the structure. The mass of masonry that spans over this opening on the interior, that is the jack arch. There had been settlement and damage, so the thing was cracked and fractured and needing repair. The potential was there for serious damage from the inside to the work of Huizar on the outside. That was another contract that Dad had out there at San José that I had also forgotten until we got to talking about it.

So I was able to contribute in my own small way to this marvel of engineering and ingenuity from the eighteenth century, helping it to continue for future generations. I think that's exciting as hell!

I don't care at all about new construction, and the path that I've taken, the wonderful experiences that I've had personally in my work, all started with the missions. My involvement with Spanish colonial architecture also traces back to them. I have done extensive work in San Juan, Puerto Rico, at El Morro, a huge, wonderful Spanish colonial fort—lost a kneecap in the process, by the way—and shortly before we moved back to San Antonio I was involved with a huge re-stuccoing project on the city walls down there in San Juan.

The interconnection of such projects to San Antonio are amazing. I'd be willing to bet that many people here have no idea that the missions ever looked different. Actually, all of these structures were stuccoed originally, but the local people have grown up seeing bare stones and grey walls. They've never seen stucco on their churches, and they'd probably be appalled at the very idea, not to mention at the possibility that those outer walls may have been painted in brightly colored designs.

Stucco or plaster is a "sacrificial coating" that's designed to be applied to the surface of stone. It weathers and fails and is reapplied, but that's how you protect the underlying structure, helping it to last for the next thousand years!

Well, down in San Juan right now, there are generations of people who have never seen stucco on the extensive system of city walls, but that's how they were originally. Anyway, I was helping the park down there, doing the design work and working with local people who work for the Park Service. Together we developed and designed the different mix designs and techniques and whatnot for this project that is going to involve *one million square feet* of stucco that has to be applied to the walls. There was also a big uproar about that!

What I've chosen to do has taken me to the U.S. Virgin Islands to work on Danish colonial properties there, and some fascinating and extremely difficult projects in very isolated places. I've done work at Fort Jefferson in the Dry Tortugas, where there is this fantastic masonry structure—seventy-six miles from Key West, Florida, on a little nine-acre sand island in the middle of the Gulf—that is the largest brick structure in the Western Hemisphere. The Park Service owns it, and it is a beautiful setting surrounded by the ocean.

I've done work on the Jefferson and Lincoln memorials in Washington, D.C., and in a number of presidential homes, all through my involvement with the National Park Service's Southeast Region. And it all comes from an appreciation of our history and of the historic structures here in San Antonio. As you say, I really did kind of fall into it, but you also make your own path, and the resources that were here, that interested me, helped me decide which way to go.

I've had this romantic notion of becoming *the* so-called expert in technical issues for masonry in Spanish colonial structures for the National Park Service. I've done quite a bit of work at St. Augustine, at the Castillo de San Marcos, and helped them with a couple of projects. I was trying to learn as much as I could about a type of concrete that the Spanish introduced to our area but that they had originally learned from the Moors. It's a type of concrete using oyster shells that was used extensively in Puerto Rico, in the Caribbean, and in the southeastern United States.

I've got a wonderful career, and I love what I do. And it all started here with the missions, growing up amongst them and around them and being curious about how some of these things were done and why! The purpose of them, of course, was to convert the natives to Catholicism and to make them part of the Church and good subjects of the King.

And there is San José, sitting out there all by itself. Imagine that here comes this band of Indians for the first time. They've never seen a mission, and they just come over the horizon, and there is San José. The effect would be the same as if some of us today stumbled upon a space vessel from some other planet! The Coahuiltecans had never seen something like that in their lives.

And for me, the wonder is to be able to occupy the same space!

Yes, you deal routinely with a level of craftsmanship and effort that is not often to be found in our daily lives.

Right. It's a tremendous feeling.

Has the bulk of your work been for the Park Service, or am I getting the wrong impression?

You know, I would have to say so, because there were several large contracts that I did privately for the Park Service even before I became an employee of the NPS. The way I came to work for the Park Service was this: I was back in San Antonio, and I had been doing contracts for them. Through that work I had gotten to know a lot of people in the Park Service.

All their contracts have a project inspector, and I had met one of them during a project up in Hampton, Virginia at Fort Monroe—it's an old Army post with a lot of historic structures, and the Army contracts with the NPS to get the historic restoration and preservation work done. The NPS, in turn, had contracted with me and Oscar Venegas to do some of the work. Anyway, we met Earl Gillespie, who was the project inspector, and when the contract was over we returned to San Antonio, and Earl went on to his next assignment. But we'd become friends, and we would keep in touch. Often he would call me with technical questions or problems, that sort of thing.

Earl was transferred to Atlanta in 1988, where they were putting together a crew of specialized craftsmen who would be based there but would go out to different parks throughout the Southeast Region and do work on historic structures. He asked if I would be interested in coming out and joining them. I turned him down, but he'd call every couple of months and renew the offer.

Then things started getting tough here in San Antonio; work started to dry up. Preservation and restoration are often regarded as a luxury, and they are among the first things to go when the economic situation is tight. After all, you know, "If a building has been there a couple of hundred years, what difference is a few more years going to make?" So I finally suggested to my key people at the time—Steven Siggins, who is my brother-in-law and had worked with me on the missions in 1979, and Baltazar Espinosa—that we travel to Atlanta and see what the possibilities were and maybe do it for a few months.

Steven was willing, but Baltazar couldn't do it. Baltazar had come over initially as an illegal, but had gotten his green card. However, he had a family of ten over the border, and he felt responsible for them, so he didn't feel he could go to Atlanta. Steven and another mason who worked for me went along. We ended up staying there for six years, and we did some fascinating things, as I've already told you.

We got quite a reputation in the Southeast Region and in at least the eastern half of the U.S. for what we were able to do out of Atlanta, and we were invited across NPS regional boundary lines to do projects. I was enjoying that quite a bit. In addition to the job satisfaction, there is a small measure of fame on a small level that comes to you. After all, the NPS has twenty thousand people in it, and for a long time it has been America's favorite government agency. After a while, people get to know who you are. And that's neat, one of the perks of the job.

Then we started going through reorganization. We were providing what we felt was an absolutely necessary service, doing this hands-on work on historic structures. The Park Service is about buildings and trees and preserving our history and our culture. But administratively we were attached to a regional office, and the goal was to decentralize as part of "reorganization and reinvention," so we were probably the first group in the NPS to get disbanded, to be affected by it. The "powers that be" felt that these individuals with their skills would be very easy to place out in the parks, far easier than some of the professionals, the white-collar people, who were in the different offices.

In the Southeast Region they were very proactive with reorganization. We were going to be on the leading edge of the whole thing so as to try to avoid the meat-ax approach to it. So we were wiped out, and all of my crew was dispersed to different parks around the region. Steven Siggins, whose family had never followed him out to Atlanta and only saw him once every six weeks or so, decided he was coming back to San Antonio regardless.

So we [NPS] made a deal with the San Antonio missions to put him on staff: we sent the park the money and the slot for a month so he could come down here and show his stuff. He did, and they fell in love with him, so they made temporary arrangements to have him continue to work there. But finally there was no more money left, and he was put on temporary furlough. I feel, though, that if he doesn't get back to work with them soon, he will do so in the future.

My goal is either to be assigned to help the man who is now conservator and chief of maintenance at the missions or to be assigned his position, if he should happen to move on.

So that's the slot you're aiming for?

Yes, but we'll have to see what happens with the Park Service and this current reorganization.

Let me ask you a question: Are you now in the employ of the NPS?

Yes.

And you have been for how long?

Six and a half years. The reason I'm here in San Antonio right now and working at Fort Sam Houston is this: reorganization was coming; we knew things were going to change, and I had a choice to make. I loved Atlanta, and I could have stayed there for another year, but after that year it was unclear what was going to happen. Either I could have limited control over where they were going to place me or I could leave it to chance. At the same time, last year our first grandbaby was born here in San Antonio.

How old did you tell me you are?

I'm forty-five.

And you have grandbabies already?

[Laughs.] Our oldest daughter is twenty-five, she's had her first child, and just a few months after that she got pregnant again! Anyway, the family situation was such that we thought the best thing was to try to get back home.

There is another group of people within the Park Service, the Williamsport Preservation Training Center from Williamsport, Maryland, who do something similar to what our group had done in the Southeast Region, going out to jobs like we did, but they also have a training aspect to their mission. They train people in the crafts, but they also train them to become exhibit specialists, which is my official job title. These are people who can do the work, but they can also design and run the surrounding framework; they provide "full service" from

beginning to end: they can put together a contract, do all the administrative stuff, and so on.

This group has been doing quite a bit of work with the Army lately,
as well as with other federal agencies who become their clients. These
agencies have historic structures that they have the obligation to
maintain and preserve. However, they often don't have the expertise or
the trained personnel to do it, so they come to the NPS.

A couple of years ago, Mike Hilger, who is a historical architect for
the Department of Defense working at Fort Sam Houston, attended a
conference in Atlanta with people from Williamsport and my supervisor in Atlanta. They mentioned my name and the fact that I was from
San Antonio. Mike immediately asked if I was related to "Boogie"
Hunt, which was my dad's nickname. It turned out that before going
to work for the Department of Defense, Mike had been in private
practice here in town and had done a number of contracts with Dad,
Raymundo, and so on.

Mike decided that what he wanted was a Park Service specialist to
come and work with him on his historic preservation program at Fort
Sam. Right soon after that, I got myself assigned to that job on a
three-year detail that just began in June of '95, through a memorandum
of agreement between the NPS and the Army. This, however, does not
keep me from going out to help parks with their preservation problems
on occasion. In fact, I just got a call from the office in San Juan, Puerto
Rico, which might mean some duty down there.

**Historic preservation is a very touchy thing, because you have to be
aware of materials and techniques used in the past *and* you have to
be aware of how to deal with those materials and techniques in the
present. How did you acquire that knowledge? From what you've
told me, it doesn't sound like you went through a formal course of
training, did you?**

No, I didn't, but I've done lots and lots of reading. I have a fairly extensive
library, and I have twenty years of practical experience, making observations as to what works and what doesn't, as to how things we've done
in the past—based on what even earlier craftsmen did two or three
hundred years ago—have held up through the years. Lots of research
has been involved.

Then there are little secrets, little tricks of the trade that may be very
simple, but you have to learn about them through practice: how to

identify the components of historic mortars, how to duplicate those mortars, how people made lime in different parts of the world, etc. I've had to learn how things were done in the past and how the resulting work can be helped to survive. And then, of course, entering into conversation with knowledgeable people, whether scholars or simple artisans, and letting them do all the talking while I do all the listening.

Another part of all this is training: I also love to pass on anything I know to anyone who cares to listen and wants to learn: other craftsmen, architects, interested lay people. I've been involved in training both with the NPS and the Department of Defense.

Is there such a thing as a training school in historic preservation, aside from this place you mentioned in Williamsport?

I don't know; my guess is that there is. I would think that the National Trust for Historic Preservation sponsors and funds a few things. There are also a number of programs that have started and failed, or have started and are still going. They are primarily in the northeast and the East Coast. Williamsburg also does some things, and there are lengthy seminars of a month or two that are staged in the summer.

But I feel that those things are more "sensitivity training" than anything else: they make you aware of historic fabric and the ideas behind historic preservation, but they can't possibly make you a mason or a carpenter or a woodworker who can carry out the job.

I don't know how much a regular blue-collar craftsman is able to attend those sorts of programs. If you talk to the average bricklayer—which is maybe a bit different from a mason—you'd find that they could care less about historic preservation. The idea of standing in one place all day long, removing this old mortar and carefully replacing it, considering the things that you are not able to do that you can do in a modern job, does not appeal to them in the least.

I, on the other hand, would view standing on a scaffold putting bricks one-over-two and two-over-one, row after row, not even having to think about what you're doing, as work suitable for a mindless robot, not a human being. So even in the masonry trade there is a division between your preservationists and your bricklayers.

I guess it requires a different consciousness of what you're doing and why you're doing it.

Right.

Now, in the specific case of the San Antonio missions, what kinds of problems do you confront from a preservation point of view?

At the San Antonio missions and everywhere, trying to make corrections to well-intentioned but disastrously inappropriate work performed in the past is a constant problem: inappropriate repairs, incompatible materials and so on that were used in the past. I could probably stumble on some inappropriate repairs that my grandfather might have done in his time. You know, "cement is our enemy!," so to speak. The old-timers always thought that the harder the better, and that is not always true. That's one of the biggest problems.

Finding the materials is another. I remember trying to find the red sandstone that the WPA collected to do the Indian quarters at San José back in the '30s. I'm not sure quite where it was retrieved from, but I had heard that there was either a quarry or a deposit of it somewhere over on Stinson Field that was used extensively, but I think that's different. Then there was the limestone and tufa that was used on the missions themselves.

But trying to preserve WPA-era-type work and not having enough material and having to go out and find it is a bugabear. I remember Betty Jo Bueché driving this big old dump truck on the other side of Elmendorf in Saspamco, where we had found some. While she steered the truck, Steven and I were walking along the dirt road, checking out the side of the road and collecting pieces of red sandstone that we found. So here you had the superintendent of a state park and two conservation specialists picking up rocks, because otherwise they couldn't do their job!

Sounds like an extreme form of self-help!

[Laughs] Yes. That's the other problem about preservation: money, funding. You have to balance trying to do everything to exact standards with practicality, and budget is always an issue. We never want to do any damage, and anything we do should be reversible.

Usually, the people with the pursestrings are (a) very practical-minded and (b) could care less about history, so when you tell them you could do it the right way, but it's going to cost one hundred thousand dollars, and you could do it this other way, which is not so good and has all sorts of drawbacks but will only cost twenty thousand dollars, you can pretty much always predict which way they would rather have you do it. [Laughs.]

You said your family worked on the drum at San José. What was involved there? And was it just at San José, or both there and at Concepción?

We did it at San José, but we also had a contract at Concepción. Steven Siggins and I installed the *canales* [water spouts or diverters] that are there right now and did a lot of pointing and repairs to the mortar at both missions.

And what exactly did you do with the drum?

We repointed it. At San Juan, the set of arches over the entrance where the bells hang was severely deteriorated and had lost a lot of the original fabric, and Dad contracted that work, and Mundo did the actual work with this limestone consolidation technique that I described earlier. We restored that feature to its original profile, and then it was all stuccoed over, which was more of Raymundo's work.

But at San José we did the jack arch behind the Rose Window—as I said—the drum, and we also worked on the flying buttresses at the granary, and I also did the interior plaster that's at the granary right now. Again, that's what is so great about this kind of work: every time I go to San José and step into the granary, there I am face to face with work of mine from years back that has stood the test.

Well, I must say that I am very impressed to see that you are not only technically involved with your work but that you are also clearly emotionally involved with what you do. There are not too many people who can have both of those things in their work.

Oh, yes, I'm lucky; I'm very fortunate.

Would you care to hazard a prediction as to where the San Antonio missions are going in the future?

Well, I certainly believe the infrastructure of the missions themselves, the physical plant, the buildings, will be there for all time. Having been gone for the last six years, I am not aware of what issues are facing them right now, or what threats. I see that Los Compadres is still active and as strong as ever, which is a great thing. I would like to see the missions become even more important to the city and to the people of San Antonio, and, of course, to our visitors.

As far as whatever politics swirl around them, that's just ebb and flow. I still don't see a lot of signage around—"This way to the missions"—and you don't seem to see or hear them mentioned much on newspapers or television, but I think they'll always be there. They've been there almost three hundred years, and there's no reason to believe that they won't in the future. What's going on right now isn't as important as what has always been!

NOTE

1. Robert Hugman was the landscape architect who designed much of San Antonio's Riverwalk.

Appendix A

The following documents are provided in lieu of the interview the author had hoped to be granted with Reverend Joseph Deane, Pastor, St. Cecilia's Church, San Antonio.

FILE COPY
LUIS TORRES
Writer, Editor, Oral Historian
3003 Whisper Lark
San Antonio, TX 78230

May 10, 1996.

Fr. Joseph Deane
St. Cecilia's Church
125 W. Whittier Street
San Antonio, TX 78210

Dear Fr. Deane,

I spent a good part of last year conducting interviews throughout the San Antonio community on the subject of the San Antonio missions. The resulting oral history collection is going to be published by the Texas Tech University Press in Lubbock.

Among my interviews, there were a few with former members of the congregation at Mission Concepcion. A central topic of those interviews was the chain of events that led to the demise of the small, but active, congregation at that mission.

For the sake of presenting as complete a picture as possible, I would appreciate the opportunity of interviewing you and getting your point of view. If you consent to be interviewed, I will have to ask you to sign the enclosed release form at the completion of the interview, something which I have asked of all my interview subjects. I would also like to take a few portrait photos of you, since all the other interviews in the book are accompanied by a portrait of the interviewee.

Since the book is now on the schedule at Texas Tech University Press, I will need to hear from you as soon as possible. I am scheduled to be out of town from May 17 to June 2, but will be in contact with you as soon as I return from my trip. I hope to hear from you on this matter as soon as possible.

Yours sincerely,

Luis Torres, Ph.D.

FILE COPY
LUIS TORRES
Writer, Editor, Oral Historian
3003 Whisper Lark
San Antonio, TX 78230

June 27, 1996.

Fr. Joseph Deane
St. Cecilia's Church
125 W. Whittier Street
San Antonio, TX 78210

Dear Fr. Deane,

You suggested in our recent telephone conversation that I should send you questions in writing, since you did not have the time to sit for a formal interview in connection with my soon-to-be-published collection of oral history interviews on the topic of the San Antonio missions. I am very interested in examining all angles on the material I am dealing with, and listening to all sides of the story to be told, so I am glad that you have acceded to answer the questions in written form, even if we cannot do the kind of interview I did with the other individuals I contacted.

Enclosed you will find my questions. Please feel free to answer at length and in as much detail as you feel necessary. If I have not provided enough space for your answer, please write on the back of the page, or add another page to the questionnaire.

I am sending you a copy of the "Use Agreement" form, a sample of which I enclosed in my previous letter. Please sign and date it, and return it to me with your answers to the questions.

For your convenience, I am enclosing a stamped self-addressed envelope you can use to return the material to me. Since I am facing publication deadlines, I hope that you will return this material to me as soon as possible.

Thank you for your cooperation.

Sincerely,

Luis Torres, Ph.D.

Fr. Joseph Deane - Written Questions

Part 1: Personal and family background.

1. Please state your full name.

2. How old are you? When and where were you born?

3. Please state your parents' names. Where were they born? What kind of work did they do?

4. How many siblings in your family? If there were several, what was your position among them? How many lived to be adults? What sort of work did they engage in?

5. Where did you get your basic education? When and where (both city and institution) did you enter seminary? When were you ordained?

6. When did you get your first parish assignment? Where was your parish located? What sort of parish was it (ethnic composition, economic characteristics of congregation, etc.)?

7. Please describe any subsequent assignments *before* you came to San Antonio.

8. When did you come to San Antonio? Describe your work *before* being assigned to the St. Cecilia's/Mission Concepción parish.

II. St. Cecilia's/Mission Concepción Parish

9. Please describe the circumstances of your assignment to this parish. Did you have any choice in the matter? Was it an assignment you relished, or were you unhappy about it?

10. The four mission parishes included in the San Antonio Missions National Historical Park are supposed to maintain "living congregations" according to the agreements between the National Park Service and the Archdiocese of San Antonio. Today, there are such "living congregations" at three of the missions, but not at Mission Concepción.

Several sources have described the situation at the mission when you took over the pastorate there as a small, but lively and very active congregation, which had expended a great deal of time and effort in sprucing up the church and its grounds and in helping their pastors in meeting all the needs of the parish. During the time you have been pastor, however, that congregation has virtually disappeared, and the only activity at the mission appears to be a monthly mass said by a priest from outside the parish.

Could you describe, in as much detail as possible, the reason—as you see it—for the disappearance of the Mission Concepción congregation?

11. Please comment at length on the following. Various sources have described your attitude towards the congregation at Mission Concepción and its members as, among other things, authoritarian, ruthless, uncompromising, and vindictive. I would appreciate hearing your side of the story, so please take as much space as you need to give your point of view.

Specifically, the following is alleged to have taken place under your administration of the parish:

a. That you took over all the parish equipment the congregation had bought for its use—folding tables and chairs, booths for parish festivals, etc.—and removed it so that it became inaccessible to its members, and that you, in effect, locked the parishioners out of their own church and parish buildings.

b. That you confiscated the congregation's treasury—funds the congregation had raised itself for its own needs—and threatened to file charges against those parishioners who objected to turning over the funds.

c. That you purposely curtailed parish activities at the mission, reducing the frequency of masses there, cancelling the special masses for Christmas or to honor Our Lady of Guadalupe, disbanding the parish choir, removing the tabernacle from the mission church, etc., and, in effect, strangling the life out of the little parish until its congregation disappeared.

d. That, when the parishioners sought assistance from the archdiocesan authorities, you retaliated against the protesters by refusing access to their children to classes in preparation for confirmation and first communion, by not allowing them to hold their children's *quinceañera* celebrations, and otherwise blocking their and their family's access to services and benefits that other parish members could expect.

12. Do you have any comments or statements you would like to make about any of the questions above?

ST. CECILIA'S CHURCH

125 W. WHITTIER STREET
SAN ANTONIO, TEXAS 78210
PHONE (512) 533-7109

June 29, 1996

Mr. Luis Torres

Dear Mr. Torres,

I do not choose to be a part of
your "Oral History of the Missions."
Your concept of history and mine do not seem
to coincide.

As Pastor of St. Cecilia's Parish, to
which Mission Conception is attached, I do
my best to serve the 1800 families in our
parish. I have four Masses each weekend,
and my ten years of service here have been
happy and fruitful. I don't think that I
need to defend myself or criticize others
for your benefit.

Sincerely yours,

Rev. Joseph Deane, Pastor

FILE COPY
LUIS TORRES
Writer, Editor, Oral Historian
3003 Whisper Lark
San Antonio, TX 78230

July 23, 1996.

Fr. Joseph Deane, Pastor
St. Cecilia's Church
125 W. Whittier Street
San Antonio, TX 78210

Dear Fr. Deane,

Thank you very much for your letter of June 29. Although you have declined to take part in my oral history of the San Antonio missions project, I appreciated your prompt response.

This letter is to let you know that I want to include the letter I received from you in an appendix to the manuscript. I hope you will have no objection to this, and, unless I hear an objection from you by August 9, I will proceed accordingly. This will allow me to meet the deadlines that the publication of the book imposes on me.

Thank you for your cooperation.

Sincerely,

Luis Torres

Note: No reply was ever received.

Appendix B

The Rose Window at Mission San José and Its Legend

The so-called Rose Window at Mission San José adorns the exterior of the sacristy window on the south wall of the church, which faces the mission plaza. The style of its decoration is labeled as Mexican Baroque, dating to the eighteenth century. The decoration of both the Rose Window and the mission church's facade are traditionally attributed to Pedro Huizar (the name is sometimes rendered *Huicar* or *Huisar*), and a local legend, continually embellished in our day by fanciful tour bus drivers, has been spun to explain the background and origin of the famous window.

An attempt to assemble some of the legend's variations turned up an interesting sampling. Stories in the *San Antonio Times-Herald* of March 18, 1928 and the *San Antonio Express* of June 9, 1936, give basically the same version: Huizar embarked for the New World with the promise of Rosa that she would be his bride after he had made his fortune. He came to San José commissioned to carve the church's facade, but soon learned that his promised had wed another man. In his grief, said the *Times-Herald*, "he plunged into the task of completing the 'rose window,' and, as history has shown so often to be the case with men bowed down in deep grief, he became inspired and exerted himself to the utmost and gave to the world his masterpiece."

The legend was further embroidered upon, and given a few twists for good measure, in the 1930s. Rosa is no longer a faithless one, but rather the victim of a shipwreck while on her way to join her beloved. Jack C. Butterfield, in "San Antonio, City of Missions," a typescript dated 1935, presents this twist, and calls the Rose Window, with considerable hyperbole, "the most notable piece of sculpture in the whole of North America, if not the New World," adding that it took Huizar five years to complete it. Butterfield goes even further afield in describing Huizar's background: "He was sculptor to the Spanish court before coming to Texas, and some of his ancestors decorated the great Palace of the Alhambra, at Granada, in Spain."

Wilma Madlem, in her 1934 publication *San José Mission—Its Legends, Lore and History*, reports that Huizar was engaged by the missionary to carve the window, which, befitting the building it was to decorate, should have "a religious character." Yet so besotted was he with love for Rosa, that his hands carved nothing but roses on the window. The last rose was carved the day Rosa was to arrive, but, instead, Huizar received a letter telling him of the shipwreck. Madlem tells us:

Now only did he realize the wrong he had done. At first the loss of Rosa seemed too great a punishment, but he swore that for her sake he would do penance. He would carve a portal for the church that would be the most beautiful in all New Spain. As the years passed, his health failed, and it was by sheer force of will that he was able to finish his penance. The work which he left the world, was indeed a penance—his soul was now ready to join his Rosa. (p. 11)

In the introduction that precedes his long poem "A Legend of the Mission San José" (no date, but likely 1935), James B. Cunningham repeats a legend about the window "said to be one of the most beautiful windows in all the world," which he claims to have heard from an "aged man who had passed the greater part of his life within the shadows of the walls of San José." According to this version, Huizar came to the New World, not seeking wealth, "for he was a famous sculptor in his native land,—being called the 'King's own Sculptor,'" but seeking to recover from some unspecified malady.

He had regained his health and was about to return to the mother country and claim his beloved, but the next caravan from Mexico City brought the news that she had died many months ago. Losing all desire to return, he determined to devote himself to beautifying and glorifying the mission, which was then under construction. Here, however, Cunningham inserts a note of mystery and mysticism:

Thirty years later, when his work was completed, one moonlit night, a troop of slow moving figures was seen passing the Mission. The last member of this mysterious band, who was clad in the gorgeous apparel of a lady of the royal Court of Spain, paused and knelt beside something that lay prone on the ground. She was heard to utter words of endearment and affection; and in a voice whose tones were as soft and sweet as the sound of a lute when the night is hushed and still, she spake of a great love that was stronger than death itself. After a few moments the strange damsel arose and disappeared.
On the next morning the body of the artist was found outstretched upon the ground and it is further told that a beautiful smile wreathed his face. He lay near that lovely window, of which one writer hath said: "If architecture is frozen music, then the window of San José is one of our loveliest songs!"
Clutched in the artist's right hand was a small golden wedding ring; but strange to say a few minutes later the ring in some way disappeared, and in spite of much search the friends of the dead Huicar could find it nowhere.

Just to be on the safe side, however, Cunningham includes that version that maintains the sculptor's young love was untrue and married another.

Closer to our day, the book *Six Missions of Texas,* produced by Dorman H. Winfrey and others in 1965, presents a version that seems to be a distillation of elements from the previously cited accounts. In this version, Huizar is a direct descendant of "the architect who designed the world-famous Alhambra, a Moorish castle and stronghold in Spain":

> An adventurer at heart, Pedro decided to come to New Spain, gain fame and fortune as a sculptor, then send to Spain for his village sweetheart, the beautiful Rosa. After reaching Mexico City, Pedro learned of the beauty of San José located on the San Antonio river and determined to journey there and link his fame to that of the famous mission by offering his talents as a sculptor to the padres. He arrived ... in the late 1780s and was assigned the task of decorating the window on the south wall of the church. The padres took for granted that the young Spaniard would carry out a religious theme. But Pedro was young [and] he was in love . . .. He determined to dedicate this window to Rosa and make it the most beautiful piece of artistry in the world. Then, with his fame established, he would send for Rosa and marry her . . . in the shadow of "his" window. (p. 162)

As Pedro came closer to completing his work, he wrote his love to embark for the New World. When he was finishing the last rose, and as he was thinking of his bride, one of the padres put a gentle hand on his shoulder and broke to him the news of her death at sea. Grief stricken, the sculptor vowed to devote the rest of his life to the church and spent the next twenty years at the mission, painting and carving its facade.

Such is the evolving legend of the Rose Window. What do we really know about Pedro Huizar? For one thing, we know that to the present day there is no documentary evidence to connect him to the Rose Window at San José. Huizar is mentioned in the historical record of the mission, but as a carpenter and surveyor, in which capacity he was responsible for surveying mission property at San José, Concepción, San Juan, and Espada during the secularization of the 1790s. At that time, he was also appointed as advisor and protector of the secularized mission Indians at San José and Concepión. Huizar received a plat of land for his services. (See: Fr. Marion A. Habig's *The Alamo Chain of Missions,* and Mary Ann Noonan Guerra's *The Missions of San Antonio.*)

The New Handbook of Texas, the accepted encyclopedic repository of knowledge about the state, has a rather lengthy entry on Huizar. He was born in Aguascalientes, Mexico (not Spain), in 1740, and was married twice, neither time to a woman named Rosa. His first wife was María de la

Trinidad Henriques, with whom he had several children. When she died, he married María Gertrudis Martínez, a widow.

No document available connects Huizar to either the Rose Window or the facade of Mission San José, although it is quite clear that he was a *vecino* of the mission—someone who lived in the area—when the two principal decorative elements of the church were being produced.

What are we to make of the Rose Window legend? Rosalind Rock, park historian at the San Antonio Missions National Historical Park, observes that the stone used for the missions was quite soft when it came out of the ground, and only hardened gradually after being exposed to the air. Given that, it is conceivable that an expert carpenter could have used his talent with wood to work this material. But until some document surfaces establishing the connection, Pedro Huizar's authorship of the Rose Window will have to remain a local tradition.

Index

San Antonio missions, xi–xiv, 1, 2, 5, 187, 214, 225, 242, 244, 246, 250–2, 262, 265, 271, 274. *See also individual listings*
San Antonio Missions National Historical Park, xi–xiv, 3, 66, 79, 86, 226, 268; church-state question, 99–101, 104: and Ebeneezer Baptist Church, 100; lines of division, 101; and Los Compadres, 110; and maintenance and conservation, 227; military and congressional chaplains, 101; at San José, 101; in Spanish colonial times, 101; and U.S. Dept. of Justice, 100 and community awareness, 113; establishment, 100, 103, 228, 271; first amendment questions, 99; General Management Plan, 104; Land Acquisition Plan, 105; NPS contribution, 226; opposition to, 77–8, 80–1, 100, 104, 105–6, 228; park office, 103, 104; Park Advisory Board, 110, 130; private funding for churches, 227; and San Juan compound trees, 79–80, 85–6; and Texas Parks and Wildlife Dept., 102; volunteer program, 111
San Antonio Police Department: cooperative agreement with park rangers, 104
San Antonio River, 70, 89, 109, 118, 121, 162, 195–6, 224, 231, 241, 246, 263; channelization, 89; fauna, 121; flood of 1921, 215; in early twentieth century, 121
San Antonio River Authority (SARA), 226; and San Juan dam, 266; sued by San Juan Ditch Association, 266
San Antonio River Corridor. *See* San Antonio River Authority (SARA)
San Fernando Cathedral, 11, 44, 146; and OSM Committee, 173; publication celebrating restoration, 246
San Isidro Labrador, 42
San José Mission Texas State Historic Outdoor Theater, 208
San José, Mission, xi, 2, 4, 6, 30, 38, 45, 88–90, 118, 122, 164, 183, 188, 194, 203–4, 208, 213, 221, 227, 241–2, 244, 274; acequia, 23, 35; Altar Society, 26; amphitheater, 178, 191, 193, 208; bell tower, 253, 261, 269; and Bexar County, 206; brick pathways, 171; *carretela*, 35;

Christmas Mass, 207; Chulita the donkey, 208, 213; church, 34, 203, 205; church bell, 34; convento, 112, 192, 206–7; dance hall, 22; division of ownership, 169; dome, 16, 269; in early twentieth century, 122; and Ethel Harris, 190, 202, 203, 212; fence, 100, 202–3; flying buttresses, 281; and Fr. Antonio Margil de Jesús, 116, 185, 186; granary (*galera*), 7, 12–5, 19, 33, 97, 193, 202–3, 205, 213, 225, 244, 265, 281; Indian quarters, 94–5, 116, 191, 193, 202, 265, 268, 272, 280; limestone cottage, 190; and Los Compadres, 104, 112; Los Pastores, 208, 242; and Madres Club, 26; masonry walls, 271; mesquites at, 41; mill, 13, 23, 203, 205, 213; as National Historic Site, 94, 97; and NPS, 91, 271; neighborhood, 124; and park board, 165; peacocks, 190, 207, 242; pottery making, 28, 205; prefecture, 202; processions, 207; Pyron Road, 202; Pyron Road gate, 203; reconstruction of church, 16, 202; roof repair funds, 179; Rose Window, 6, 206, 225, 272–3, 281, 290–2; ruins, 33; sacristy, 28, 33; and San Antonio Conservation Society, 94, 229, 242; *San José Story, The*, 208; school, 191; as state park, 94, 102, 165, 169, 188, 190–1, 205, 261, 268: administrative staff, 191; Advisory Board, 168, 175; church-state question, 169, 203; and Hemisfair, 168; funding, 102; jurisdictions, 203; mission and parish, 175; origin of, 202; and OSM, 175; superintendents, 91, 98; visitation traffic, 192, 205–6 termites, 183; and walls, 17, 21, 35, 213: wall quarters construction, 202–3, 272; and WPA, 175,194, 265, 267, 280; and YCC, 268;
San Juan Ditch Corporation, 107–9; Ditch Association: *v. River Authority*, 266
San Juan, Mission, xi, 38–40, 45, 60, 65–7, 73, 83–5, 125, 146, 165–6, 168, 183, 185, 263; acequia, 40, 62, 72, 107, 263: and community cohesion, 109; dam destroyed, 107, 109, 266; repair and maintenance, 265

𝒴

𝒵